Confessions
and Declarations
of Multicolored Men

Post-Jim Crow (?) and still integrating

Frederick Douglass Alcorn
(Papa Son Tate's Grandson)

VERNON PRESS

www.vernonpress.com

In the Americas:
Vernon Press
1000 N West Street,
Suite 1200, Wilmington,
Delaware 19801
United States

In the rest of the world
Vernon Press
C/ Sancti Espiritu 17,
Malaga, 29006
Spain

Library of Congress Control Number: 2016935308

ISBN: 978-1-62273-080-3

Dedication

This book is dedicated to Mama, Ms. Thelma Louise Tate Alcorn, also known as "Aunt T" to my first cousins, and as "Thelmoo" to her Sista Ruby, and best girlfriend, my second Mama, Ms. Helen Knox; and to my Daddy, Mr. Frederick Huffman Alcorn, who instilled the value of listening, observing, and studying what is going on in my surroundings as critical to the accumulation of self-understanding.

I love u

To the ***Bloods*** Southeast Asia

Preface

In the study this work is based upon, I set out to explore the function of *habitus* as it concerns self-actualization regarding learning and academic success among a small group of Black African American, bi-multi-racial males. There was this *undergirding interest* to see if there was an awareness among these men of their manly inclinations, tendencies, predispositions relative to their quest and discipline for learning, to academically achieve, to be educated; i.e. in a seamless sense of masculinity amidst a quest for learnedness as a natural part of their sense of manliness and sexuality. Habitus, as the conveyor of dispositions, inclinations, and tendencies, I thought could be the construct with which to shelter and reveal being as man and being educated as the fabric of manliness.

What I discovered was that although the Nigerian born participant was the only one that confessed to being directly aware and embracing of *the educated – manly self* as one, all the other participants became curious about this, as they reflectively came to realize the presence of manliness in their quest for learnedness, were in fact one. In other words, as all participants proceeded during their respective interview session they demonstrated astuteness about how their racialized-masculinity and manhood inclination and tendencies were in fact present in their quest for learnedness, education, and understanding. The perspectives they presented accounted for this, in analytical collaboration and integration with the literature.

I learnt that these men sanctioned their ethnic-cultural heritages as being an important – relevant part of their lives, as part of a diverse society. Moreover, that they endorsed education as life-long natural part of their lives that was not controlled and mandated via institutional requirements, but believed as essential to their existence and contribution to society. Education it seems is psychological and social-culturally woven throughout their sense of masculinity, manhood, and sexuality, i.e., one can be learned and sexy at the same time, one does not have to exclude the other, or cancel out the other. In conjunction, these men of color were concerned about the "Stereotype Threat" named and evidenced by Hall (1990), not just for themselves but also among their ethnic-cultural brethren.

Courtenay's (2000) study regarding how constructions of masculinity influenced men's differentiated approaches to health and well-being, helped me to realize in the analysis of participants' response, the role that social construction played in the defining, developing, and enactment of their masculinity, manhood, and sexuality, and the influence of factors such as ethnic-cultural, race, social-economic status, and cultural capital, contributed to that social construction. Very importantly, this included the social construction of world view, and respect for education as being centric in their lives. So, can the social constructions of masculinity influence men's differentiated approaches to education? Do factors such as race, the persistence of institutional racism, social-economic wherewithal, ethnic-cultural affiliation, attitudes and efforts involving degrees of participation in learning activities, influence the social construction of one masculinity, manliness, and sexuality?

I would argue yes, that this is not a leap, as literacy regarding the importance of health and well-being is intimately tied to one's sense, cultivation, and habited accumulation of self, within one's social-gendered-racialized skin, in a culturally coveted biological and cognitive intra-interactive merger.

Table of Contents

Prelude

*What many men today are missing is themselves, the
complex and unique experience of self that has been
rerouted and suppressed in the name of work, war,
and the arduous task of "being a man." This mandate
to repress or obliterate anything and everything ex-
pansive or off the grid has defined generations, so
much so that most men cannot even perceive the ex-
tent to which they have been robbed (Walker, p. 5,
2004).*

What sista Walker most disturbingly and insightfully declares and
points to is the question: when the hell do you get to yourself with all that
other social-gendered-manning up this and that stuff, that is already laid
out there and for you? You know you can get in your own way and not
even know it, because you are "manning up" to status quo. Then to there
are those unconscious, conscious practices and strategies among those
folks who are purposefully trying to do it, that is, intentionally read and
status you as some kinda Black African American or racially mixed blend-
ed radical, ungrateful thug, or an unpatriotic so and so. Of course, in all
this so-called manly declaration and heterogeneously sanctioned innuen-
does there is the need to work on avoiding backfiring in our own face, that
includes, most certainly yours truly. Under such historically pressured
social ascription, the consideration and pursuit of defining and enacting
progressive Black masculinities, manhood, and sexuality (Mutua, 2006), is
a moving target among us if you want in. But get in we must.

Most certainly, this is true in the area of gaining an education that for
all intent and purpose should be the fabric of our-self. What I am talking
about is the seamless merger of masculinity, manhood, and sexuality, (the
physical, the phrased in maturity, collaborating with the sexual responsibility); like being joined at the hip and the mind. Put another way, what I
am saying is a seamless merger where working on being learned is the
fabric of a self-gendered existence that is progressively defined and ethi-
cally sustained by multicolored men as: non-sexist, anti-racist, interculturally literate, and not stuck in some heterogeneously old timey shit. Like
Isley brothers sang - "I... (weeee) got work to do."

Early Testimony

*Like professor poet brotherman Sekou Sundiata
spoke-sang – "Somewhere in America tonight there are
those loving the past just so long as it ain't history."*

Among others, un-under-knowingly, my existence was silently and
sometime more loudly gendered and racialized after birth as I-we came
into the view our history of becoming; and I of course had no words or
thoughts for it. (As a side but important note - I do recall my Aunt Bert, in
an earnest attempt to warn her son, my 1st cuz Arnett, off from becoming
an early daddy, you need to "play the field." While my Mama planted some
kinda unknown boogie man seed in my head that prompted a reflex action
leading to my jumping up, and thus I did not have any kind of you know
what intimacy, until I was just past eighteen years of age).

School learning, family and neighborhood life was useless in this regard. Useless in the sense that I was not consciously aware enough to put
the two together in both social-cultural - historical proximity; race and
gender, that is. But, I did come to sense us and we-ness that I was wrapped
in. I believe that I was acting on inner impulse with sexuality taking the
lead. I fostered roles from my parents who were beautiful dark brown and
lighter brown skinned, both worked outside the home, but the cooking
was primarily done by my father, while both engaged in cleaning our
home, with me learning my chores as responsibility. I sought to emulate
social-behavioral roles from older jitter-bug homeboys in my neighborhood and that of my cuz's north Philly project dwellings.

Both Mama and Daddy spent quality time-tending to my Grandma
Agnes, Daddy's mama, who was home-bound. Daddy was a boarding
house baby resident from Baltimore at one time. But, to announce, from
segregated neighborhoods of North, South, West Philly, and Germantown,
I witnessed, felt, and socially-psychologically digested the ritual of everyday working woman/man; to include church-going, strong civic manners,
neighborhood-community compassion - street and police alertness, a
respectful cooperation. For instance, my Mama was a neighborhood block
chairperson. *"Hello Freddy, Hello Mr. Wellman;" "Hi Mr. Knox, "Freddy, how
you doing;" "Hey Ms. Highsmith, Hi Freddy, How's your Mama doing?"
"Good x-cross country running the other day Freddy, Thank you, Mr. Highsmith." "Fred Alcorn, I know your Mama would want you to keep up on*

your grades better than this," "Yes Mr. Young, she would." (Mr. Young was one of two physical educational - health teachers, and athletic team coaches. They lived in the same segregated neighborhoods of West Philly that we did).

My evolving discovery of being raced and gendered simultaneously, was initially more sharply brought into focus and awareness during my very brief hiatus down south at a "Black" traditional college; where ROTC was mandatory for two years during early years of the Vietnam War, along with a standing threat that if you fell before a C/2.0 GPA average you would be drafted right off campus. This was in writing and told to me verbally in a one on one meeting with the ROTC commandant. I had a number of these one on one meetings because I refused to go to military ROTC classes and scheduled formations in uniform. I was one trifling student, I have always been unsettled and resistant to organizational cultural systems and standard operating procedures. (My best friend homeboy, who is presently a teacher coach in the Baltimore school district, informed me that not long after my departure a series of campus protests occurred against mandatory ROTC among traditional "Black" colleges, as we socially referred to them during that time).

The educational experience at Norfolk State College, the fall of 1967, in a setting of predominately Black educators, administrators, military instructors, and students of all shades, inaugurated my senses with all kinds of wonderment about possibilities that I was not yet ready to process nor recognize. But unbeknownst to me the social-cultural construction of self and reality sent me off on a totally different trajectory where I began to realize the racial-gendered particularities of me and my home-boy's existence. (And by the way, as a side note just so you know, a number of Historical "Black Colleges and Universities" are conservatively toned, particularly when it comes to the intersected topic of race/ethnicity/gender, social-economic inequities, and social justice, Dr. Boyce Watkins, 2015).

This episode in my social realty, launched the quest to deconstruct my existence while still experiencing it in relationship with self and others. I began to do, think, critique, wonder and be anxious about, and perform while being more purposefully cognize about myself as a Black man becoming; regarding forward directional thought and imagination in contemplation and study for enhanced learnedness and purpose. I did this in view and pursued understanding based upon what historian John Hope Franklin declared as, "America's false start." A false start that a great number of European Americans, people of color among them, believe and when surveyed pooled, indicated, and thereby denied, the advent of any tampered with conditions and returns for themselves.

With the Vietnam experience among my brotha's self-declared and recognized themselves as "Bloods," I began to say out loud with others, and critique my existence, observations, and experiences in the historical-contemporary context of my ethnic-cultural point of reference group regarding our psychohistorical and materialistic circumstance, and peculiarities. All this was under the public perceptions of how I/we were being looked upon, and how we looked upon ourselves. My emotions, anger, and intuitive mind, became newly attuned to social-political contradictions and rights to self-empowerment beyond sexual and physical prowess, and male-centered tantrums such as I didn't get my way. (Perhaps in youth the informed good-lookin' out up-bring that my parents, family elders, adult neighbors, and extended significant others, engaged in with me was their attempt to give me a calmer place at figuring things out on the run as was needed. *Asante* (thank you) for that).

Understand that things about race in my growing up time and even years after were not audible nor cognitive to me. I don't remember hearing it directly as it was concealed relative to in the group term Negro, the unspoken social taboos and socially cultural awkward interactions (the emphasis not placed on the action), in so-called school integrated space. Here we meant one another daily for school hours then went back to our racial-social and class segregated neighborhood enclaves. So race to me was this under named presence, (like James Baldwin said No Name in the street) that was experienced-perceived via differentiation marked by phenotype, clothing, language-behavioral styles, temperament, your assigned - associated academic track frame of mind and reference, and construed social reality, that you carried around with you. (Habitus)? In other words, race-gender-sexuality, and social economic class differentiations, were viewed in relationship and in association with other things, relative to physical and social proximity to sources and people of authority and power, and sources sought and found to experience self-empowerment.

Certainly, I others of my friends and peers experienced male unspoken pressure and anxiety about manning up that was emotionally laden and time consuming, along with sexual harassment bullying, particularly, in jr. high school space, if you attempted to help one be any kind of a serious student. The social assumption floating around was that you were a punk, sissy, or some kinda smart guy if you engaged in study. In a capitalistic heterogeneous dominated society, there has been the psychological pressure for manliness to connect economic wherewithal with social persona; the dollar and materialistic got-ness of it. I mean manliness, masculinity, and sexuality are literally wore like a suit tailored to meet the scope and nature of racialized-gendered; assimilatory heterogeneous demands and taunts of expectations. Then to there is the advent of experiencing confidence and trust that you can compete, struggle, succeed, work through it...the racialized gendered contradictions. Eventually, many who turned out to be my closet friends, wondered into organizing themselves (I among them) into an all-male home-made Black fraternity called Kappa Phi Delta, (K, Phi, D), as did others to include the sista's. This I believe in retrospect somewhat warded off social demons of Jim Crow segregation - racialized gendered societal social differentials, neighborhood gitter-bugging, public school academic tracking. Black African American culture it seems formed degrees of social-cultural insularity. I do believe, in some ways social-cultural development and outlook as Black African American, bi-multi-males, among folks of people of color, can liked to being situated on a diving board extended out-over a pool of assimilatory racialized-gender-class and stereotyped, "body scripted" expectations/demands, via "mainstream culture" in this country. I contend that our persona, socialized development, and world view, are trespassed upon by race, intersecting with phenotype, gender, masculinity, manhood, and social-economic circumstance. As Jackson, II, (2005), explained/asserted,

> *Socially, the body facilitates the perpetuation of ascriptive devises used to assign meanings to ingroups and outgroups; it serves to jog the personal memories of cultural interactants, to remind them visually of the constitutive (power to assign) discourses that provide form and structure to their social cognitions about racialized bodies.*

Jackson went on to comprehensively explain how the action of ascription is applied and supplied by body during intra-interpersonal interactions, which is treated discursively like text, interpreted and read by interactants. Put another way, the racialized gendered body phenotype, social-cultural in-group and out-group's experiences, and frame of reference, act collaboratively in pronounced and subtle meaning making ways through the ascription of body type, that is used discursively from topic to topic, situational setting to setting. A key point here is the power, i.e., the financial wherewithal, knowledge and news making-presentation, and political-legal clout, relative to the historical precedence of dominant inter-group power relations in U.S. society, and among historically western dominate nations period. In other words, to make things stick in people minds that forge habits, frame of reference rationalizing, about what is being said, claimed, of eventful occurrence by whom about who - among what ethnic-culture group(s) of people concerned. In this case I am speaking to and about multicolored men, brown, black, bi-multiethnic, of varying shades of complexions, orientations and experiences, relative to their social-cultural reality, with respect to their equality of rights.

I came to know that, and as did my cousin, homeboys, other kinfolks and among peers, that we lived and moved back and forth in and out of primarily Black folk's neighborhoods, in Philadelphia, while witnessing European American ethnics, Jewish, Italian, German, Polish inter-ethnics owning the stores in my neighborhood, and the supermarket directly behind my row house home. (No ill thought in mind or intended). For instance, we knew to stay out of or moved quickly through the neighborhood called "Little Italy" off of Gerald Ave. It was just where our heads were at in those days.

In the vicinity of my neighborhood in the Northern part of West Philly, eventually we had one African American grocery store deli – owned and operated by Mr. Cane and family, down the street and around the corner. Prior to that in the fifties there were Black barbershops intimately dug into the lower part of a row house but mostly on street corners. Very importantly, there were Black women owned beauty parlors in my neighborhood at main street locations, and in backrooms off kitchens. I recall spending time with my Mama at her "beauty appointments," as they were called when I was younger. I do recall a Chinese family who had a laundry in the lower part of their home, there was a beaded covered door entrance inside the store that someone would emerge from when you entered the store; an intercultural encounter. You could look through and see into some of their living space. Things were so intimate and face to face back then. There was this constant experiencing of one another's presence. I learned and enjoyed making runs there for the short time I got to know my Daddy to get his shirts, before he passed. (My eyes cloud with the fog of tears).

Integration back then essentially amounted to passing through European American neighborhoods on the way to another segregated Black neighborhood South or North Philly to visit relative and friends. Integration occurred for me when I visited Dr. Louis A. Chase, the interculturally astute Jewish doctor who delivered me and was our home/office visit family doctor, or when we went to Gimbel Brothers, Lit Brothers, or Straw-bridge and Clothier department stores, all European American owed. (Where at one-point Mama could not try on the clothes for fitting and by my birthright I as well). Then there was the street market in South Philly full of fresh fruit, meat, bread, etc. vendors, European American owed. None of this, to repeat, none this was even hinted to me and other of my friends, and cousins of my age. And that to me is the scary thing about this thing called integration, segregation, and of course at the top of the A list, assimilation, you subconsciously associate these things in forming your view of social reality relative to your place in it. The ability, motivation, and urgencies to critique and respond to issues of what was going on around me, before I came in direct contact with the physical, cultural, and spiritual world beyond where I was, and of course the dominant political power relations of it all, did not start to emerge, or I should say dribbled out of me, as noted previously, upon my departure from the neighbor-hood.

In October 1963, my first year at Overbrook High School in West Philly, James Baldwin, writer and social activist had a talk with teachers and he said this: "*The paradox of education is precisely this – that as one begins to become conscious one begins to examine the society in which he is being educated*". In direct view of this I argue that --- an assimilated education and process of schooling does not prompt nor help you to become criti-cally conscious of the society in which you are being educated about until you start tripping over societal contradictions about your existence, in this case I'm referring to Black African American, bi-multi-racialized males.

This to me most certainly includes the intimate and needed cultivat-ing merger of one's social gendered existence and sense of sexuality with becoming progressive and learned. Hence, the more I and ***among*** my friends and peers became aware of manly pursuits, in heterogeneously ascripted gendered self-awareness, the more to some degrees, education and classroom learning and academic achievement became disconnected from our-my daily view in the construction who we were being and be-coming at this point in our lives. Very importantly, there was the social-political, perceptional, and behavioral overt and subtleties of segregation – integration struggles occurring all around us.

Let me be clear, I am not saying that education, classroom learning, and academic achievement were misnomers, as it concerns having no place in our lives. I/we knew and "felt" ☺ (I think old schoolers get my drift), the seriousness of education and attentive participation in schooling to engage in self-opportunities to learn and grow early on. For instance, throughout segregated Black neighborhoods I frequented in West Philly and among North Philly row house streets and projects, from elementary through jr. high school, I witnessed-heard parent-extended family member **homework calls and yells**, from porches, along with street hunt and find walks and authoritative struts, and siblings carriers of get your butt home now, with I'm gonna tell Mama, Daddy, or who-ever was in care-charge, warning messages. What I am saying is that as one begins to realize (become conscious as Mr. Baldwin may put it) existence in societal experiences, there is the critical need for cultivating attitudes and understanding relevant to the seamless merger of masculinity, manhood, and sexuality and learnedness.

As I have worked and talked among Black African American, bi-multi-racial males, there is seemingly this same unknowingness and more pronounced disconnect, regarding manly or gendered inclinations and dispositions regarding how they self-actualize as males specific to working on the seamless merger between becoming learned and working to academically achieve, as one with evolving self-masculinity, manhood, and sexuality. For me and others among my friends and peers, one piece of masculinity, manhood, and sexuality, was in the gym, on sports teams, in competition, and running the streets with swagger, which got traded-off each and every time I entered the classroom.   Manhood was self-consciously checked at the door of the classroom period as it became a predisposition that needed to stay with me. (I carried this attitude with me to college on a sports scholarship and lasted as long as *two-cents*. At one point my track coach walked into my health education class and asked the professor how my homeboy and I were doing. To this she stated well, "Jackson is doing alright, Alcorn is just occupying space"). It has taken me over thirty years to really initiate working on undoing this fragmentation and disconnect. When it comes to being a man, establishing your gender orientation period, the seamless merger with creating the educated self, in the broadest sense of the word, as part of the human fabric of who we are, there are those among who are simply punking out or, too frustrated and disaffected to try, or is it simply not being put out there in cultural context?

In general, I contend that this is not part of Western societal cultural orientation and approaches in the process of schooling and education, i.e., a seamless merger with masculinity, manhood, and sexuality within group ethnic-cultural context and within the structuring of social reality. Very saliently, let me preface all of the preceding discussion by this thesis caveat: *It is within a societal pressure cooker-comfort zone assimilatory process, that Black African American, bi-multi-racial males have to negoti-ate.* It is like we have to lower our cultural profile in public sphere. You know, when growing up in Philly my parents and among my friends and peer parents, significant adult relative others, and neighborhood elder's period, that there was always this concern about us young boys keeping a low profile in the streets, and in public sphere. This was a major *testy stressful bone of contention* socializing point, for my Mama, Daddy, Ms. Helen, Mama-best girlfriend, and my second Mama, and Black elder's period.

In a racialized gendered society among whose citizens there are those who are still instinctively susceptible to identifying with pathological and assimilated stereotypes and the profiling amongst Black African American, bi-multi-racial males, the implication can prove to tantamount to intellec-tual, cognitive, and physical suicide, *if* I may be so dramatic. There is, for instance, this hegemonic bad dude archetype that is still pervasively allur-ing among a heterogeneous European American culturally dominant soci-ety, that is old-school and non-progressive.

In this book voices speak unapologetically about grappling with the psycho-historical complexity and issues of racialized masculinity and eth-nic-cultural heritage among Black African American, bi-multi-racial males relative to the norming and storming of masculinity, manhood, and sexu-ality. The multicolored young adult men in this book were part of a genera-tion born post-civil rights overt struggle/protest, coming of age during the so-colorblind anti-affirmative action anything, and conservative blown back response under Reagonomics and Bush *Era.* From these presidential administration's, there was and continues to be in complex ways, and coached in innocent patriotic stances, a debunking of social-economic-liberatory civil and legislative advocacy. (You know what is said about assumptions). That along with the racial-gendered coded fear mongering rehetoric, and I must say, a privatizing push of higher education learning that contributed to today's student ill-affordability - debt crisis issues.

The men in this book are on a similar path of thoughts, experiences, and perceptions about race-gender in their lives and the world around them, join others of similar mindset and body of experiences. I heard hurt, pride, love of la familia and the pursuit of learnedness in their voices while simultaneously critiquing the multiculturally complex society that they are imbued in, which among who members for the most part, per-ceive and believe the state and articulation masculinity, manhood, and sexuality is simply....... gender-universal.

Say What!?

As Vershawn Ashanti Young (2007) most forthrightly stated, the full achievement of Brown (1954 decision striking down school segregation), "was deferred because the progress toward making race not matter stopped when the focus shifted from color to performance."

With the introduction of civil rights laws, the integration of theirs, mine, and other multicolored men's - masculinity, manhood, and sexuality came under wider public eyeballing via various societal institutions, and intimate social circumstance. This can be contrasted to the physical-psychologically overt cultural cleansing conditions under chattel - caged slavery, and further oppressive and suppressive conditions under Jim Crow segregated social-racialized society *de jure* and *de facto* contractual arrangements. (I invite you to read the work by Scott Poulson-Bryant entitled: *Hung, A Meditation on the Measure of Black men in America*, (2005).

In others words, race, racialized unconscious/conscious perceptions and judgments were/are no longer confined to our phenotypical markings, alerting folks to our self-recognized or not, ancestral ethnic connections to Africa and (forced-forged), non-immigrant developed ethnicity in this country. I assert that such perceptions and judgements are unconsciously/purposefully used to debunk and relegate us through outright ascription. But to performance evaluation and perceptional tastes of public and private venues, which provide opportunities to conceal and justify racialized-gendered judgmental-ness and stereotyping under performance as technical competency and its antecedents. Said plainly, race is still there/here, *it just ain't said out loud and plainly.* But yet in still, there are those folks who take to social media tweets to and Facebook with taunts and insults. For instance, most abstruse to discern, there are the mean spirited digs made among certain university college students which embed racialized micro-aggressions to be discovered within their course evaluative remarks and ratings among professors and instructors of color.

With the invention and propagating social-economic, psychological, physical-biological, and political, effects of race and racism, we have gone from one dichotomized extreme of admittance-justification to - *it no longer ain't so and I can't see it.* I invite you to give this a read, consider or most directly contemplate how, the un-under stated hard-headed *normalcy* of racialized gendered heterogeneity unrealized, in denial, and/or saturating in blissful ignorance,continues to be perpetuated in a multiculturally diverse society in dire need of accessing and then realizing its' humanity.

Or is it simply - a man is a man is a man?

This ink is for them and their brethren.

To the Bloods of Southeast Asia

Definition of Key Terms and Concepts used therein.

I have chosen to provide the definition section of strategic terms and concepts used, placed upfront, as a point of reference. *Asante* (Thank you).

Habitus: Habitus, is a "system of lasting transposable dispositions," inclinations, and tendencies in choice making, the integration of past experiences with present situations, and conditions to assist in what style of behavioral action to engage in (Bourdieu, 1971, p. 83). Habitus functions "as a matrix of perceptions, apperceptions (conscious synthesis awareness) whereby new experience is merged with the residuum or past ones to make possible the "achievement of infinitely diversified tasks" (p.83). Among styles of engaging in masculine attitudes, behaviors, language, and performance practice, habitus stands as the major determinant, i.e., social player.

Bourdieu (1991) maintained that a person's habitus is affected most by what is compatible with the person's past experiences or options made available within socioeconomic, materialistic (physical surroundings), institutional arrangements, and present circumstance. Culture, racialized gender, ethnicity, hegemonic masculinity are all informants of habitus.

Swartz (1997) drew on the work of Bourdieu to remind educators that "not all social experiences teach people what may or may not be possible; agency is intertwined with and perhaps limited by past experiences." This is particularly relevant to hierarchal caste society in a capitalistic dominant society such as the U.S., where social-economic status affects social-psychological and cognitive views and perceptions of self in relationship to others, (world view - interpersonal and intra-inter group power relations and sense of empowerment).

Black African American: This concept is used to refer to United States forced-forged citizens of African ancestry, (called Black American if you so choose), who are descendants of African slaves who were kidnapped, forced into slavery, experienced ethnic-cultural erasure, brutality, and forced assimilation marked by access to limited controlled literacy. Use of the group ethnic – cultural name African American or Black American is still controversial in the literature (Salmon, 1996, Koroma, 2003). As discussed among Black or African Americans, there is preference and rationalization regarding how to self-reference themselves ethnically. For the purpose of this study I will use the terms Black American and African American interchangeably, and in combination of one another as a seamless but social-political-psychological challenging merger. (*It is crowded up in here, say's I to myself*).

Black African American Masculinity:

> *Depending on who you ask, the black man, as an American concept at least, was invented sometime around 1633, around the time—less than twenty years after the first Dutch ships brought Africans to pick tobacco and rice on the Southern plantations of the New World—that a Virginia court decided that any child born to a slave mother was also, alas, considered a slave (Poulson-Bryant, 2005, p.16).*

Black masculinity involves self-perceived – accumulated socialized ways and perceptions of expressing one's gender-sexuality relative to ethnic-culture, the pseudo social political construct of race, to include the phenomenon of "racialized gender." Gender identity involves the consideration of masculine and feminine assigned role behaviors and the emerging characteristics generated from those socialization efforts, within an ascribed heterosexual dominant society. These include but are not limited to: Black English/Standard English styles of non-verbal and verbal interpersonal communication; the use of more standardized English diction, assimilated behavioral posturing and attitudes; and the development and use of strategic adaptive styles of revealing and performing attributes and characteristics believed to be manly, in response to perceived and real ecologically raced-based social circumstances. Richardson (2007) told us that Black masculinity in the U.S. has a hierarchal geographic dimension to it, as he examined the understanding of "black male southerners as inferior and undesirable models of black masculinity within such racial hierarchies based on geography" (pp. 2-3); while Wallace (2002) revealed subtle, complex, and provocative challenges of "Black Male Specularity" (p.19), i.e., mirror/photographic lens portraying, seeing, and perceiving of Black males via the refractive lens of a camera that portrays mirrored characteristics to be reflected on within one's mind's eye.

Clatterbaugh (1990) said that describing masculinity is a difficult task. For example, he stated that there is a question, gender-wise, regarding what men are, i.e., what constitutes being a man. What further complicates describing and/or defining the construct of masculinity is identifiable social reality, political, and psychological experiences of member connected with ethnic cultural group cultures within a racialized U. S. society. Gilmore in his book entitled: *Manhood in the Making, Cultural Concepts of Masculinity,* (1990), appeared to set the construct of manhood within cultural concepts relative to masculinity. One could then question – is manhood making, i.e., development and representation a part of masculinity? The implication here and with Clatterbaugh is that masculinity is representative of something broader, more comprehensive or sophisticated than the term manhood. Then there is masculinity and manhood discussed within feminist culture relative to term the patriarch, which is described and discussed as societal systematic male power domination of and over women.

Bi-Multi-Racial: Are individuals *who* are the children of an "interracial parent lineage," (Grant & Ladson-Billings, (Eds), 1997, p. 31). Interracial parent(s) can themselves hold bi-multi-racial ethnicities from their parents, grand-parents, great-grand-parents, and intergenerational lineages. Bi-multi-racial individuals experience and negotiate the effects of not fitting into demographic categorical or societal this or that ascribed categorical markers of race, ethnicity, culture, class intersection.

"Progressive Black Masculinities:" Progressive Black Masculinities embodies and actively stands again social structures of domination; they are both antiracist and anti-sexist, affirm maleness and recognize the humanity in men. Still further, progressive black masculinities are not predicated based upon the subordination of others; "progressive black masculinities are men who take an active and ethical stance against all social systems of domination act" (Mutua, 2006, p.7), and who act in concert with others in activities against institutionalized racism, sexism, homophobia, heterosexism, and structural inequality that form and sustain systems of domination.

Intersectional Theory (Intersectionality): In her work on Critical Race Theory, Crenshaw (1986) coined the concept "intersectionality" as a methodological approach to comprehensive examination of how race, gender, and class oppression sources interact and intersect. This method avoids the trappings of the one phenomenon at a time either/or dichotomy of race or gender, race or class by viewing and studying multiple forces at work in *convergence.*

Multidimensionality Theory: Mutua (2006) explained that multidimensionality theory directed a focus on various and multiple social structures that oppress and constrain the agency (capacity) of individuals and groups in "uniquely distinctive ways" (p.23), relative to the ability to develop and make choices. A principal ideology of multidimensionality is that a male of color could be privileged by heterosexual patriarchal gender membership, while at the same time be oppressed, or feel the effect of racialized gender and ethnic-culture.

Racialized Gender: Few (2007) defined and discussed racialized gender as a concept that embodies the critical analysis as the concurrent intersection of race and gender processes on individuals, families, and communities. Racialized gender regards studying the effect of social-cultural experiences, sexually ascribed expectations, and self-societal awareness of racial makers on the individual concerned.

World View: Koltko-Rivera (2004) said that world view "is a set of assumptions about physical and social reality that may have powerful effects on cognition and behavior" (p. 3).

Sue (1975) and Jackson (1975) define world view as how a person perceives self in relationship to the world view, nature, organizational institutions, and groups of people. (Sources and perception of self-empowerment are influenced by world view) World view is highly correlated with a person's social-cultural upbringing, education, and life experiences.

Psychohistorical Experiences: is concerned with the study and suppositions regarding the impact of historical events on people (DeMause, 1975).

Self-Action Research: is a technique of engaging in self-analysis to include self-interrogation. I am suggesting *turning the action* in action research on one's self in order to find techniques with which to more effectively self-actualize positive healthy ways, relative to past-present social-situational challenges and conditions in a U.S. multicultural society.

Survival Thrust: Generally speaking, survival thrust are ways in which an individual - group of people drive or orient themselves to continue; that is, reasoned ways, habits, ideological basis for purpose of existence given circumstance and condition of materialistic, nature, and social-economic - cultural reality (Adapted from Baldwin, 1992).

Chapter One
Background Script
Layin' in the cut

July 25, 2014

Dear Mr. Baldwin, This new century has already turn 14+ corners. Dear sir, I am so glad to finally make your acquaintance. I missed and I miss you both. My sincere apologies but I did not find you until the 1990's. By then I had experienced service in a war zone, being racialized by police enforcement officers twice while in service to this government's country, and one of those times involved my being placed in a room stripped and served down to my underwear, I was too tired to protest as I was on a 7/11 leave from Nam. I simply placed these events in the recesses of my mind. But out of the blue or gray, there they were just staring me in the face. I dam near starting crying of embarrassment and anger for such rude treatment, as I remembered how dutiful I had behaved while sneering on the inside.

But, I know as among a ton of European Americans and a conservative supportive cast among people of color would say, they were just doing their job, stopping blaming us White folks, and the presence of our culture for things not going right, fix Black culture, that what you really need to do. This is what I have read, heard out loud on the news, for instance, like from this European American women pundit commenter, who was a former teacher education in an urban area. She literally stereotyped Black culture as a culture that blames what she said "Whitey," for group problems and challenges, live and in living color with a finger up in the brotha guest's face. I do believe Mr. Baldwin that there has festered in this country among certain European Americans and their cast of assimilated allies, a social resentment that has fed their attitudes, behavioral responses and reactions, and informs their political decision making mentality, regarding any form of protest for social justice and calling out loud attention to racialized contradictions in U.S. society. I clearly now understand the term "eat it."

One thing that I learned from the Black African American elders I grew up around, witnessed, and read about was that over time, they knew how to give critical analysis, discuss contradiction, and give praise and appreciation regarding this country all within the same what comes to mind cultural peopled framework. They are not, and I still see this capacity among Black folks, just either-or thinker, or with us or against us posturers. There is a big difference between running-around blaming folks as in thought-less complaint than it is in critically calling out social injustice as democracy in error.

I unnervingly wonder with prongs of anxiety and disappointment if we have entered a modern day Willie Lynching, gun fighter street executions, where the meat flesh of young Black males is left lying in the street in un-spoken protest, in the face of juried members and prosecution that sanction the death of young Black men, at the hands of the nation's marshal Dillon's; gun smoke gets in your eyes clouds your mind like "the shadow."

These and other thoughts and experiences such as walking away from a scholarship funded education at a traditional "Black" College, Norfolk State, really added to my upset-ness. You see to know that you existed and I was unaware, that you had performed such insightful under-realized human civil rights advocacy and eye-popping critiques of Black people's lives in struggles, contradiction, and protest, in written and spoken voice, during such heralding times, really pisses me off. Why hadn't I been introduced to you through my schooling, or was it simply that I wasn't paying attention, which could have been the case. But yet I now know what I didn't back then, that we were steeped in segregated dominant cultural book learning and linear old school teaching strategies, and as in jr. high the use of humil-iation as punishment. I can't help but continuously attempt to re-imagine myself back then, in the sixties and seventies, possessed with some degree of cardinal knowledge of your existence and literary work, and how and if it would have veered the path that I was on.

The fact that I was bliss in my ignorance does nothing to appease a case of teenage day-dreaming, assimilated schooling, be tix and between racial-ized segregation right in front of integration. There was though, I must ad-mit, my constant preoccupation with sex-uality (hours in front of the mir-ror and corn starching my shirts), and the pursuit of neighborhood sista's; neighborhood being in whatever Black segregated neighborhood I was in. I was in a word running the streets, as much as I could get away with – with-out upsetting my Mama or Aunt Bert, my cousin Arnett's Mama, to one point of bushing with jitterbugging, as not in the dance, but in the slang way for gang or as the elders would say, hard-heading. Mama once said to me sports and running saved my butt. So your work Nobody Knows My Name, , more notes of a native son (1961), really grabbed me and won't let go. It is fortunate that I worked on trying not to envision what amounts to me as carrying around manhood like a concealed weapon, I hate bullying period, and to me taunting people because of raced looks, cash flow situa-

tions, sexuality, is bullying. In angry moments it calls me to pay attention. Because of the way I left the neighborhood, in yet another time of war, like so many others, I am like a kid in a man's body still trying to figure out past-tense the meaning of and conditions of those earlier 50's and 60's experiences.

Segregation was living like somebody pulled the shades down over my eyes. But, then to the cultural insularity of Black neighborhood s in Philly and down south in Castle Hayne-Wilmington North Carolina, gave me a front row seat as an edifying witness to working women and man grounded in Dr. Rev. Richard Allen's AME churches and various other churches of spirituality in the Black community. With all my faults I do believe at the very least I am anchored in decency and civility, that surrounds my critique of democracy's, concerns about the equality of humanity, opportunity, and protest anger. I know that I have much work to do.

I came to know that as a Black male of African ancestry (a Negro male) via slavery, that historically and contemporarily, I must weigh in on the presence and constant reshaping of subtle and pronounced European American dominant social structures, such as, educational institutions (by their strong control and sway of political, capitalistic economic, media resources and peopled personal sources). This has become part of the daily contemplation on my existence. It is no happen-stance and simple such individuals wherewithal that intergroup power arrangements stand the way they are, with a hunch among certain somebodies hiding within the shadow of those arrangements in claimed innocence beyond reproach taking pot shots at social justice and economic inequality protest efforts. They do so while standing in seduction to integration's declarations-and assumed normalcy of social – private intimacy; as the heir to social justice, civil rights, and the continued need to struggle for equality of opportunity in this multicultural nation-state.

I have come to the conclusion that I cannot afford to avoid jumping in on the occurrence of constitutional contradictions (a phrase jump to action by Frederick Douglass) that amount to me as equality of opportunity issues which are raced, gendered, and classed interwoven like twine. Factual and potential pull over beat-down, abusive threat power gritting (stare down's and glace looks) and/or death by law enforcement in this country of Black African American, bi-multi-racial males, occupies my social reality, like a game of dead-block on Frazier street. I don't care how much training they take law enforcement police through, there is difficulty in providing training for any person that brings racialized gendered baggage and/or conserva-

tive socialized manliness and mentality period, that merged with either you/me, this/or that, us vs. them, attitudes and below anger psychics in with them. They need to be screened out at the front door like Mama's rule, don't bring no cussing, fussing, or confusion into this house, on the porch, or on this landing. Not happening. Seems no different than among – I say among – the nasty White dudes we faced in the military.

Mr. Baldwin I am not simply running around wanting to make things up, or say that I am not grateful for citizen-membership in this country, that I have birthright and invested in, but when it comes to race, gender-sexuality, class, religious spirituality choices, the somebody's among certain ethnic-group persuasions are always trying to make what's crooked straight, even when the facts are against them. Our self-interest and good will people in non-Western countries, are killing us, particularly in those continuous them-vs us scenarios, even when it is so obvious to democracy, that we were hooking up with the wrong regime, government leadership, class of rich folks. At any rate poor and struggling folks got no relief and most times get played on like Malcom in the middle.

So, in a sense that maybe, though time-wise saying this to you now, makes no sense, you contributed to saving my life Mr. Baldwin. Your work and gutsy living of sexuality-personhood that others placed you be tix and between (for their own sanity and this or that rationalizing), was beyond the pale standard of the American ideal of manhood and the cultural taboos within the Black community. It contributed to my eventually opening doors I had shut my mind's eye too long ago and ones that I never knew existed. Moving my lips in said thought out loud when they would have remained shut and in simplistic compliance. Subsequently, I say with all my heart and soul, thank you so much Mr. Baldwin, you have been my gateway to critiquing the man in me in the social reality of real time; to imaging myself more than what is expected and required of me in a complicated assimilatory otherness kind of democracy, with all its' materialistic and violently driven vices.

Yours truly,

Frederick Douglass Alcorn, Son Tate's grandson.

I read one of Mr. Baldwin's essays where he was talking about the controversial Black English argument and he said, "People evolve a language in order to be able to *describe* and thus *control* their circumstances, or in order *not to be submerged by a reality that they cannot articulate,* (and if they cannot articulate it then they are submerged)."

I do think that in part this is an act of realized or subconscious resistance, seeking purposefully to breathe, think, normalize an existence as not to get crunched and taken for granted.

Language (verbal, non-verbal, written) is that part of us we use to think and express our interpretation of the world and our experiences/existence in it. Turning a corner, one could apply this assertion in thinking about masculinity-manhood-sexuality making, in this case, among Black, African American, bi-multi-racial males. They, we, work at developing linguistic style and language ability in ways that describe, mediate, and manage the circumstances of our social reality; some of us bend backward in our thinking as an instructive posture for the present. The multicolored men that I talk with refused to be submerged in social-political and the social complexity of economic positionality and circumstance that they could not articulate. Entailed in their perspectives based upon the self-knowledge of themselves in the world and social reality, it was revealed how they live double conscious lives synthesized in guarded moments, where they are not just quiet by dispositional ways, but by frame of reference, (the body of information, knowledge, and experiences that are called upon in response to social reality and interpretation). As such, requiring them to work at carving out and negotiating predominately European American social, political, work, policed, and legislated spaces. They did not speak in any way that was accusing, but simply about reality as they perceived and experienced it in relationship to and with others people. Their insights are illuminated by Clark (2002) who said taken jointly that the concept Black masculinity brings forth an overabundance of impassioned, conflicted, and often at odds responses. Clark's assertion to me is analogous and in collaboration with Henry Louis Gates, Jr. (1997) authored work adeptly entitled: *"Thirteen Ways of Looking at a Black Man."*

This book revealed the autobiographical and deft social essays among Black males such as James Baldwin and Bill T. Jones regarding the racial gendered complexity, the contradictions, anxious moments, and successes of being a Black man; hence ways of looking at and perceiving Black African American males not as human beings mired in crisis. Yet, on the other hand, crisis issues of negative disproportionality in health, life expectancy, un-underemployment, school lateness, suspension, drop-out truancy numbers in school, incarceration, racial profiling, do stubbornly exist. It seems then when there is controversy involving a Black man, multicolored

men, there is always the danger of a sharp edged knife of criticism or stereotypical comments being unleashed, maybe that's why the men that I
talked with worked hard to blend but not bend to the ramifications and
unspoken expectation 's of what I call America's social cultural assimilatory contract.

Perhaps one could say there are those among Black and African American, bi-multi racial males, who are facing crisis but somehow alluding its'
devastating grief and consequence, which Jackson II and Hopson (2011)
provocatively asserted that there is this "debilitating pain that accompany
Black masculinity in America" (p. 3). Because no matter how successful
you are in this materialistic capitalistically controlled democracy, it is argumentative that the epidemiological related issues among Black African
American males in categories of health, mental health have been mani-
festing or more directly, festering, in this racialized gender hierarchical
society for centuries, (Crothers, (2008), Hall, 2006; and Watkins, 2012).
Now to be simply declared among some as erased, along with declaring
"The End of Racism" (D'Souza, 1996), joined by others who refer to themselves as "racial realist," with a sweep of European American and supporting cast of assimilated scholars, cultural pundits, and critics' hands.

Then again, there is the existence of the double standards thesis regarding race, sexuality, and class, among people in U.S. society which en-
genders a perceptional outlook from a public-private platform to comfortably view and interact with Black African American, bi-multi-racial males,
outside of entertainment, incarceration, the military, law enforcement, in
everyday life path crossing.[1]   This is the space Ellison, in his poignantly
complex book, *Invisible Man* (1952), told us that when a society is hin-
dered with peculiar historical stereotypical perceptions, dispositions, and
inclinations affected by race, this and that categories of gender status, and
ethnic-culture looked upon as physical makers, one can be rendered invis-

---

[1] Darron Smith (2012) argued that President Obama had to maintain a disciplined
composure not just as the Commander-in-Chief, but at the "risk of being perceived
as 'too black' and angry, even during times in the debates where it was necessary to
engage in assertive response" (p.2). Although the events were interpersonal and

intercultural most of the listening audience to include the predominantly European
American media representatives, would not acknowledge or admit out loud that
this was a mono-cultural public event, where so-called "mainstream rules" of
communication (universal) were the norm of expectation; hence, a double-
standard.

ible except in certain areas of human activities, circumstance, and conditions.

Fundamentally then, we can still be placed in otherness, wrapped safely in declaration 's of colorblind and all-ness diversity, as to relegated to a wannabe form of liberatory public space. Requiring, if we wish to continue beyond the necessity of autopilot biological function, for us to engage in private in head strategizing regarding how act in public space; as what our masculinity, manhood, and sexuality amounts to are acceptable forms of assimilatory kinds of European American – Whiteness. But there is of course the right to reject such impositions that have been devised and exercised historically among Black African American, bi-multi-racial males, as sista Dr. Sherene Razack (1999) would say while, "looking White people in the eye."

People see you in society but don't understand certain of your dispositions, inclinations, views, and attitudes that seem to be uncharacteristically *ungrateful* for someone who as descended from slavery and Jim Crow de facto and de jure segregated time, that no longer exists as a visible representation seeable to the naked eye, having been congressionally, begrudgingly anointed with civil rights. Begrudgingly, because for some unexplainable reasons the only way to cope or fathom this is by declaring the "end of racism" or we *is* now in post-race American times. Ellison did point out via his main character, that he was not complaining or protesting, but that this state of existence he admitted was "most often rather wearing on the nerves" (p.3). I don't know, but taking a wild guess perhaps he was alluding to hypertension.

Not to belabor the point, nor to imply that Black African American, bi-multi-racial males are ascribed, that is, assigned to crisis status, but to reiterate, there exists statistical categories of *negative* disproportionality relative to the health, well-being, employed/employable, education, incarceration, and social-economic status, that are salient and compelling to pay attention to. Put another way, studies, reports, and articles, that speak to the quality of life among Black African American males in U.S. society divulge qualitative and statistical evidence and perspective showing their disproportionate presence among negative health, life-expectancy, education, adjudication and adult incarceration, and un-underemployment social-cultural indicators (Centers for Disease Control & Prevention, 2010, Black, 1997, Davis, 1998, Gadson, 2006, Head, 2006, Johnson, 2010). One such eye-opening term coined years ago by Gibbs (1988), was the "new morbidity," life-threatening behavioral habitus among young Black males via homicide, suicide, accidents.

Along these same lines Rios (2009) had conducted a study arguing the negative disproportionate effects of incarceration among young Black and Latino males regarding the social-cultural construction of their masculine inclination and tendencies, and manhood practices. He claimed such experience has resulted in "the production of a hypermasculinity that obstructs desistance social mobility" (p. 150). Harris (2000) quoted in Rios (2009) defined hypermasculinity "as the exaggerated exhibition of physical strength and personal aggression that is often a response to a gender threat expressed through the physical (I would add psychological) and sexual domination of others" (p. 151). Rios contended that the criminal justice systems' "pipeline encourages expression of hypermasculinity by threatening and confusing young men's masculinity" (p.151). I concur and add that lack of legislative mandate and preparedness by state, local, and federal lawmakers and administrators, to more aggressively fund, plan, and conduct systemically reliable culturally responsive approaches to the full inventive *scope* and *nature* of what rehabilitation is supposed to mean, in a democratically multicultural cultural society such as ours, sustains and exacerbates this developmental phenomenon.

There is the impact of in head-self and societal tainting that needs to be recognized/weighed in on, as the result of the incarceration experience and/or general contact with the criminal justice system and law enforcement. Not to speak of the *injustice* racialized gender decision making that occurs within the justice system. The mind can take but so many images, commentaries, over-heard remarks, blank face staring, along with law enforcement police killing deaths and threat power behaviors, before it impacts our gender-making attitudes and behaviors about self and our chances in society to pursuit a quality of life existence, without distrustful general outlooks. Oh yeah, this is me with all my politeness, civil obedience, I do not trust police people, just as much as believe in their necessity. Yeah uh huh, somebody always trying to make their crooked look straight.

I have no problem saying that there have been many flames and sparks that have been and continues to be doused with self-doubt, ethnic-culturally racialized self-loathing, inward-outbound anger, and magical assimilatory acts of economic class escapism, among multicolored men throughout the communities in this country. Like Mystikal belts out – "you keep bumping me against the wall," *but you ain't seen bouncing back.*

Hargrow (2001), in an article discussing African American racial development, observed that African American men constitute 47% of African American people in the country, but hold fewer political positions of power. Next, although more African American men are attending post-secondary schools, their numbers are small. Hargrow said, "African American men suffer physically and psychologically," as it concerned health related issues (p.1). Parham and McDavis (1987) argued that despite the gains of civil rights and anti-discriminatory laws, Black males were at-risk in the categories of internal and external factors concerning life expectancy, un-underemployment, and raising suicide rates. Brother Head (2004) spoke about increased rates of depression and suicide among upwardly mobile Black men and social economically disadvantaged Black men, himself included in all this. For instance, Head stated that "Upwardly mobile Black men are confronted with the pressures of working in business and corporate structures dominated by Whites" (p.26). Moreover, he pointed out that "Black men must also realize that their success in the world of work is often tied to their ability to assimilate their values, behaviors, appearance, and life-styles into what the White culture deems legitimate" (p.26). Hence, it is implied that Black males must confront racialized gendered stress producing perceptions, thoughts, and circumstance regarding whether or not they are compromising their cultural selves, their sense of dignity, worth, empowerment, well-being-ness.

Parham and McDavis asserted that "Black men may feel a sense of internalized anxiety, anger, frustration, and resentment because of withheld promotions, dead-end jobs, lack of policy-making power, and the necessity for them to have a 'dual identity" (p.26). These authors argued that the identification, study, and realizations of these psychological factors and circumstance, hold implications for mental health practitioners in public schools, institutions of higher education, community based agencies, and social service agencies, and moreover, among parents of Black children. Lastly, the authors noted the underrepresentation of "Blacks" in mental health counseling as an issue.

Know that, the complexity and subtle day-to-day conditions under which Black African American, bi-multi-racial males construct and respond to their social realities does not occur in a social-economic and political vacuum. For instance, Hogan (2001) stated that a condition of acquiescence among "ordinary people exists in the form of positively supporting an unequal social and economic system" that he called a "culture of conformism of social consent" (p.1). Hogan argued that a disproportionately unequal distribution of national wealth exists, (further exacerbated by the latest recession), but people still acquiesce to this condition intellectually as well as practically. I mention this because this claimed condition of acquiescence exists in the face of dogmatic ideological reasoning involved in social everyday discourse.

This daily discourse contains stereotypical lexicon regarding people of color, women, and sexual minorities, relative to people's perception and construction of social reality amidst intergroup power relationships not readily recognized and/or simply denied, in historical and real-time. Hogan argued that "it seems likely that everyone in the United States, whether White or Black has a category of common beliefs about" Blacks in their lexical entry (single word meaning developing into a phrase) for "Black." This category might include, for example, "lazy" (pp. 120-121). [2]Rome (2004) in a study regarding the establishment of the Black male criminal stereotype, contended that negative stereotypes many people have of Black men as criminals were "created to a degree by the mass media" (p.1). Lexicon stereotype exists relative to individual and group stereotype threat (Steele & Aronson, 1995), and their stereotypical vulnerability.

According to Norguera (1997), rates of unemployment for males of African American descent "are higher now than they were 30 years ago" (pp. 2-3). Suicide and rates of depression are disturbingly on rapid rise among Black males (Poussaint & Alexander, 2000). Head, as cited previously, called the rise of depression among Black men a "silent epidemic," as depression largely goes mistreated, untreated, and unspoken about because of adherence to the *silent undeclared masculine I'm too tuff code* among males of African American descent. In this regard, Canada (1998) said that Black boys are "conditioned not to let on that it hurts. They are taught by coaches to play with pain." Still further, they "are told by parents that they shouldn't cry" (p. 11). Then to, they watch their heroes on the big screen getting punched and kicked and shot, and while the heroes might let out a groan or yell, they observe that they never cry (pp. 11-12). During my 60's growing up time in South, North, and West Philadelphia, PA, there were

---

[2] The author noted that the lexicon entry of lazy as a common belief out there in society in general but for the cognitive tendency toward "confirmatory bias) (the tendency among people to favor information that confirms their beliefs) (p. 121). In the case of confirmatory bias there stood the likelihood that Blacks or Mexicans being stereotyped as lazy, as the Hogan pointed out that, any person not doing his or her work is likely to be more important "than any number of persons doing their work—a point that does not affect Whites as there is no relevant lexicalized property that might be accessed to categorize them as "lazy" (p. 121).

those older teenage brother jitter-bugs who engaged in laugh-crying when in a fight and they were getting hurt in public (Alcorn, 1994). In the face of this, "what are the conditions under which we reproduce strong black men, self-respecting black men, self-regarding black men, self-loving black men, who recognize they're in a *kind of war"* (West, 2008, p. x)?

West's conscious Black man question/declaration is timely, as somehow my critical and oftentimes times disturbing reflection about war as sanctioned violence (James, 1996), intertwines itself with my evolving understanding of gender socialization, its definitions, beliefs, imaging, and enacting, in private places - public spheres. This includes knowledge regarding the mutilating tree and truck lynching of Black women, men, elders, and children in U.S. society. (The incontestable song "Strange Fruit" was transformed from the poem written by Abel Meeropol (1939), a White Jewish high school teacher in protest against the lynching of Black people occurring primarily in the South).

My thoughts are a daily ritual of fear, anger, redemption, and compassion. It is this reflection that raised my conscious mind to a renewed awakening regarding the subtle, alluring, and demanding presence/role that Black masculinity making plays in my life, and I would dare say among fellow African American/inter-ethnic males. That for us, there is politics and social-cultural and racial demands of cultural existence within a multicultural society that is racially-gendered, polarized, and hierarchical.

Cooper (2006) contended that poplar representations of heterosexual Black men are bipolar, as there are alternative images between a "Bad Black man, who is crime-prone and hypersexual, and a Good Black, who distances himself from blackness and associates with white norm" (p. 853). He explained that "the threat of the Bad Black man label provides heterosexual black men with an assimilationist incentive to perform our identities consistent with the Good Black Man image" (p.853). He posited that the reason for bipolar Black masculinity is that it exists to resolve the White mainstreams' post-civil rights anxiety (cognitive dissonance). The cause of this anxiety "results from the conflict between the nation's relatively recent determination that some black men merit inclusion into the mainstream and it's no longer-standing belief that most black men should be excluded" (p.853). In the midst of this society anxiety, the social reality that "Working man" (Perkins, 1991), and I would add-combine "Working Women," are no longer a regular fixture in urban neighborhoods (Alcorn, 1994).

I argue that Black African American and bi-multi-racial males, consciously and subconsciously, are subject to bipolar masculinity making among themselves, when engaging in the assimilatory cultural trade-offs in mainstream America. I suggest that Cooper's argumentative heterosexual Black men bipolar masculinity making thesis, and Du Bois thesis of two-warring souls (from his seminal historical work: "*The Souls of Black Folks,*" 1903), are over-lapping. Both amount to an assimilation acculturation struggle, in which assimilation pays, (it seems to some psychologically and economically), while acculturation limits conditional equality of opportunity chances, as acculturation as opposite of assimilation, would promote the stereotypical "Bad Nigger," the crime prone Black man, the revolutionary Bloods (Wallace, 1984), from the civil rights and the Vietnam War Era. To wit, there is the *angry Black man* that is still referenced in mainstream media today, in the imagination among U.S. citizenry with limited degrees of intercultural literacy, in our multicultural society.

Under the bipolar thesis we have two manifestations of ethnic-cultural group exceptionality. There is the acceptance of conformity to the dominant rule or patterns demanded by assimilation of a conservative nature and simultaneously acculturation efforts used to engage in nonconformity to the dominant rule or patterns demanded by assimilation. Acculturation efforts involve more critical examination and interaction when faced with the demands and undeclared but societal expected normalcy of assimilation; that is, an accounting for of democracy, capitalism, and the social humanity for an equality of existence.

Thus, it follows that one kind of uniqueness I am referring to among Black African American, bi-multi-racial males is that we separate ourselves in terms of how we relate or un-relate to African American culture or Black American culture while we are immersed in and of a Eurocentrically dominant so-called "I'm just-American" society, which to me incurs some degree of social-psychological struggle or utility of cognitive energy.

Such ethnic-cultural historical exceptionality in the presence of crisis suggests that Black African American, bi-multi-racial males are all over the social-cultural ecological terrain and/or landscape as it concerns how we define, construct, and attempt to enact and represent our masculinity, manhood, sexuality, and sexual orientation in public and private spheres; we are not constrained and constricted within the undeclared normative positioning of "White heterosexuality" (Chandler, 2007, p.1). As Chandler deftly pointed out, Black males have come to perform gender in "unique and diverse ways" (p. 2), and that it is salient to examine the "context that produces particular gender performance in African American males" (p.2). In other words, it calls for looking inside the numbers that represent the demographics to see how those among Black African American, bi-multi-racial males are working to identify and realize ways to be healthy and progressive in cultural context, while others have the potential to do so, and work to find out what's stopping them. In part, this requires formulating inquiry that involves identifying and exploring ways in which the construction and response to social reality occurs given the historical-contemporary circumstance of racialized-gendered and patriarchal demands, contributing to the formation of habitus.

Very importantly, the formulation of inquiry should be motivated by the fundamental aim of prompting self-social-psychological reform activities among Black African American, bi-multi-racial males, that involves their working to develop healthy or healthier social-culturally responsive and progressive ways of engaging in masculinity, manhood, sexuality, and sexual orientation, while under past-present loud and subtler social siege in public sphere. Overarchingly, the formulation of inquiry should be framed in consideration of various areas of human activities - the law, economics, politics, education, public-private job markets, anti-government White supremacy circles.

Hall (1997) contested that the social-cultural daily experiences of biracial-ness (I would add multi-racial ness) masculinity and maleness identity development is socially psychologically challenging in the face of a historical racial-gendered Black/White categorical dichotomy. (In other words bi-multi-don't fit, like what are you anyway, or those polite but rude blank face stares in public). This complexity, in consideration of identity development, is subject to subconscious and conscious observations among people during interpersonal-cultural social interactions in the public sphere of still eurocentrically dominated integrated space.

This consideration concerns skin-tone, phenotypical features such as hair texture and facial features, linguistic tones and styles, racialized gendered ideological points of view, socializing and educational experiences (or lack thereof) regarding inter-ethnic-group power relations, and sources and acts of empowerment, heterogeneous expectations, that do not readily place bi-multi-racial males within the Black/White racial-gendered dichotomy. [3]

Such socially conditioned perception and assumptions also involves "threat stereotyping" (Steele, 1995), in areas such as intellectual cognitive ability limits, social-cultural linguistic and behavior expectations, that hold mental health and well-being challenges for bi-multi-racial males in the identity development of masculinity and manhood (quiet self-doubt is and can be the elephant in the room). Hall asserted that, "The need of bi-racial males for a separate identity contrasts with the degree to which race remains a cultural imperative" (p. 74).

My discussion about these study interview findings is not about the numbers per se, it is about literately going inside the numbers, to inquire, examine, and discuss the role of masculinity, manhood, and sexuality that held implications concerning social-psychological, identity development, mental health and well-being, and their social construction of reality, for a group of adult Black African American, bi-multi-racial males. I asked them to speak and frame their perspectives in contrast-comparison with the literature about other of their brethren. Fundamentally, I sought to engage in an effort to capture the understanding, perspective, habits, and emotional states of minds of participating adult males via self-reflective discourse within the context of their racialized gendered experiences.

---

[3] Squires (2002) conducted a study aimed at rethinking the scope and nature of Black Public Sphere by introducing vocabulary that allowed for a broader more comprehensive and inclusive identification and examination for multiple public spheres via an "exploration of the history of the African American public sphere" (p. 446). The author- pointed out that people of color, women, sexual minorities, religious minorities, and "immigrant groups have created coexisting counterpublics in reaction to the exclusionary politics of dominant public sphere and the state" (p.446). Squires referred to public sphere as "physical or mediated spaces where people gather and share information, debate opinions, and tease out their political interests and social [cultural] needs with other participants" (p.448). For example, in the segregated Black enclave of West Philadelphia during the 1960s my mother, Mrs. Thelma L. Alcorn, served as a block neighborhood captain facilitating meetings at our home in which people engaged in discussion and identified issue/needs of the neighborhood to be communicated to City Hall. Squire explained that at "different times in history, African Americans have been forced into enclaves by repressive state policies," and had to use such enclave spaces to "create discursive strategies and gather oppositional resources" (p. 458); for example, AME and Baptist churches and homes in the South during the civil rights era.

Invisibility is a dangerous and painful condition. When those who have power to name and to socially construct reality choose not to see you or hear you, whether you are dark-skinned, old, disabled, female, or speak with a different accent or dialect than theirs, when someone with the authority of a teacher, say, describe the world and you are not in it, there is a moment of psychic disequilibrium [cognitive dissonance], as if you looked into a mirror and saw nothing. Yet you know you exist and others like you, that this is a game with mirrors; [now you me now you don't]. It takes some strength of soul—and not just individual strength, but collective understanding---to resist this void, this nonbeing, into which you are thrust, and to stand up, demanding to be seen and heard. (Rich, 1986, p. 119)

Chapter Two
Voices in Related Literature

In this chapter a discussion of Black masculinity and manhood occurs in mixture with social, psychological, and political human constructs such as race, culture, gender, and worldview. It begins with a talk about a sociological term called habitus, as it concerns, predispositions that form within us in and response to various social-cultural and democratic living conditions, and life experiences in the neighborhoods, cities, towns, and world of nature around us.

Exploring the Meaning of Habitus

In his works entitled *Outline of a History of Practice* (1977), Bourdieu in search of what regulates human action and interaction that formulates style and intentions, purported in part that habitus was:

> *The conditionings associated with a particular class of conditions of existence produce habitus, systems of durable, transposable, dispositions, structured structures predisposed to functions as structuring structures, that is, as principle which organizes and generates practices and representations that can be objectively adapted to their outcomes without presupposing a conscious aiming at ends. (p. 52)*

Bourdieu stated that "In short, being a product of a particular class of regularities, that habitus tends to generate all the reasonable, common sense behaviors" (p. 55). Swartz (2002) stated that concept of habitus is derived from the "Latin word habere meaning" to have or to hold (p. 615). According to Swartz the growth of this concept was expanded and popularized out of Bourdieu's interest in exploring the question: "*how is human action regulated*" (p. 615)? Moreover, he stated that Bourdieu's concept of habitus is rooted in a theory of action. My introduction to the term habitus arrived as a result of being invited to develop an introductory elective course at a 4- year university exploring the meaning of Black manhood in the United States. The term habitus was intriguing because of my understanding of Black manhood enactment via such things like non-verbal and verbal interpersonal communicative styles of speaking, non-verbal expression of body language, attitudes about urban street life, expression and kinds of personality characteristics among Black men that I had direct experience with, viewed, read and studied about, and simply observed. Manly styles and how you viewed, thought of, and acted out yourself in an integrated setting was generally different than it was in segregated settings. And therein lied some of the rub, i.e., complexity of manning up with your sexuality, your intellect, your body, and language, while shifting back and forth between integrated space and segregated space and all the social materialistic, experiences, expectations, within the shifting and eventful space of public sphere-private thoughts.

Romaine (1999), discussed how gender has an inherently communicative process. Not only do we communicate gender, but we also do it, we socially construct and enact gender predominantly through conversation and discourse; then to there is more formally reflective talk in study and analysis. But know that one's sexuality-gender orientation and gender stance, is always present and in one's mind's eye and that of others, even when not fully aware.

Our social-cultural activities are related to forming of habits as routine and strategic ways of being present and in responding. For example, there were the circumstances that took place in racially segregated community neighborhoods of Philadelphia, PA that I grew up in from which I developed predispositions about people in places, events, and experiences that I carried with me. Thus, I related the term habitus to developing and emerging manly tendencies (inclinations that become part of one's, for example, sexual persona, temperament) to and think-act of self in relationship and response to what is going-on around the self, for instance, in comparison and contrast with other individuals, particularly, as it concerns in ethnic-cultural, social-economic, group context. (There is the conscious and subconscious accumulative experiences of positionality. When it comes to this the development and cultivating implementation of self-action research hold utility here). This comparison and contrast work includes, and I consider this to be very important, in various situations and under differentiating social-ecological conditions during intra-personal, interpersonal-cultural-gender interactions with others.

Habitus then is within the thought process, attitudinal dispositions, and behavioral persona of the individual concerned derived within geographic space and under social-ecological conditions experienced. Habitus makes available a cadre of past experiences from circumstances, conditions, and situations that can and do serve present perceptions and actions, Compton-Lilly (2009).

I. Social Cultural Sites and Circumstances that Affect the Forming of Habitus

According to Bourdieu (1977) "structures constitutive of a particular type of environment" (p.107), that is, material conditions relative to existence, such as "characteristics of class" produce habitus; "systems of durable, transportable (mobile- transferable) dispositions" (p.107). Bourdieu, in his discussion of habitus, emphasized that his theory of habitus is not based upon behavioral determinism, (cause and effect), but occurs as predispositions, that is, inclinations, or tendencies that produce social cultural practices and perceptions in individuals. In other words, habitus is inclinations and/or tendencies experienced and shaped relative to material conditions that can be, for example, characteristic of intra-personal-interpersonal social economic class experiences. These inclinations and/or tendencies are revealed in perceptions, thoughts, and actions that are resilient and enduring in the individual concerned; habitus is brought to new places and circumstances. Moreover, it *appears* from the description of habitus that in some sense it can be a collaborator of intuitiveness, which is, knowing something instinctively without it consciously being discovered. This perhaps raises the question that if one demonstrates a particular instinct that demonstrates characteristics of durability and mobility can this instinct be characteristic of habitus? Put another way, can tendency or inclination collaborate with instinct to respond to the presence of certain similar conditions and circumstance from the past, such as, those that are racialized? Lau (2004) argued that Husserl revived the medieval pedagogic term habitus for this *intuitive sense*. Lau stated, "in an intuitive sense, habitus works as automatically as bodily motor skills" (p.376).

Grenfell and James (1998), discussed how habitus provided insurance that there was an "active presence of past experiences" in the form of blueprints of perception, thought and action" (p.14). A question that comes to mind is, what about group subjugating psychohistorical experiences under circumstance and condition such as slavery, being pseudo free in a hostile and peculiar circumstance of White supremacy, next Jim Crow, then desegregation and integration, neighborhood displacement from urban gentrification?

According to Grenfell and James, habitus makes possible for the individual the tendency to engage in creative perceptions, thoughts, and action responsive to the space-time conditions and circumstance concerned. Then too it appears that habitus exists in the mind of the individual in response to and as a part of social reality; as in the subconscious
mind, that lies between the conscious and unconscious mind. So, when
people recognize the social reality that they are in or similarities of it, habitus (tendencies and inclinations) can assist by providing social-cultural
messages in the form of awareness and thoughts that allows them not to
feel totally estranged from that social reality (Bourdieu, in an interview
with Wacquant, 1993). Grenfell and James (2004) further stated that "if
habitus is ontologically specific [the nature of being and existing], universally shaped, can only be actualized through individuals and individual
instances; in other words, social action always have a time and a place" (p.
388).

Relevantly, ontology involves group cultural beliefs and assumptions
regarding existence. Nobles (1989), in part of his definition of culture, aptly stated that the human activity of culture provided "a general design for
living and patterns for interpreting reality" (p. 6). Moreover, is it purported
that culture presents itself as an accumulation of nuances specific to interpreting social and natural reality, it seems to follow that culture both
joins and influences the forming of habitus in a reciprocal relationship
(Personal communication, Jose Vasquez and Benjamin Rhodes May, 2012).

The presence of culture theorized by Bourdieu (1984) via his concept
of "cultural capital" was part of his discussions regarding cultural production (p.241). Generally speaking, Bourdieu's concept of cultural capital
had to do with the availability of social assets. The point is that culture
produces and provides designs for living as a human activity and is influenced by and in turn influences the existence of habitus reciprocally. Culture is a social-construct, with economic, materialistic, racial, political,
and law/legal, among other ramifications for human activities, such as,
thinking, perception, attitude, and behavior, that we look to in forming,
managing, and guiding the social-psychological, sexual and personality
characteristic of our existence.

Given the role of culture, it seems important to consider what informs
habitus within a given social reality. For example, social-cultural gender
socializing occurs in response to heterogeneous beliefs in raising a person
in accordance to biological apparatus. In U.S. society, ethnic-culturally
nuanced socializing occurs under capitalistic materialistic conditions and

social economic circumstance that is racialized (hooks, 1989; Marimba, 1994; Mills, 1997; West, 1993). Since habitus continues to inform individuals in the present situation and place, given the preceding named conditions and circumstance, what implication does habitus hold relative to socializing, for instance, via parenting and in formulating curriculum, approaches to teaching and learning, and rules for managing attitudes and behaviors in educational institutions (private and public)? I would argue that naming and interrogating self, regarding who and what are the informants of habitus, relative to individual-group valuation, is both relevant and salient to one's well-being-ness.

Wallace (2002), in his comprehensive treatise on the subject topic of Black masculinity in the "literature and culture" between 1775-1995, revealed the challenges and paradoxes of constructing, developing, defining, and fundamentally recognizing the existence of Black masculine identity on its own terms, and how it has been submerged within universality of masculine studies within a White male patriarchal dominant society. Put another way, Wallace mapped out practical efforts found in the Black masculine literary works and cultural history revealing and discussing the negotiating and survival thrust strategies that Black men engaged in to insert and invent themselves in "American culture" (p.5). This is not an indictment but fact of social-reality that what is today called Black culture or African American culture, and therefore, the construction of Black masculinity and the enactment of manhood, was rooted and invented under extremely challenging and difficult conditions in U.S. society. There stood and stands the challenge of historical displacement as forced descendants from African tribal nations, and the need and efforts to invent themselves in a culture of ethnic hybridity that privileged the forming of a White collective among European immigrants who called themselves as Wise (2008) has referred to as "just American."

Historically, masculinity in U.S. society has generally been subconsciously judged in view of a dominant White male heterosexual ideation and value structure that is deemed universal and all other male ethnic-cultural constructs stand in comparison to it, (Byrd & Guy-Sheftall, 2001; hooks, 2004; Hurt, 2006; Madhubuti, 1991; Mutua, 2006; Staples, 1982; Wallace, 2002). Robinson (2000) stated that a prevailing narrative regarding the decline of White males in post 60s era America was developing an accounting for "historical, social, and political decentering of what was once considered the normative of American culture" (p.2).

According to Robinson this narrative articulated that "in wake of the civil rights movement" (p.2), and with the growth of women's liberation, gay liberation movements, and with the growing visibility of ethnic and racial diversity in U.S. society, White men began to be decentered. Said differently, major narratives read that the social, political, economic, intellectual, and so on, positionality of heterogeneous White masculinity and manhood that was dominant, as in central to what was considered to be normative North American culture in the United States, had been decentered.

It appears then that among changing demographics, the decentering of power is central to reasons why a large number of heterogeneous White/European American males in U.S. society (particularly among working class and economically struggling males in the south, southwest, and Midwest regions of the country), there are those who dogmatically stick to conservative and ultra-conservative partisan political ideology. There are those among this group of males who aggressively desire and respond in an attempt to protect, maintain, and regain perceived status losses, as an empowering source of self-hood, which is perceived to be under-siege (Kennedy, 1996). Of salient note, there has been a shift within the influential centrality of White male habitus as a standard for universal masculinity, manhood, and sexuality. After all, as Wideman (1990) so adeptly put out there in his chillingly powerful provocative book *Philadelphia Fire* – "MPT" Money Power Things are at stake.

An important question is where is the social-cultural positionality among Black African American, bi-multi-racial males, in the wake of this decentering? It is noticeable to recall that, White European male patriarchal masculinity and enactment of manhood has historically been used among Black African American males (and males of color) to compare and contrast their hierarchical position in "mainstream" society and among men. Whether one is up or down in the manly and class scheme of things, thug or not thug, independent or dependent is often in times, and place (historically and in real time) in comparison and contrast with Black African American males. (Does the term whipping post remind you of anything)?

In reference to normalcy in seamless social-psychological integration with positionality, hooks (2004) consistently and courageously argued, reminded, and pointed to what she called the "life threatening choke-hold that patriarchal masculinity imposes on black men" (p. xiv), that present challenges to reconstructing a healthier and more *progressive* Black masculinity and enactment of manhood. Collins (2006), too asserted, and rightfully so, that "men do immense damage to themselves, to women, and to children, all under the banner of protecting their manhood" (p. 91). Collins pointed to the "need to tell the difference between strength and dominance in progressive black masculinities" (p. 91), that artfully constructs black masculinities that are "not predicated on the dominance and exploitation of others" (p. 91). The value logic underlying hooks' and Collins' arguments are that it is healthier, culturally empowering, and a more progressive place for Black men to stand outside of and apart from the dominant patriarchal construct in U.S. society and globally.

Very poignantly, hooks pointed to and explained that the beginning ethos of Black masculinity took shape under the oppressive and suppressive yoke of "plantation patriarchy" (p.1); as part of a system of capitalism and White supremacy, something that to this day that is generally suppressed and/or dismissed as being temporally irrelevant to the defining, developing, and enactment of ethnic-cultural masculinity and manhood among Black African American males. hooks (1992) argued the longevity and dogma of patriarchal domination collaborated with racism in U.S. society that was aided and abetted by White supremacy.

In today's materialistically driven consumer society, being educated and learned is the broadest sense outside of work, is not readily promoted, accessible, and easily understood nor seen as attractive to one's manliness, sexual persona, or one's physical stature, particularly when this has to compete with social-economic poverty, that is, "the promotion of addiction as the free enterprise system that works to provide unprecedented wealth to a few and short-terms solace from collective pain for many" (hooks 2004, p. xiv).

Booker (2000) argued that throughout U.S. history there has been this expectation among White Americans that Black males were not expected to "fulfill the ideal male gender role" (p. ix). Booker stated that it has been "made abundantly clear that severe repercussions would follow if they [Black males] made serious and steadfast efforts to live up to the white standards of masculinity" (p. ix); this amidst historical and contemporary characterization theories of self-hatred, anger, emasculation, and hypermasculinity (Ransby & Matthews, 1993).

One should wonder is this repercussion thesis still true today, and if so, what form does it take and under what circumstance are repercussions accountable in recognizable ways? Hence among Black males, like the working men in my family and neighborhoods, who worked to define and establish their existence in empowered ways, there has been societal push back among European Americans, relative to shifts in positionality in power sharing, for example, in various spheres of private – public sector positions of responsibility, power, and authority. (The president of the United States as bi-racial male of African-European American ethnicity).

Anecdotally speaking, there has historically been this *watch your public behavior warning* in reference to Black males as part of our socialization, and how we needed to consider this in construction and response to social reality (Alcorn, 1994). Darron (2012) contended in his blog that during the recent Presidential elections (particularly during the series of debates) President Obama had to "play it cool and maintain a calm demeanor" (p. 1), not just as an expectation of demonstrating the persona of a national leader, but to avoid the trapping (ambushing) of stereotypical blow-back regarding "being too black"(p.1). Moreover, there was also the danger of being touted as the angry Black man within the context of works by psychiatrists Grier and Cobb (1968) in their provocative book entitled: *Black Rage*. In *Black Rage*, the authors argued the psycho-historical influence/effects of racism, upon the physical, psychological well-being, disposition, worldview, and survival thrust among the past-contemporary lives of African Americans.

In essence, the implication of the findings from the from the book Black Rage spoke to inclinations and tendencies (habitus) among Black African Americans regarding the internalization anger that was harmful to their physical-biological and mental health, particularly when it goes undetected and suppressed and unprocessed in unhealthy ways. The paradoxical social expectation under the Western ideation of masculine and manhood is that men are supposed defend themselves and their rights so basically they have a free license to get angry (Wilkins, 2012); what a social mind bending paradox. There is the challenge/issue then of forging a positionality of social-culturally legitimate space in a multicultural society that is still dominated by so-called mainstream culture, for the defining, enacting, and developing of Black African American, bi-multi-racial masculinity and manhood that is not confined to the fields of entertainment, sports, images within pop culture and hip hop.

Finally, Bourdieu, in Eisenburg, (2008), was noted as discussing habitus as ways that individuals figure out and make decisions on what future actions to take "based on existing rules and values representing existing conditions" (p.2). If conditions real and/or perceived, to varying degrees, continue to be racialized, then it would follow that habitus takes place under such conditions. From the preceding discussion, it appears that defining and conceptualizing the forming of habitus among individuals is not formed in a social-cultural vacuum that is issue free; the social-psychological activity of habitus is subject to social-ecological sources and phenomena such as White supremacy, racism, classism, sexism, homophobia, educational inequality, urban and rural poverty, and other social-cultural human phenomena, developmental choices and influences.

What is relevant to consider in the literature regarding the subject of habitus, specific to this study, has to do with considering and recognizing the conditions and circumstances under which Black American, African American, and bi-multi-racial males have had to define, develop, and strive to enact/represent their masculinity and manhood, that is, their manly tendencies and inclinations. Hecht, Collier, & Ribeau's (1993) study regarding African American communication, group perspective, and ways of interpreting and responding to social reality, suggest that intra-interpersonal communication styles are a conduit through which habitus is seen and heard. Romaine (1999), asserted that gender is "inherently a communicative process" (p.2).

II.   Organizational/Institutional Habitus

What also appeared in the literature that is central to the shaping of habitus is location-space, particularly as it concerns positionality of the individual in contact with organizational and institutional structures, their rules, standard operation procedures (contextualized), and policies for managing, directing, framing and sanctioning the conduct of activities. Slater (2001) in the conduct of a study regarding "personal change and change within organization" (i.e., collaboration between a public school system and university for the purpose of building and establishing a public elementary school on a university campus), used the concept of habitus as an investigative tool looking at habitus in organizations. The investigative activity in part looked at the interaction of habitus between individuals from both organizations who were engaged in collaborative transformation project work.

Slater examined why such collaborative partnership ventures between school and individual universities waver, why people resist change, and "what conditions are necessary in human systems to effect systemically planned change" (p. 12). Slater stated that "resistance to change results in cultural and social reproduction of the status quo and an ideology of ac-

ceptance that is embedded in the habitus of operation of the organization" (p.12). A compelling question posed by the investigator was, "Why
must habitus be overcome?" As in this case habitus was said to be a "formidable impediment" to transformative movement that could make future planning possible (p.12). In this regard, the researcher engaged in
analytical discussion concerning "the overcoming of organizational habitus" (p. 13), as a barrier to developing effective collaborative relationships
responsive to the notion of community (p.13).

Since habitus is a response to material structural condition and political circumstance by individuals and individuals in groups, habitus has
systemic and organizational attributes. Najarian (2005), in a discussion
exploring how kind of ways one's habitus and cultural capital affect the
relationship between schooling and work, argued that there is a "myth of
meritocracy" (p. 14) based upon the belief that *free will* allows the individual concerned regardless of social-economic or cultural group ascribed
membership to achieve any desired status in society (p. 14). Meritocracy is
a fundamental argument and belief of those in US society who profess
rugged individualism as a tool for gaining equality of opportunity (Stewart
& Bennett, 1991). This is a corner belief of manliness. The authors stated
that such an assumption ignored social factors within Western society that
constrains and challenges the individual; I would add most prominently
the individual in ethnic-cultural group(s). Najarian also stated that "theorists working independently of educational research have developed the
notions of "habitus" and "cultural capital" that described the social factors
that come to bear on personal decisions made by cultural actors" (p. 1).
Najarian said,

> *students' habitus and cultural capital in fact con-*
> *stricts their perceptions of schooling, consequently*
> *limiting their vocational possibilities beyond educa-*
> *tion. The connection between schooling and work*
> *thus becomes one of social reproduction, rather than*
> *upward mobility. (p.1)*

Along this line of thinking, habitus is a set of dispositions or inclinations that predispose the student's concerned approach and attitude toward schooling and personal education in relationship to other possibilities in life in certain ways, that are brought to the experience of schooling
and education. In concert with this, Najarian held that

in some capacity, there is a dependent relationship be-
tween one's habitus and one's cultural capital a cul-
turally underprivileged individual will generally be
predisposed to socially reproduce underprivileged cir-
cumstances by making decisions in line with an un-
derprivileged habitus. (p. 2)

Based upon Najarian's position, habitus in organization and institution can effect a student's degree of aspiration, in this case self-imposing a glass ceiling or inhibiting engaging in the pursuit of healthy learning productivity. Very importantly, the impact of organizational and societal structures should be considered as it concerns the shaping of individual habitus within ethnic-cultural groups, intersecting with social-economic class status, in gender identity.

Finally, a continued point to consider is once the condition of habitus becomes a particular way of thinking and acting, habitus is then the psychological and perceptual house in which one resides in, so to speak, looking out at the world, responding to it, so awareness of self in habitus in relationship to how one is being glazed upon and perceived seems pertinent to pay attention to. A salient question relative to habitus as it concerns manhood making or orientation is: What sources inform the habitus of Black masculinity, which is, manly tendencies, manly persona, gender orientation wants, and desires?

Donald and Wingfield (2008) stated that "in a racially stratified society, organizational habitus may produce different outcomes for racial minorities than it does for whites" (p.31). These authors argued that: "one such example of difference is a minority's sense of (in) visibility not only among students, but among faculty members as well" (p. 31). Very pointedly, the authors argued that "organizational habitus of predominantly white institutions are often ripe for facilitating institutional racism" (p.31). Gibson (2009) discussed the implications regarding the shortage of Black male teachers in education and learning issues faced by Black male students, arguing in part that the "presence of an anti-education culture" (p. 207) on the rise in the Black community is a contributing factor. Is this then a contributing factor regarding the impact of organizational habitus in predominantly White institutions, as studied by Donald and Wingfield?

What seems relevant to consider regarding organizational habitus is that if the implication holds that race as a social and political construct, along with other social-psychological constructs and activities, interact

with individuals' conscious and subconscious in ways relative to the perceiving of reality, then most certainly such social constructs can inform
and shape individuals' habitus in organizations and in public-private
sphere. Hence, as it has been pointed out that individuals bring habitus
from social-cultural experiences with them into organizations. Organizational habitus then holds implications for the work of multiculturalists,
diversity and social justice activist and theorists, educators, mental health
practitioners, administrators-managers, and school boards members.

In further consideration of the shaping of individual habitus, it is implied that when the self's mental state goes untreated or experiences acts
of self-medicating, the habitus of self re-norms itself and becomes part of
and culprit in its own shift in mental states and ways of perceiving reality
(Rhodes and Vasquez, personal communication, July 28, 2012). Like Head
stated in his poignant book entitled *Black Men and Depression: Saving Our
Lives, Healing Our Families and Friends* (2004), "We call depression the
blues in the black community," (p. 3); the blues grew up in Jim Crow culture of *de jure* and *de facto* segregation. The blues is a state of habitus.
Renalls (2006) declared that habitus is a mixture of deep values that defines a person's point of view towards, for example, schooling. In other
words, people can and do, to varying degrees, internalize the experiences
of their own cultural group and formulate expectations based on them (p.
24); that is via the activity of meaning making in cultural context. (People
frame answers and responses in part from social cultural experiences).

Hovat and Antonio (1999) asserted that external factors such as race
and ethnic-culture should be built-into analytical research regarding organizational habitus. The authors conducted a study focusing on how
race and class "influenced school experiences of six African American high
school seniors who attended a predominantly white, elite, independent
secondary school" (p. 317). In their study they found utility in Bourdieu's
conceptual approach to habitus, saying that it had been a proven tool in
"how interactions influence individual dispositions and preferences,
which in turn affect how individuals interact with their social world"
(p.319). However, the researchers chose also to utilize the conceptual view
of "organizational habitus" postulated by McDonough (1997, p.319), to
study how the organizational process of schooling influenced students'
lives.

As maintained by Hovat & Antonio organizational habitus is a "set of
class based dispositions, perceptions, and appreciations transmitted to
individuals in a common organizational culture" (p. 320). Still further, the

authors were interested in how organizational habitus influenced social interactions. Significantly, they chose to integrate Bourdieu's conceptual approach to habitus with McDonough's "organizational habitus." McDonough approach enabled them to study and reveal "how the race-and-class based dispositions, practices, and rules of organization structure, legitimated action" (p. 339). I suggest that the conceptual framework from their study and findings, based upon Bourdieu's theory of habitus and McDonough's conceptualization of organization habitus, could hold possibilities for examining the complex and fluid scope and nature of masculinity-making among Black American, African American and biracial males, relative to manly tendencies towards learning, schooling, and educational success.

In their study Hovat and Antonia claimed that the school's organizational habitus was "classist-elitist," racialized, and possessed an atmosphere of "narcissistic entitlement" among its' administrators, teachers, students, and parents" (p. 326). That is to say, their findings pointed out that the six African American students in the study had to adopt a brand of survival thrust strategies in ways that caused these students to pay a heavy psychological price in working at- fitting into a dominant European American presence and institutional structure of arrangements and social cultural attitudinal, communicative, cognitive, and behavioral nuances. These authors asserted that the students they studied were compelled to do this as part of their efforts to experience learning, academic achievement, and levels of social acceptance in such a privileged environment.

Diamond, Randolph & Spillane (2004) conducted a study that focused on the student demographics of low-income African American students in urban elementary school districts. The authors discussed the quality of teachers' expectations toward students associated with a reduction of their sense of responsibility for student learning. Their thesis was that the degree of teacher expectations and reduced sense of responsibility for student learning among this student demographic, were anchored in "school-based organizational habitus through which expectations of students become embedded in schools" (p. 75). Put another way, they argued that "teachers' sense of responsibility for student learning was connected with their beliefs about students' academic abilities through a set of organizationally embedded expectations regarding what is possible for students from particular backgrounds" (p.76). These same authors viewed in part, studies in the literature that were in concert with their claim that "teachers often view low-income and African American students as less capable of high academic achievement than their white counterparts" (p. 77). Their findings suggested that,

- Race and social class demography of the schools studied is associated with teachers' and administrators' general beliefs about students.

- When they analyzed their data by school separately, they found that beliefs about students varied by school's composition.

- Data patterns emerged in majority White and majority Chinese schools showing 71% of teachers' emphasized students' assets over their deficits; this was compared to only 23% of the teachers in African American schools.

- Social class composition of student populations appears to impact teachers' assessments of students across ethnic-cultural-racial demographics (p.77).

Finally, data from their study showed that teachers' beliefs about students were patterned by race and social class composition of student demographics, and that school micro political contexts were influenced by schools' race and class compositions by way of school-based organizational habitus.

A final significant point regarding habitus specific to Bourdieu's definition, is that, habitus is a way that individual actors figure out and determine future actions on the face of existing norms, rules, and values; this is strategic to work at ascertaining what works and what doesn't. This implies that one engages in gender-identity making and enactment in part from perceived options and views regarding what it means to be or become a "man." From this position forming habitus would involve worldview perceptions and survival thrust strategizing occurring in interaction with neighborhood social-economic ecological conditions.

Consequently, I would argue that among Black American males it can be further said that habitus in actuality informs present (but does not serve as determinants) perceptions, attitudinal, and behavioral responses to social-cultural interactions in institutional circumstances. This is relative to, for example, education, community, and social and work related experiences; given the particular states of racial-class ecology they live in, and on the face of group psycho-historical experiences. Namely, that is to say, the literature reviewed suggested that the construction of habitus is not shaped in a societal vacuum. Communication styles, literacy, introspective thoughts, respond to social reality that is socially, politically, and economically gendered-racialized, and as such, all this informs habitus and habitus replies in the form of human tendencies and inclinations.

My contention, is that, in U.S. society among Black African American, bi-multi-males, habitus relative to masculinity making, interacts and evolves under the dominant shadow of a European American patriarch. Hooks, (2004) again, adamantly and analytically presented argument that preconceived views exist within a "White-supremacist capitalist patriarchal culture" (p. 82), that projects a stereotype of Black males as possessing a sexualized expression and aggressiveness for sex, that is both hated and desired.

III. Black Masculinity and Manhood in U. S. Society

The purpose of this section is to explore the literature as it is associated with Black masculinity and manhood emphasizing them as a social process with psychological, ethnic-cultural, and racialized ramifications and complexities in their ongoing construction, understanding, and performance. Put another way, exploring perceptions and circumstances surrounding black masculinity and manhood identification, construction, and enactment.

> *The United States was also created out of the doctrine of natural rights, whose restrictive application was continually eroded by the struggles of the excluded: first the European "others," and the other "others" down to our own day. (Winant, 1998, p.87)*

Lemelle (2009) argued that a major problem, among others, concerning how the construct of gender, with regard to how masculinities are studied, "has been the tendency to ignore the idea that social status is necessarily a relational process" (p.8). Lemelle informs us that social roles are generated in society; this makes power as sanctioned, associated, and exercised with the roles critical to pay attention too. From this position masculinity and manhood as a social process is also concerned with how individuals and individuals in ethnic-cultural groups relate to and perceive one another in the context of social reality. This systemically in-

cludes experiences with materialism and various institutions in the society at large. Very importantly, this involves perceptual - social tendancies
among people to compare and contrast each other in association via phe-
notypes based upon racial aesthetics relative to gender and social-
economic wherewithal. (Ego-baited jealousies preside here).

J.A. Rogers, who from the West Indies, during the turn of the 20th century talked about the role of aesthetics relative to race, sexuality, the body,
within the context of racial intermixing, relative to racism, sexism, conquest, and colonializing subjugation, in his well-documented three vol-
umes of Sex and Race. It is through the social process of direct and indirect interaction and in imagination that the inventive construct of *race*
subconsciously and consciously became "the main characteristic most
Americans use to classify each other," within the context of power and
control as impacted intergroup power – and sources of empowerment
relationships (Roberts, 2011, p.1). Further, Roberts declared that race (as
put to one's phenotypical features, color tone of skin, and as a social fallacy, contributed to a mark of lower or limited intelligence) is the initial
thing that is noticed in coming in proximity with a stranger in the public.
But very strikingly Roberts observed that race, like citizenship "is a political system that governs people by sorting them into social groupings
based upon invented biological demarcations" (p.2). For Roberts, then,
race is a "political category that has been disguised as a biological one" (p.
2). Very saliently, Roberts argued that race as a political category is misperceived in U.S. society as a social construct. Hence from this perspective, U.S. society "determines the consequences of this natural inher-
itance," that is, race as social construction (p.2).

The implication of this consequence, according to Roberts is that the
contradiction of perceiving race as a social and biological construct is not
readily consciously realized as a continued part of social reality. One of
the ramifications of non-awareness and denial of not perceiving race as a
political entity in this society is that hierarchical intergroup power relationships based upon historical-contemporary dominate group relationship, is received and critiqued as a natural order of things, and thus social-
economic inequalities are simply viewed as lack of individual "boot strap"
initiative; (which is fundamental to the valuation of self-interest). You
know, the free-market and lack of individualism self-valuation, so you
have no one to blame or take issue with but generally yourself. As Roberts
masterfully stated,

> We know race is a political grouping because it has
> political roots in slavery and colonialism, it served a
> political function over the four hundred years since its
> inception, and its boundary lines—how many races
> there are and who belongs to each one have shifted
> over time and across nation to suit those political
> purposes. (p.5)

Most prominently, the deceitful and abstruse construct of race converges in the literature socially, psychologically, economically, and politically with perception, thought, and imagination among individuals and individuals in ethnic-cultural groups, to include the valuation belief and favored socialized pursuant strategy of self-interest (Dalal, 2002; Brown, Carnoy, Currie, Duster, Oppenheimer, Schultz, & Wellman 2003; Lui, Robles, Leondar-Wright, Brewer, & Adamson, with United for a Fair Economy, 2006; Mincy, 2006; Poussaint and Alexander, 2000; Olsen, 1997; Staple, 1982).

Mills (1997) presented a thesis purporting the existence of a "Racial Contract" that determined "(p. 9) who gets what, economically, and that this same contract is an exploitative one. Mills stated that most critical race theorists argued that race does exist as a social-political determinant and therefore racialized contractual attitudes and behaviors take on social-political features. Generally speaking, Mills alleged that the Racial Contract consisted of a set of informal or formal agreements which set limits on people based upon racial phenotype, ethnic-cultural heritage, their affiliations, self-identity, self and group social-cultural ideological beliefs and epistemology, and interpersonal-cultural communication styles. To wit, the Racial Contract established and influenced transactional power relations and assumptions about the intellectual capacity and moral standings between White European Americans and individuals who were categorized as non-white.

Historically, in accordance with the Racial Contract, which joins/merges with the "Social Contract" Pateman (2007), non-whites had been subordinated, for instance, morally, sexually, and intellectually. The Racial Contract then serves as a form of *de facto* and/or *de jure* rules of engagement that are consciously and unconsciously present to regulate intercultural-racial-social interactions that privilege White European Americans over non-whites relative to intergroup power relations, in the categorical duality of interactions (Tilly, 1999). Here too, Mills further argued that non-whites are the "objects rather than the subject of the agreement" (p.12).

Finally, in accordance with the theoretical undergirding of the Racial Contract, race exists through social reality and is not intrinsic or natural-istic (biologically determined). However, the existence of such a contract would affect cognitive appraisal of others, potentially impacting biological and mental health, and decision making. When it comes to equal of op-portunity as a social justice standard in U.S. society, there exists an abdica-tion of responsibility among its citizenry to a multicultural democracy.

Given the phenomenon of race, and the purported presence of such constructs as the Racial and Social Contract, has there ever been social-cultural, psychological, spiritual, and behavioral room in the so-called universality of masculinity, and historical sanctioned beliefs regarding heterogeneous dominant standards of masculinity and manhood, for the construction of masculinity, manhood, sexual formation, of progressive Black African American, bi-multi racial identities? What complicates this more is that in the same breath one must ask what is or constitutes, for example, Black identity, and why is there such struggle among Black Afri-can Americans that causes some to scurry away from it and into the raw clutches of Eurocentric assimilation, while others stand idly by wishing the demise of Black identity and culture perhaps rationalizing that its ex-istence was shaky or embarrassing to begin with? Woodson (1933) argued this in part in his seminal works *The Miseducation of the Negro. What is a brotha to do in all this!? I'm just sayin.* Please pardon my frivolousness.

Adeptly, Harper (1996) declared that masculinity and manhood is called into question under the guise of "authenticity" regarding African American identity particularly when the sexual identity of the Black male concerned is suggested or declared as possessing a *feminine identity and persona*, or used in derogatory declarations as failure to be a man. He acutely discusses the ping pong ball like informed debates regarding what to call and declares ourselves to be, Negro, Black, African American, Col-ored historically and contemporarily. (I was surprised that my Mama who was born at right after the turn of the 20th century self-referenced herself as Black and used the term Black people, but when it came to any refer-ence to African, she simply said, "that happened a long time ago").

Harper purported that by interrogating the dominant presence of con-ventional masculinity specific to established "conceptions of blackness" (p. ix), his investigation in actuality constituted a "critique of masculinism in African American culture" concurrently (p. ix). In other words, by interrogating forms of dominant conventional masculinity, he concurrently critiqued the conceptualizing of masculinity and manhood within the context of Black American culture and the Black community.

Harper also argued the presence of historical-contemporary *paradoxical* and *anxiety* producing issues and circumstances involved in the construction and enactment of Black masculinity among its "diverse representations" relative to conceptualizing Black identity (p. x). In U.S. society Black masculinity and manhood is not just a product of biologically assigned heterogeneous determinism, but it is a product of the politics of racialized gender within the framework of intergroup power relations, to include the Eurocentric valuation of the pursuit of self-interest, and what is considered to be acts/status of personal empowerment, and protection against racism.

Franklin (1999) discussed findings from a therapist case study purporting that among Black men there are those who possessed perspective concerning experiences with cross-racial encounters, suggesting that their racial identity development was in actuality fundamental to their "personal identity, and served as a buffer against racism" (p. 761). The suggestion here is racialization of self has been internalized within psychics. He went on to say that having an awareness of the dynamic intersection between racism, invisibility syndrome (i.e., psychological experiences whereby the individual concerned feels that one's personal identity and ability was diluted by racism in numerous incidents of interpersonal cultural interactions), and racial identity development, could be found helpful in the counseling process when interviewing African American men.

In the literature then, there is ongoing argument and evidence that the historical subject of Black masculinity and manhood includes the topic of the social understanding of the body as a site of power, empowerment, and patriarchal dominance (meaning the characteristic of power by men in a culture), to include the body as a site of subordination, insubordination, exploitation, entertainment, and labor (John, 2007; Lemelle, 1997; Mutua, 2006; Summers, 2004: Wallace, 2002). People read the body and engage in body ascription (projection) in collaboration with racialized gendered-sexuality association and treatment, group-societal psychohistorical experiences, intra-interpersonal cultural expectations and stereotypes.

Richardson (2007) stated that Black American men "have been one of the most visible and topical categories in the nation's media over a decade in light of a range of issues" (p. 17). According to this author, by geographic regions, the South has been influential in establishing stereotypical characters within Black masculinity such as "Uncle Tom," and the myth of "black rapist" (pp. 5-6). Very importantly, Richardson acknowledged that there is a need to consider the stereotypical historical images of Black masculinity beyond the regions in the South that contribute to the construction of "black masculinity in the United States that has yet to be acknowledged" (p.6). Put another way, race and geography matter in examining the circumstances under which the social construction of Black African American masculinity takes place, and the complexity regarding why, how, and in what forms racialized gendered stereotypes persist about Black African American males.

For example, Richardson described an incident where stereotypical off-color remarks were made by a prominent White male during a CNN interview, basely aimed at belittling Tiger Woods in view of his success in professional championship golf, particularly at such a young age. Although the author pointed directly to the racialized remarks that were made, (i.e., "these condescending remarks reveal anxiety about a minority man's inroads into a sport conventionally dominated by White men," (p. 230), I maintain that his example holds broader implications regarding the occurrence of Black and bi-multi-racial males making advances into various professional occupations and political office that had been historically dominated among White males. That is, such movement can and is perceived as threatening to their sense of masculinity relative to the Western masculine ideation of dominance, competitiveness, and authority.

This is another example regarding the occurrence regarding social-cultural and political transformation within the U.S. as a multicultural society, among people of color, women, and sexual minorities, and the kinds of push-back among White males, White women, and assimilated like-minded people of color, because of the perceived threat of decentering White males, and therefore what has been referred to as Whiteness, Eurocentricity, and mainstream culture, as the social-economic-political-cultural center of U.S. society. The centering I speak to has to do with having exclusive dominance and control over resources, their allocation, access, media production, and governmental affairs. In keeping with Richard, it recommended that eras and regions (time and space) and conditions in U. S. society should be regarded in examining contributing factors and influences in the construction of Black African American, bi-multi-masculinity and manhood and sexuality, and how they are perceived, socially constructed, and held more broadly among men of color.

Speaking more about transformation, Bush (1999) in his review of the literature, focused on forces that produced change regarding Black manhood in the U.S. He stated that there were "socio-historical circumstances and sociopolitical movements" that begged the question, *"Have Black males gained their manhood?"* In a similar view, coincidentally, Harper (1996) posed a question in the title to his work, *"Are we not men"*? Harper explained that the implication of the question recognizes the hegemonic dynamics in the United States that denies some males the social mobility to be "viewed by society as men despite their biological sex" (p.1). Harper used what he referred to as conventional masculinity, and pointed to African American culture as a frame of reference in his analysis of Black masculinity and manhood. A step further, Bush's question also implied the involvement of Eurocentric hegemony historically that produced and/or contributed to socio-historical, political, social economic circumstance that held and still holds implications for the forming, defining, and enacting of Black masculinity, manhood, and sexuality within social-psychological and political intersection.

Relevant hereto is that Bush pointed out the social movements discussed by Pleck and & Pleck (1980) regarding the engenderment of "male sex roles and altered definitions of manhood, i.e., the women's movement, the gay liberation movement, and the men's movement" (p.1). Specific to Black males Bush included "the Black Power Movement, Civil Rights, and the African-centered Movement" (p.1). Is this regard I would offer that during the 60s era Black power movement and civil rights there are references to this era depicting it as the "Black cultural revolution." During the Black cultural revolution, which was spawned quite literally out of the civil rights movement, while embodying the Black Power Movement, among Blacks there was a reassessment of personal-ethnic-cultural group aesthetics of beauty regarding their phenotypical features, hair type and sculpturing, styles of clothing, seeking and importing colors, patterns, from the nation-states of Africa, reinvented in response to historical-economic-political circumstances here. Controversially, according to Bush, slavery was a socio-historical and political circumstance that had an effect upon the construction of Black manhood and sexuality.

According to Emerson Whitted, (personal communication, March, 30, 2011), a retired elder social studies-agricultural educator and African American social justice and cultural history advocate, who has resided in Castle Hayne, North Carolina, since his birth in the early 1940's, there were numerous times that he encountered among African American youth/students who displayed and verbalized embarrassment regarding having any connection with ancestry of enslaved Africans, while also feeling uncomfortable and estranged from talk about Jim Crow segregation and the civil rights movement. Mr. Whitted explained that students had difficulty in developing and finding, let alone giving student voice relative to the human and social injustices regarding these history events. Moreover, since this was down South there was the historical proximity that added social-psychological complexity to his observation.

The implication here too is that --- *how* can one holistically conceptualize and establish realistic healthy gender sexual identity when historical ancestral and elder family roots are denied or belittled? But yet, I would argue that there has never really be an *en* mass systemically established social and/or formal educated process for Black African and bi-multicultural Americans to engage in, regarding studying and fathoming the scope and nature of slavery, emancipation, Jim Crow segregation, civil and human rights. (Argumentatively, we have been *short cut off at the knees* intra-interculturally, throughout our physical, psychological, self-group cultural, social economic, and civil human rights history, here in this part of the Americas, as a reinvented group of people in this country; as non-immigrants, among migrants, and among ethnic-cultural groups of people from historical conquest and dominant cultural treaty arrangements).

So, I find it odd, unsettling, and simply disturbing that, for instance, those among social political pundits, academicians, politicians, supreme court justices, and individuals who wield considerable voice, resources, and power in this country, that refuse to recognize let only contemplate with any kind of social reality or simple humanity, regarding the role and impact of White supremacy with regards to enslavement, *de jure* release, segregation, civil-rights integration, relative to historical conquest-aggressive military-government and capitalistic supported expansionism, that has been incurred upon people of color in this country. There has never been a systemic social-educational and apologetic accounting for, simply temporal assumptions and declarations, along with racialized silly-grams of "get over it."

In regards to Mr. Whitted's informed observations previously discussed, a survival thrust strategy of denying and distancing self from those ancestral roots is historically-contemporarily in play. Among Black African American, bi-multi-racial males, a survival thrust strategy in general has been socially and psychologically crafted in route regarding the establishing developing and crafting of masculinity, manhood, and sexuality within self-identity, under oppressive and suppressive circumstance and capitalistic materialism, to be enacted beyond a "shadow of doubt" that "I AM A MAN" Hurt (2007). Perhaps, such circumstances and conditions historically contributed to the prompting of overplay on the processes and demonstration of Western patriarchal heterogeneous standards of defining and enacting characteristics of masculinity, manhood, and sexuality.

Johns (2007) also discussed Black masculine identity as a product of U.S history, noting that "the concept of black masculine identity was fashioned during and codified after the formal collapse of the American institution of slavery" (p.1). His investigation argued in part that historical-contemporary dominant stereotypical imaging continues, contributing to the compromise of efforts aimed at assisting adolescent Black males to develop healthy and progressively empowering construction of Black masculinity and manhood identities. He further argued that there continues to be an overreliance on, for example, sports and entertainment performance as acceptable sites of Black masculinity and manhood making, and an over-pronunciation (reliance of expectation) of the hood segregated urban and rural geographic areas - where the culturally expressive persona among Black males as a diverse ethnic-cultural group, can be viewed or imaged at a comfortable distance; save in gentrification. Most directly, his analysis spoke to gender as racialized while demanding or at the very least, *coveting* heterogeneous conventional masculine performance and manhood roles as most desirable, natural, with biblical interpretative reasoning, i.e., Western and Eastern religious denomination sanctioning of male dominance and dominion over women period.

A. Racialized Gender

In the politics and social realities of public sphere the visibility of the gendered body is subject of dominant heterosexuality as a fundamental frame of reference, and ascribed expectation, via binary (female-male) appearance and sexual persona, that is, if you look like a man act like one; if you look like a women same thing, what then if you feel like neither or vice-versa, or both? (Jose Vasquez, Benjamin Rhodes, & Dwight Randolph, personal communication, July 18, 2012). Black masculinity racialized, within the construct of conventional Western masculinity, is still reamed in a rigid heterogeneous conventional version of manhood. Black feminist thought has provided compelling, provocative, analytically and factually reasoned, and comprehensive knowledge regarding the intersecting construct of "racialized gender"; that joins other social-political makers in our milieu of social reality daily (Boris, 2003; Few 2007). Few (2007) stated that "racialized gender" is a sociological construct that refers to the synchronized effects of race and gender "processes on individuals, families, and communities" (p.1). Further, Few pointed out that multiracial feminists and ethnic scholars have written extensively about racialized gender particularly as it relates to "social construction practices on the individual" (p.1).

Collins (1998) conceptualized and argued the intersectionality of race, class, and gender, that is, social class affairs and gender inequality as "descriptive variables attached to individuals" (p. 1), that is, "reinserted into existing theoretical models on the family" (p. 27). Collins asserted that gender ideology created ideals about femininity as well as conceptualizing masculinity. From the perspective of intersectionality, gender identity is socially constructed racialized, and enacted in response to social reality. Gender ideology cannot simply be universally applied as a common set of descriptive social characteristics regarding biological determinism of persons who are deemed women and men, but a complexity of variables involving sexual identity and persona, race, ethnic-culture, group psycho-historical experiences, and politics, as the *body is politic;* along with whose knowledge say's so.

Moreover, there is the presence of habitus to consider in the shaping and forming of tendencies and inclination among individuals and individuals in groups regarding sexuality and persona, in the face of institutional practices, policies, and the materialistic conditions under which habitus is formed.

Very saliently, according to Collins (2006),

> *For African Americans the relationships between gender and race is intensified, producing a Black gender ideology that shapes ideas about Black masculinity and Black femininity. This Black gender ideology is not simply a benign set of ideas affecting individual African American women and men. Instead, it is used to justify patterns of opportunity and discrimination that African American women and men encounter in schools, jobs, government agencies, and other American institutions. (p.6)*

Put another way, as Collins argued, sexuality is not simply a state of biological functionality but a systemic set of ideas and practices that are deeply implicated in "shaping American social inequalities" (p.6); the politics and social ideological influences of heterogeneous sexuality must be weighed and attended to in the fathoming of Black gender ideology.

Race and gender carry with them physical, psychological, social ramifications specific to self-identity/conceptual perception and interactions with self and others; and in the perception of otherness, that could be, the degree of worth or condition of being different, for instance, as deemed exotic or strange as discussed by Fusco (1995) in her works, *English is Broken Here, Notes on Cultural Fusion in the Americas.* Fusco stated, in referring to the history of Black people in her Cuban familia (family), referenced a popular refrain from the Abakua religion: "Chivo que rompe tambor, con su pellejo paga," which she said that the literal translation was, "the goat that breaks the drum will have to pay with his skin" (p. 21).

Fusco went on to state that,

> *I keep thinking about that refrain as I listen to how and why black vernacular cultures have so many explanation for the critical positions black people adopt within identity and community. Black popular cultures, especially musical cultures, have generated an abundance of archetypes that embrace dissonance and contend with internal difference, these I take to be semantic residues of histories of contradiction and conflict. Maybe one of these days our intellectual debates will catch up with our popular cultural ability to engage in dissent, without defensiveness that continuously rears its head in other spheres. (p.21)*

I argue that slavery, conquest, immigration, (non-immigrate), migration, and anti-immigrant issues are burdensome social-cultural, physical, and psychological markers of otherness among Black American, Mexicans, and Latinos, while they are embarrassing to others, in particular those who strive to be assimilated and conservative in their social-political beliefs and approaches to life. All these events and issues most certainly carry with them the markers of racialized gender. Fusco declared that "if we take the implications of recognizing difference seriously, then we must understand that the designation of and even the very concern with Otherness are culturally relative" (p. 103).

Fusco also asserted that "the multicultural paradigm as we know it demands that its Others (which constitutes most of the world) conform to recognizable standards of difference that rarely questioned the power relations that define those distinctions" (p. 103). Moreover, she said this conformity represents the most fundamental flaw of multiculturalism. In the literature, (Main, 2000, Gomez-Pena, 2006), described how otherness is present in contemporary immigration issues, which involves being the target of anti-immigrant stereotypical discriminatory thoughts about Mexican illegal immigrants and native born Mexican U.S. citizens. These too provide evidence of the continued prominence of physical racial and ethnic cultural markers of otherness. Engendered racialized bodies, marked with class differences, serve as sites of labor ripe for self-exploitative conformism to a society of class and racialized gendered rationalizing (Alcoff, 2006).

B. The Body as Socialized and Marked by Racial Phenotype that is Subconsciously and Consciously Contrasted

Boris (2003) argued that "race and class themselves are both engendered identities and categories of analysis. Bodies have created a realm upon which racialized gendered as well as class is inscribed, constructed, made, and remade" (p.9). From the literature it is implied and argued that our bodies are visibly and socially involved in interpersonal cultural interactions and thus subject to considerations regarding racialized gender presence, public gaze, and personal feelings regarding conscious and subconscious degrees of, for instance, empowerment, self-worth, and beauty (Collins, 2006; Hecht, Collier, & Ribeau, 1993; Hurt, 1996; Richardson, 2007; Sewell, 1997). Moore (2010) discussed how among Black males there are those who have historically attempted to position themselves via their body to prove their worth not only specific to the disciplines of manliness but citizenship. For example, Moore stated that during the 19th century antebellum period, John B. Bailey, who was a "black sparring professor" lacked federal citizenship. In response to his racialized gender situation he "positioned himself in the physical culture movement during the 19th century to prove his middle-class fitness for manhood rights. Moreover, during the 1880s, when middle-class men began to perceive a "rough working-class masculinity as powerfully attractive" (p. 2), Black prizefight-ers "found an avenue to assert and prove their manliness across racial and class lines" (p.2). Given the intense race hate climate of Boston during the mid-19th century, Black males sought ways to demonstrate that they pos-sessed the required discipline "for citizenship" (p.2). Another historical example of proving masculine worth for citizenship was a sturdy demon-stration of patriotism; there was the formation of an all-Black militia called the "Massasoit Guards" (p.2). The militia provided opportunities for Black males to "perform disciplined military training drills and demonstrate a structured regiment in front of white naysayers who doubted the capabili-ties of the black body" (p.2).

> By the time that the Black man was able to attach the word "free" to the words that already described and defined him—let's say, officially speaking, in 1865 or so—he had already been so culturally entrenched as some objective "other," a creation of the collective im-agination of white men who had as much of an eco-nomic reason to set him free as they had to keep him enslaved, that the act of existing, of living day-to-day became the sole task of like (Poulson-Bryant, 2005, p.17).

Poulson-Bryant, author of the provocative book entitled *Hung, A Medi-tation on the Measure of Black Men in America* (2005), merged the remind-er of Black men being literally lynched (hung) from trees, *w*ith the stereo-typical story of possessing hyper-sexual prowess and persona; this being built around social-psychological invention of the so-called large penis size, and advent of racialized anxiety among a White southern populace. Poulson-Bryant explained how it is easy to bury such myth within "*the measuring up game*" (p. 2), of one's manhood among males, with curiosity and some expectation talk among women, and man-up talk among Black males. Accordingly, he stated, "it is the metaphorical power of a penis's size that gives it the psychological weight that men lug (drag) into rela-tionships with women and with each other" (p.2).

Hung carries the weight, burden, and the falsity embedded in racial-ized gender clouded by the allure of sexuality of one's persona. Anecdo-tally, among Black male service members during the Vietnam War there were those service members that talked about encounters at various clubs and bars at R&R locations, such as, in Taiwan, where among working women there were those who would not approach them because of the *stereotypical myth of hyper-sexuality and over endowment of penis size.* (Nothing to brag about and the fact that this was another in line of war time man's club for their sexual release and pleasure). Several interviewees in this study discussed personal experiences about inter-ethnic racial encounters with European American women students where curiosity was expressed regarding penis size and/or hyper-sexuality in love making or copulating. In this lays an inkling sample calling attention to the historical stereotype of Black masculinity and manhood as a social-biological construct marked by race.

Historically among Euro-Americans there were those who worked to both ethnic-culturally strip and to propagate the reinvention of Africans and their descendants in this country. Du bois (1947), in his essay entitled "Can the Negro Expect Freedom by 1965? - asked, "How far will...young Negroes consider that their primary duty is toward the cultural group which they represent and which created them" (pp. 4-6)? His question implied duality-acculturation, assimilation-conformism, and the right and necessity of possessing group culture as a critical frame of reference. hooks (2004) provocatively stated that, among Black males in this country whether incarcerated or not, they "have been forced at some point in his life to hold back the self he wanted to express, to repress and contain for fear of being attacked, slaughtered, or destroyed" (p. xii). Furthermore, according to hooks, Black men have, in historical context, been "seen as animals, brutes, natural born rapists, and murderers," and have had no real say when it comes to the way they are represented (p.xii). Finally, hooks believed that "negative stereotypes about the nature of black masculinity continue to undermine the identities black men are allowed to fashion for themselves" (p.xii).

According to Ross (1998) the mass media (*now prominently situated within social media*), has become the country's largest exporter of the images and voice bits of Black American males who have figured prominently into the desirability and profitability of mass culture "free enterprise style" (p.598). In other words, it is suggested that Black American males hold "high social visibility" disproportionately in sports, popular music, the military, and entertainment in general. In this post-*de jure* Jim Crow/Civil Rights era of the 21st century, televised "Representations of Blackness," (Gray, 1995, p.xxi), bring racialized images and voice bits into the homes, movie theaters, sports arenas, and into the psyches of millions of older and younger viewers and listeners; thus entering into the imagination and subconscious minds of the listeners and viewers concerned.

Ross argued that the sports industry has become too much of a prominent one dimensional zone for the desired construction of male identity, esteem, and image making. He also argued that, the "global media" (p. 599), has become overly reliant upon perceiving and portraying the iconography of African American men in the post-civil rights and post-cold war era, as the emerging reigning symbol of aggressive American manliness" (p. 599).

An implication of this line of reasoning and assertion is that Black masculinity, the Black male body, gets sampled and admired for sculptured haircuts, clothing, social-linguistic styles of talk, walk, and posturing, entertaining sports exploits, among youth domestically and globally (Dyson, 1996); but generally speaking, not for intellect, cognitive reasoning, leadership, being courageous, trustworthy. On the other hand, there is limited and no sampling from the pool of Black males who engage in articulate, well-informed, thoughtful, and culturally conscious discourse, who are working men of various professions and occupations.

Among European Americans, one may find confused blank faced stares, Malcolm X type references, and angry fearful comments that the Black male is too aggressive, too sensitive, playing that so-called race card, a discerningly smooth talker, in other words there is limited or no sampling among intellectual men of color, to be touted nationally in media iconography, save Dr. King, and now President Obama who unbeknown to many is under-racialized-gendered siege (Cooper, 2006; White and Cones III, 1999). It is no wonder that Cooper maintained that "popular representations of heterosexual black men are bipolar" (p. 853).

Lastly, regarding Cooper's thesis cited previously there are the presentations of images,

> *Between a Bad Black Man who is crime-prone and hypersexual and a Good Black Man who distance himself from blackness and associates with White norms. The threat of the Bad Black Man label provides heterogeneous Black men with an assimilationist incentive to perform our identities consistent with the Good Black Man image." (p.853)*

Brown (2011) pointed to the works of Jackson (2006) regarding the scripting of the Black masculine Body" (p. 151). Jackson (2006) in his thought-provoking learned book entitled: *Scripting the Black Masculine Body* argued that,

> a "mass-mediated depictions of culturally and racial-
> ly different human beings encourage people to re-
> spond to the differences rather than to the similarities.
> There is a hyperawareness, for example, of the nega-
> tive inscriptions associated with the Black masculine
> body as criminal, angry, and incapacitated. (p.2.)

Brown stated that for African Americans difference is defined through phenotypical features, such as skin tone, hair texture, and facial features. According to Brown, "social prescriptions are worldviews that devalue and perpetuate negative and stereotypical images toward the Black body" (p. 153). Furthermore, social prescriptions of the Black body have historically served as a devalued marker in comparison and contrast with European Americans. Brown said, "scripting is the process of an individual placing his or her own worldview onto another---a worldview that perpetuates negative assumptions, characteristics, and behaviors of African Americans" (p.153). Moreover, Brown argued that contextually within the mass media the conduct of scripting represents the placement of the mass media meanings "on the Black body and a portrayal of how those bodies match the script imposed upon them" (p.152). Thus, according to Brown scripting is evidenced in "how the media defines, interprets and constructs Black bodies" (p.152). However, scripting as Brown discussed, is not solely an intercultural act via dominant culture as the only source. Brown, drawing from the work of Aldridge (2007), stated that "African Americans themselves engage in inscriptions, which is another reason why the images continue to be found in contemporary society" (p.157). For example, stereotyped names, house "n" Uncle Tom, "he's an old Tom," along with a sampling of belittling words in an attempt to negatively associate say, hair texture, dark skin tone, or strong African facial features, in relationship with behavior or devalued looks, are historical to the Black community, within the broader context of dominant cultural social-economic-political experiences and worldview.

Richardson (2007) in his works entitled: *Black Masculinity and the U.S. South: From Uncle Tom to Gangsta*, examined the elucidation of Black male southerners "as inferior and undesirable modes of Black masculinity within such racial hierarchies based on geography" (p. 2); he exposed regional to national stereotypes of Black masculinity and manhood temporally. For instance, he examined and revealed how the Uncle Tom character on "theatrical and minstrel circuits, epitomized an innocuous and neutered model of Black masculine body" (p. 3). Richardson asserted that critics have shown that this portrayal "grossly contradicted Uncle Tom's original literary characterization in Harriet Beecher Stowe's *Uncle Tom's Cabin* (1852) as a strong, muscular man" (p. 3).

> *The point of view was that slaves were not persons but property; and laws should protect the ownership of such property, should protect the Whites against any dangers that were likely to arise from the presence of large numbers of Negroes, and should maintain a position of due subordination on the part of the slaves in order that the optimum of discipline and work could be achieved (Franklin, 1969, pp. 187-188).*

According to Cooper's bipolar Black masculinity thesis, there exists in response to resolving "White Mainstream's post-civil rights", an uneasiness regarding *which* Black men "merit inclusion," that is, what Black men make the cut to fit into the assimilationist ideal (2006, p. 853)? "Bipolar depictions justify the status quo to the exclusion of most black men into jail or the lower-classes and the inclusion of only a token few white-acting Black men into mainstream" (p. 853). Critically, Cooper maintained that there exists a hierarchical rank ordering of bodies regarding a "Western epistemological system of ranking identity characteristics in the scaling of bodies against a norm and organizing society according to the resulting hierarchies" (p. 857). Cooper asserted that "the assumption that identity hierarchies are inevitable" provided underlying support for the existence of "racism, sexism, homophobia, and other forms of oppression" (p. 857).

Bipolar Black masculinity involves the seduction of heterogeneous Black men to participate in such an arrangement via *assimilationist compensation*. Assimilationist compensation entails "accepting the right to subordinate others as compensation for our own subordination" (p.853).

It appears that bipolar Black masculinity is analogous to Du Bois's duality in that acculturation and assimilation-conforming are boundary lines of demarcation within societal identity hierarchies. Within bipolar

Black masculinity, assimilation-conformity compensation represents the scaling of bodies (and minds) in terms of a sense of worth and degree of acceptance, that are sought to receive forms of social-psychological, political, and/or monetary payment. In the case of Black masculinity and manhood, societal identity hierarchies have to do with the cultural identification, perceiving, and experience among Black males who do or do not identify with, borrowing from Young, (2011), "white European male norms of reason and respectability" (p.286). Namely, the paradoxical and complex circumstance of defining, constructing, and enacting gender identity and sexuality among Black African Americans grew out of the subjugating experience of slavery and Jim Crow segregation, the subversive attacking against Black Reconstruction, and racialized-gendered informed interpersonal-cultural interactions, as historically culturally anchored in the southern region, and southwestern State of Texas.

For instance, from evidence and informed perspectives in the literature, I contend that the experience of assimilation-acculturation pre and post-civil rights era is socially, politically, and *aesthetically* paradoxical because Black African Americans have had to work at contextualizing meaning and purpose of their cultural existence and a sense of worth as individuals, as property once enslaved, then freed to experience *de facto* and de jure segregation, and the social-economic, racialized-gender, and political dynamics and circumstance of integration.

This has occurred while experiencing *difference and otherness* (within and without) that included eras where voluntary European immigrants and conquerors screened and rejected one another relative to their ethnic-cultural heritage, phenotype and language, subject to American citizenship, and who was naturally "American" (in the Northern part of the Americas now known as the United States); as established by conquest, civil revolutionary war, and the instituting of the Declaration of Independence and other legal constitutional documents and edicts, such as, "manifest destiny." Moreover, I would argue that a state of *de facto* violence has been socially and psychological festering particularly among this country's European American males that were promulgated via Western ideology regarding masculine ideation and gendered socialization, sanctioned under the rights to keep and bear arms.

In further considering Ross there is the work of Shilling (2003), on the body in social theory. Shilling discussed the position of the body in pop culture and cited that there is a "massive rise of the body in customer culture as a bearer of symbolic value" in relationship with self-identity. (p.2).

Further, he noted the symbolic value as a "practical recognition of the significance of bodies both as personal resources and symbols [that] give off messages about self-identity" (p.4). Moreover, Shilling stated that the "body as a project varies along racial, ethnic, and class lines of sexuality" involved "individuals being aware of and actively concerned about the management, maintenance and appearance of their bodies" (p.4). In addition, Shilling stated that the body is a project that varies along racial, ethnic, and class lines of sexuality that concerned individuals being aware of and actively engaged in the management, maintenance, and appearance of their bodies, should pay critical attention to. Finally, he stated that this awareness entails "a practical recognition of the significance of bodies both as personal resources and symbols that give off messages about their self-identity" (p.4).

Shilling's work suggested that the body as personal resource is employed in the self- expression of identity, and in the establishment within the construct of societal ascribed and achieved masculine identity and manhood enactment. Very importantly, the sociology, (in part the study of social logic with examination of social cultural behavior in public sphere and domain), of the body, concerning the subject of Black masculinity and manhood development, appears to play a significant role with regards to racialized gendered development amid Black Americans and males of color. For instance, there is the self-societal view among Black African American, bi-multi-racial males regarding their phenotypical features that can and is subconsciously and consciously present in nonverbal-verbal communicative styles of expression; relative to interpersonal-cultural interactions between people. There is, anecdotally speaking, the public glaze and out-right stare and frown, (Fusco, 1995; Smith, 2012), that my wife, who is Chicana (Mexican American), and light complexioned, and I, as an African American and brown complexioned, have received in the public settings.

From Shilling's work and the previous literature reviewed, I would maintain that it is plausible that there is a heightened awareness regarding the phenotypical features among males of color, particularly if their acculturation and/or assimilation posturing is part of a negotiated goal of interpreting and structuring a response to social cultural reality. Acculturation posturing refers to accessing the use of ethnic-cultural knowledge and interests, that is a part of cognitive conceptualizing and presentation of knowledge during interpersonal cultural interactions. Like it or not, our skin is likened to a suit of clothing carrying historical-contemporary social-cultural, political, intimate connotations and curiosities, subject to major areas of human societal activities, to include actions, such as, sanctioning, judging, punishing, incarcerating, social gendered subjugation, exclusion, and comfort zone conditional expectation and acceptance.

From this review of the literature, it is maintained that the body is so-cial among Black males and is subject to how they are imagined, thought about and discussed, and entered into the subconscious minds among citizens at large. The process or phenomenon of the body as social con-tinues in a post-civil rights Black African American historical era, in the face of changing attitudes among our increasingly diverse younger ethnic-cultural and inter-multi-racial demographics, particularly among groups of color.

What adds to the complexity regarding the phenomenon of the body as social, is a reliance on non-judgmental attitudes and perceptions blurred by beliefs and self-declarative posturing behind naïve presump-tive ideology of colorblindness; now decades old. Colorblindness is thought to cut through, for instance, the social-economic and politically mesmerizing racialized-gendered subtleties of integration, and assimilat-ed views and stances on democracy. Very strikingly, it is supposed to do so despite a lack of or in the absent of, borrowing from what Dr. Derrick Bell (1980) defined and evolved in legal race critical studies, "interest conver-gence" essentially say's what do European Americans – White people get out of supporting racial justice, "what's in it for them?" For that matter, assimilated conservative folks of color. Or what might be said by the indi-vidual citizen, what's in it for me?

There also doggedly stands a lack of recognition, study, and engage-ment regarding the role/strategy social – intra-interpersonal literacy is-sues. I would strongly suggest that this is acute, particularly given histori-cal-contemporary mainstream normed struggles in major areas of human societal areas of activities in public sphere, over intergroup power rela-tions, and the role of social justice relative to self-group empowerment, and most assuredly, humanity. For example, Baker, Jr. (1995) stated that as the results of the Rock Hill, South Carolina Nine, Black youth, to include four members of the Student Non-Violent Coordinating Committee (SNCC), who conducted freedom and equality protest activities, in White-controlled space in public sphere, "a new moment of the black public sphere had been instituted" (p.19). (Prior to this protest there was the 1971 protest by what became known as the "Wilmington Ten," Wilming-ton, North Carolina School District, another moment of the Black public sphere).

Relative to the Black masculine body as social Ross (1998) stated,

It is not just white boys from the suburbs who don hip-hop clothes, shave their heads, and step with macho urban bounce; boys from across the world also can be found mimicking the gestures, styles, and lingos invented by and thus associated with young African American men. And yet, amidst this astonishing proliferation of Black male fullness (myth of the over-sized penis) and Black men figured as the brash plenitude of nationalizable commodities, the rhetoric and realities of Black men's disembodiment intensify. (p.602)

In reference to the body as social, Bourdieu (2001) stated, in his treatise entitled *Masculine Dominance*, that:

The social world constructs the body as a sexually defined reality and as a depository of sexually defining principle of vision and division. This embodied social programme of perception is applied to all things of the world and firstly to the body itself, in its biological reality. It is this programme which constructs the difference between the biological sexes in conformity with the principles of a mythic vision of the world rooted in the arbitrary relationship of domination of men over women, it-self inscribed, with the division of labour, in the reality of the social order. (p.11)

Bourdieu went on to say that biological differences between the sexes gave rise to the natural assumption of socially constructed differences between genders, and thus differences in gendered socializing practices among groups of people. Drawing from Bourdieu, I surmise that the interpreting of the body, within the context of ethnic-cultural hierarchies, race, sexuality, aesthetics, social-capitalism, and materialism, has historically generated/influenced socializing, self-contrasting perceptional, and behavioral practices relative to Black masculinity, manhood, sexual identity development and "strategic" styles of enactment. These self-contrasting perceptional and behavioral practices are relevant to the development of manly tendencies in sexuality and racialized gendered identity, and most importantly, conscious/unconscious tendencies and choices as to how to accept, relate, or reject association with one's ethnic-cultural group(s), Wilson (1992).

What is salient to consider regarding this study, is that the body is poli-tic come to life in the delegating of differences among men and between men and women involving their sexuality via biological apparatus, within their *social skin*; while at the same time serving as sites of power, empow-erment, dominance, oppression, and subordination (Hill-Collins, 2000, 2006; hooks 2004; Wallace, 2002; UpChurch, 1997).

In regards to the intra-interpersonal cultural perception of the skin as social, Breland (1997) conducted a two-state study *among* 200 African American adolescents regarding the hypotheses: "(1) *perceptions of com-petence*, (2) *that African Americans' self-esteem, ethnic identity, and use of strategies for coping with cultural diversity affect individual skin tone bias*" (p.1). Study results indicated that African Americans viewed "*lighter skinned group members as being more competent*;" additionally, "the study demonstrated that African Americans view attractive group members as more competent than unattractive members" (p.1). However, Breland not-ed that although African Americans demonstrated skin tone bias, "the reasons and processes by which such occurs remain unknown," as it was found that study results did not indicate that "self-esteem, ethnic identity, and use of coping strategies affected the skin tone bias viability" (p.1).

C. Black Men, Brown Shaded Skin: Their/Our Con-ceptualization and Enactment

Hooks and West, and other scholars of Black African American descent, have *historical* roots in contemplating social-civil-human justice activities within the diversity of Black African American communities and the pub-lic sphere of society at large. Broaching multiple areas of human activi-ties, those involved in this salient enterprise sought to explore, identify, and redress interest-issues related to gender, race, ethnicity, class, and cultural areas of specific to Black African American communities, within the context and political realities of diverse domestic and world societies. Whiting and Lewis (2008) stated that masculinity by Black people have a long and well-documented history; according to these authors, "questions regarding manhood have been under investigation since emancipation" (p.1). Wallace (2002) pointed out that earlier than the "mid-nineties not even the new wave of U.S. masculinity studies", and the post-men's movement, "seemed capable of imaging black men paradigmatically "at the center" of their critical contemplations or "giving any more than the most peripheral acknowledgement to the racial contingencies of the American masculine "ideal" (pp. 2-3).

Saint-Aubin (1994) in his work in which he examined why Black masculinity and "the way that the experiences and the representation of the experiences of black men seem to problematize existing theory" (p. 1055) in masculinity studies, stated that,

> *In the men's movement and in many of the studies of masculinity, in spite of lip service to policies and practices sensitive to differences in class and race, some men are still marginalized. In a culture so clearly defined by and so self-conscious about race, one might expect attention to be paid to the position of men of color because one would expect any discourse on masculinity to be radically inflected by a focus on rather than a mere appendage of non-white men. Yet, precisely these men who are marginalized; therefore, scant attention if any is paid to the inter-articulation between racial and sexual ideology. (p. 1056)*

That is to say, Black African American and bi-multi-racial males are subject to examination through the analytical filters under a European American frame of reference or what is touted as universal masculinity studies. This declared universality, is supposedly inclusive of all males, regardless of the cultural social-psychohistorical experiences in view of social-political circumstances throughout the history of this democratic nation state.

Hunter and Davis (1994) argued that "the meaning of manhood has been treated as largely unidimensional (one-dimensional) and universal ---man as economic provider and as head of family. Further they said, "What Black men are and what they should be is measured against the status and privilege of White male" (p. 20). The investigators also stated that as a result, "we know little about *how Black men define themselves* either *within or beyond conventional notions of masculinity and manhood*" (p.20). This point regarding universality stands in historical-contemporary contradiction to the still emerging existence of Black men as a diverse demographic now with generations of experiencing social, racialized gendered complexities into a post-civil rights, among whose citizens are engaging in microaggressive push-back in response to earlier social-justice of equality gains and when presence-past issues are raised. (The normality surrounding the universality of masculinity and manhood and the natural right of men has been and is thought to be sublime across ethnic-cultures historically).

It has been asserted in the literature that during daily social interaction and in scholarly context, Black African American, bi-multi-racial males have been discussing, perceiving, explaining, and performing, who we are, want to be, and the circumstance of how and why we exist in this country (Belton, 1996; Byrd and Guy-Sheftall, 2001; Carroll, 1995; Dyson, 2007; Head, 2004; White & Cones, 1999).

Black males have and continue to work at carving out cultural space for existence on their own terms in the personal and public sphere, located in various organizational institutions/industries and social-multicultural settings. In other words, they work at defining, interpreting, explaining, and substantiating their right to be visible on their own cultural terms, (Gates, Jr., 1997; Harper, 1996; Price, 2000; Shelton and Seller, 2000; Young, 2007, Lemelle, Jr., 2010). However, and with this caveat, how aware are Black African American, bi-multi-racial males, thereby conversant about the self as relevant to ethnic-cultural affiliation and racialized gender, regarding how it affects the degree and depth of this kind of work and effort? I would add, that this question is particularly relevant as it concerns the need to develop more progressive non-sexist defining, enacting, and critiquing the gendered self in cultural and intercultural context and interactions with others. This includes, for example, the presentation and negotiation of their worldview and perspective in the face of real possibilities of eliciting subconscious and/or racially conditioned closed mindedness among members of the society at large during intercultural class, and gender, and so forth, interactions, such as those punctuated by racial microaggressions.

A study conducted of 124 young adult Black men by Mahik, Pierre, & Wan (2006) "indicated that self-esteem was positively related to participants' internalization of racial identity attitudes and negatively related to conformity to traditional masculine norms in the dominant culture of the United States" (p.1). Carby (1998), in her study regarding the nature of Black masculinity construction in "historical moments," (p. 2), stated that Du Bois believed his striving to serve the advancement of his race informed his development as a man embodied in the term "Race Man" (p. 9-10). Du Bois sought to expend concentrated time and space on developing and expanding his intellectual development and directing his knowledge not just as an intellectual person, but as a Race Man; I would assert that this was a male gendered declaration. As per Carby, "Du bois constructed particular personal, political, and social characteristics of a racialized masculinity to articulate his definition of black leadership" (p.11); this involved sexist heterogeneous rationalization when it came to Black African American women and the Black struggle. Carby went on to say that Du Bois was concerned with planting ideals of life, thrift, and civilization among the community of Negro Black men, that would hopefully filter through overtime to the masses of Black people as examples of moral living. Very pointedly, Carby analyzed Du Bois' authored work, The Souls of Black Folks, arguing that his project comes up short, in that Du Bois failed to imagine and declare Black women into the "sphere of intellectual equality" (p.9). Du Bois failure to consider and involve Black women, perhaps had to do with the sense and practice of his manly tendencies, inclinations, pre-dispositions specific to conventional patriarchal standards for manhood. This, particularly given the overtly racist bent times he was present in and the temporal proximity to slavery, and then it's *de jure* proclaimed end that rolled right into Jim Crow segregation's social-political contract.

Collins (2006) stated that meanings associated with Black masculinity in the US were analogous to a narrow huddle "of controlling images" within a broader framework granting varying values assigned to "racially distinctive forms of masculinity" (p.75). According to Collins these racially distinctive manifestations of masculinity resided along a continuum raising critical questions regarding attributes of Black masculinity portraying weakness.

For example,

> *is weakness associated with an inability to control violent impulses, sexual urges, or their black female heterosexual partners, or a weakness attributed to men whose lack of education, employment patterns, and criminal records relegate them to inferior social spaces? (p.75)*

On the other position of the continuum there was the representation of Black males who "posed no threat to White society" (p.75). Collins argued that negative representations, that is, stereotypes of Black men as being portrayed and perceived as oversexed, docile, threatening, suave communicators, were populated in American science and societal imagination long after Black males' post-emancipation into contemporary representations of Black men portrayed as "rapists and thugs" (p.75). She pointed out that Black men are debilitated and *inhibited* by such images, and the "underlying vision of masculinity as dominance" (p.75). [4]

In sum, do such images represent the unconscious desired expectations *a*mong members of the dominant society which amount to the dichotomized option of the "Good Negro" who is rendered as an "acceptable image" for Black males, in order to avoid or to psychologically compensate for the image of "the "Bad Negro" who characterizes "all the anxieties, fears, and stereotypes toward black masculinity?" Recall that Brown (2005) claimed that historically, from the *so-called* settlement of the country, there have been societal pressures to dominate and control Black people, particularly as it concerned posing a threat to dominant life, property and cultural interests and values.

According to Mutua (2006) hegemonic masculinity (i.e., masculinity as dominant and the American ideal of manhood) has been successfully argued by feminists as "binary and dichotomous thinking that is endemic to Western thought" (p.12). Binary representations as the result of dichotomous thinking are not side by side equal but "hierarchical with the first being desirable and positionality, and the second being undesirable and a corrupted position" (p.12). For instance, there are dualities of good-evil, male- female, and heterosexual-homosexual. Still further, there are categorical traits assigned to each set of these dualities. Mutua stated, "Many of the messages men hear about what it means to be a man, particularly those associated with ideal masculinity, may be harmful to them and psychologically and socially problematic" (p. 15). For example, from Ross (1998) I garnered ideas about how the images of Black men via mass media domestically and globally can arrive in the imagination and real-time perception of others regarding African American males. These recorded live images and sounds, along with edited pictures and sound bites, carry with them the constant potential of the ideal and profit-driven appearance of what is means to be a man. On film, television, various social media devises, computer, and so on, "iconography" of super entertainers, hip

---

[4] In the readings of work by Patricia Hill Collins and bell hooks they both demonstrated themselves as dauntless intrepid scholars with unwavering working agendas for social-equality and justice, who acknowledged the state and ill-logic of patriarchal hegemony in collaboration with historical White supremacy.

hop artists, athletes among African American males are in your face up close and personal. Ross strongly proclaimed that global media has become "overly determined by the iconography of African American men in the post-civil rights and post-cold war moment, similarly, that the figure of the Black man has emerged as a reigning symbol of aggressive American manliness" (p.601).

One of the implications of Ross's analytical perspective is that among Black and Brown men even when in public settings outside of sports and entertainment, there is the potential for them of gaining the self-perception and/or self-conscious feelings of being involved in spectator sports. Spectator sports allows those among men of color to be perceptually viewed, imaged, and interacted with-within a safe comfort zone place. From the preceding literature on Black masculinity, it can be suggested that among those Black males empowered via the military and sports that hold a conservative "Good Negro" sway would most likely meet the perceptional approval among European Americans and assimilated like-minded people of color, particularly those among the wealthy and elite corporate owners.

Both Collins and Mutua have argued that Black males need to avoid the trappings imposed by the rigidity of binary representation that drive the unrealistic structuring and interpersonal-relationship strategizing based upon the *American ideal of manhood*. As Courtenay (2000) discussed in his analysis of male construction of masculinity attitudes and approaches towards well-being, dominant masculinities not only involve degrees of interpersonal power practices directed at women, but work to subordinate lower-class and marginalized masculinities in their exercise of degrees of power, such as those of "gay, rural, or lower-class men" (p.1391). It would follow that exercising degrees of power in the construction and performance of masculinity results in the forming of inclinations (as in habitus), regarding styles and strategies for working to experience empowerment within a variety of settings, conditions, and places.

Courtenay further observed that "physical dominance and violence are easily accessible resources for structuring, negotiating and sustaining masculinities, particularly among men, who because of their social positioning, lack less dangerous means" (p. 1391); if it is physical then it is connected with psychological violence and/or the threat of either.

It should be considered from this perspective that lacking less *dangerous means*, involves the deficiency of financial and social-cultural capital to exact a sophisticated, propagandized, and covert means of configuring and reconfiguring masculine dominance in social-political arenas; thus, the ability to impact multiple ethnic-cultural, class, sexual gender groups of people. Unfortunately, this dominant masculinity socializing and valuation thesis, includes support and conformity from among heterogeneous women of a conservative mindset in particular. For example, in the critical controversial arena of abortion rights to choose, there are women who support conservative males' position to deny women that right (Maddow, 2012).

In response to the paradigm of Western heterogeneous male dominance ideology, and the paradox of racialized gender, Collins said that "Progressive black masculinities require rejecting not only the images currently associated with black masculinity but also the structural power relations associated with them" (p.75). Mutua stated that "Progressive black masculinities, for instance, take an active and ethical stand against all social structures of domination, that are anti-racist, pro-feminist, and are not based on the subordination of others as the "reigning symbol of aggressive American manliness," (p. 599).

Billson (1996) developed identity archetypes presented in a paradigm called "strategic styles" of manhood making among urban situated young African American males. Billson drew on data from Harvard University Pathway to Identity Project to explore and study five young Black males who grew up in a Northeastern city during the 1960s and 1970s racial upheaval and cultural response for change; hence the term response to social reality. In actuality, it can be said that strategic styles speak to the development of manly tendencies in response to social reality as habitus of Black masculinity making. In part this involves survival thrust, the ways that one constructs and adapts to organize and deal with social-cultural reality. Pants sagging, which is not new in the history of clothes wearing among Black men in African American cultural vogue, is more strategic to masculinity styling than to the "what' as in what one is wearing; it is more to the how as in symbolic interaction (Men of Color, 1998).

Hammond and Mattis (2005) conducted a study entitled *"Being a Man about it, Manhood Meaning among African American Men"* (p. 114). Included in their study was a discussion regarding the provocative Moynihan Report of 1965. The report was conducted during the early years of the military draft and Vietnam conflict whereby a finding of this study listed a claim that, *"African American manhood was reviewed as a "problem"* (p. 115). Findings for this report characterized Black men as trouble-some or

contrary, and focused mostly on their presumed abnegation of family responsibilities; it was a racially exacerbating and social culturally illiterate
report. hooks (2004), in her cultural critique of the "Moynihan Report" on
the "Negro Family, asserted that findings from this generated racialized
views that Black men were being "emasculated" (viewed as being ineffec-
tual and/or powerless) because of Black women being viewed as matri-
archs; thereby raising a false racialized gendered dichotomy. hooks adeptly pointed out that "participating in the armed forces was one way for
black men to reclaim their patriarchal status" (p.12). Put another way,
manhood (personally and publically realized) could be reclaimed via participation in an organization where global armed violence was sanctioned.
Data analysis from the Hammond and Mattis study generated 15 categorical areas of manhood making among African American participants, such
as,

- Responsibility – accountability: taking, handling and having an
  awareness of one's responsibility to self, family, and others.

- Providing – way-making: a provider for self, family, and making
  ways available for others financially or otherwise.

- Moral rectitude-virtues: striving to engage life in a morally upright
  fashion.

- Surviving-overcoming: enduring and striving to persevere in the
  face of challenges.

- Self-appreciation-awareness: possessing an emotional appreciation of self and having an appreciation for one's race and history
  (p.114).

The authors stated that findings showed that participants augmented
traditional conceptualizations of masculinity by capturing a greater depth
and range of meaning that African American men assigned to manhood.
Furthermore, since results from the study could not be encapsulated in
the 15 categories, four major thematically descriptive discussion points
were formulated from their data analysis specifically regarding how participants in the study viewed defining African American manhood:

- Manhood as an Interconnected State of Being: participants generally constructed manhood as best understood as an interconnection between self, family, and others.

- Manhood as a Fluid Developmental Process: manhood is fluid and adaptive; for example, the importance of ascertaining positive manhood traits over time.

- Manhood as a Proactive Course: establishing a proactive course of action means anticipating potential barriers and threats to one's identity as well as ensuring its maintenance by initiating a set of positive life actions.

- Manhood as a Redemptive Process: there were narrative responses among the study participants that implied that manhood offers several opportunities for redemption, i.e., there is opportunity to rectify one's past behavior and "recouping one's humanity through active family and civic participation" (pp. 122-124).

Finally, the authors believed that manhood meaning making (self-definition and enactment) among African American men "appears to be multidimensional in nature" (p. 125), also maintaining among other suggestions for future study, that there is a need to focus on the exploration of sociological issues Black men confront "as they attempt to actualize their masculinity" (p. 125).

D. Performing Black Masculinity

> *My collaborator, Guillermo Gomez-Pena, and I were intrigued by the legacy of performing the identity of an Other for a white audience, sensing its implications for us as performance artists dealing with cultural identity in the present. Had things changed, we wondered (Fusco, 1995, p. 37)?*

Butler (1999) stated that "performativity is not a singular act, but a repetition and a ritual, which achieves its effects through its naturalization in the context of a body, understood, in part, as a culturally sustained temporal duration" (p. xv). As a sustained temporal duration, repetition of time, I suggest habitus plays an intricate role in performativity.

Chandler (2007) cited Schechner (2002) as suggesting performativity involves two elements. Element 1 is that performativity is a method of "constructing reality" such in classroom teaching or lecturing in front of an audience (p.57). Recall the Shakespearean saying "the entire world is a stage and we are mere actors" (Shakespeare in Hope's study of rhetoric, 1999). Secondly, "performativity characterizes the practice of recycling behaviors for the purposes of embodying particular kinds of performances in everyday life" (p.57). An example was cited regarding ritualized behavior in a decision to wear wedding bands to create a "reality called marriage" (p.57). The author gave an example regarding how the wearing of rings was part of demonstration, belief, self-reminder, and public announcement of a formal partnership. This partnership involves negotiating and constructing social-cultural reality in regards to being considerate, respectful, and responsible, as part of the symbolic, psychological, and physical bond toward one another. Here too, I would suggest that the symbol of a ring, for instance in the wearing of ethnic – cultural group jewelry, can initiate symbolic interpersonal-cultural perceptions in the public sphere, particularly given the visibility of racial phenotypical features as generally perceived as the other, member of a racial minority group, or relative to the concept of otherness.

Chandler pointed out that the simple act of saying something out loud involves performativity. I suggest that given the literature on the influences of race, ethnicity, and gender on the self -perception and exploration of identity, interpersonal intercultural communication is part of performativity, and relevant to and within, the symbolic interaction theory. Hecht, Collier, and Ribeau (1993), in their investigative analysis of African American communication, stated that, "Cultural communication is a system of interdependent patterns of conduct (conversation) and interpretation (code) that are used by a group of people to define their personhood and reinforce group identity" (p. 29).

"Code or style switching" (p. 89) is involved in cultural communication (performativity) as a situational response to the conditions of materialistic social reality in the context of dominant group power relations and socializing influences within a multi-cultural society. In their study regarding ethnicity, identity, and cultural interpretation of African American communication, Hecht et al, cited findings from their study that participants felt it was salient for them to be understood during interpersonal-cultural communication encounters relative to the goal of communicating with clarity of meaning. Code or style switching is what I refer to as "cultural commuting" (Alcorn, 1994, pp. 42-43). Generally speaking, cultural commuting involves making perceptual, attitudinal, listening, and linguistic adaptations in moving between interpersonal intercultural situational interactions relative to space and location. According to Seymour and

Seymour (1979) in Hecht et al, among African Americans there are three kinds of styles or code switchers. In *one* group it is asserted that the lesser degree of education plays a role when present in situations where "Mainstream Standard English" is sanctioned; the *second* group are those among African Americans who are proficient in and preferred speaking Mainstream Standard English, but find difficulty in social-cultural situations where "Black English is preferred." Lastly, there are those among African Americans who are educated and can use both (p.89). Said differently, this final group can engage cultural commuting as I noted previously.

Borrowing a concept from Shade (1989) in reference to cultural world view, from her work, *Culture, Style, and the Educative Process*, all three group's linguistic choices and/or efforts involve engaging in situational "cognitive appraisal" (p. 63), as a part of their habitus shaped by the construction and response to social reality. In sum, it appears that code switching involves a response to the dynamics of intergroup ethnic-cultural, gender, class, and racialized power relations and locus of control perceptions.

One of the suggestions from findings in Chandler's (2011) study is that "African American males perform their masculinities as a result of, and between various tensions. Tensions revealed were inward and outward" (p. 66). The locations of these tensions were sets that were both inward and outward.

> *First, masculinities are performed in certain ways a as result of the dominant society's expectations of Black Male Pathology. This also fed into the second tension, which I termed "The Judging Act:" negotiating life between the dominant society's characterization of normalcy and what I term the "Organic Self." I define the Organic Self as the conscious performance of identity that represents what a person believes to be his authentic identity. As well, respondents routinely articulated the third tension, which I termed the "Me against the World" tension. (p.66)*

Finally, Chandler pointed out that study respondents clearly indicated that they generally lived in a "survival and defensive mode" (p.66).

Baldwin (1976), in his investigation of African American personality identified the presence of what he called "Survival Thrust" (p.?). Generally speaking, survival thrust, as noted previously, means how one develops and organizes strategies to social-culturally and psychologically to survive in various settings; moreover, survival thrust is a response to perceived social-materialistic reality and conditions. Baldwin's survival thrust appears to be contextually akin to the survival and defensive mode named in Chandler's study.

Staples (1992), in his provocative social essay entitled "Just Walk on By: A Black Man Ponders his Power to Alter Public Space," discussed how his presence and that of Black males in general "can alter public space in some ugly ways" (p. 103). The author discussed how his existence, and those among Black males in public space, frightens and/or unnerves certain individuals across race-gender-class lines.

E. Black Masculinity and Manhood in Educational Context

Like Mirza (1999) so pointedly stated,

> *Black masculinity is not something we consciously talk about much in academic study. We find a gaping absence on the subject in our research on education or writing in sociology [outside of pronouns he, his, him, in reference to something that occurred]. What we find is that the blanket of black masculinity that envelops and shapes our very Whiteness, seeps unconsciously onto the front pages of our daily newspapers. With an almost acceptable normativity, we read, [view, listen] with deadpan regularity, about the rise of black male exclusions in school, disproportionate incarceration, academic under-achievement and truancy as pre cursors to prison, and higher than average rates of un [under] employment. (p.139)*

The author went on to discuss how culturally conditioned assumptions rise up in interpersonal-cultural racialized gendered conversations associating Black males with father-parenting absenteeism, violent deaths, drugs, crime, under-education, hyperactively-sexed, physical-aptitude, Black English-Standard English speaker, and I add being "thugged-out"(Amah, 2008). That is to say, recognizing and addressing the construct of Black masculinity is not more readily recognized, and studied to be better understood as directly associated with learning, academic study, and achievement. What appears to be studied and discussed more regularly in the literature are cited findings relative to the subject of education and schooling is academic underachievement results related issues.

Suppositions and claims from research findings regarding the why and what of the attitudes and behavioral result are not more readily available with regard to analyzing and considering social construction of Black masculinity itself, and its relevancy to forming of habitus, the social construction of reality and response among Black African American, bi-multiracial males, particularly, given the history of racialized gendered and European American masculine ideation in this country.

What is more readily stated and therefore accessible in the literature are studies and media reports pointing out that Black males are underachieving, truant, and dropping-out under the comfort zone term of, for instance, the achievement opportunity gap, more recently and realistically referred to as non-engagement.

Laubscher (2005) stated that contemporary psychological theory and research regarding African American men are overwhelmingly cast in crisis terms, that "the social science literature in general and psychology in particular characterize the African American man as one beset by a multitude of problems" (p.111). At issue here, among others, as pointed out by Ross (1998), is the limited research presence on successful Black male college students. For example, according to a U.S. Census Bureau report (2001) cited in Spradley (2001) "the number of black males 25 years old and over enrolled in college has increased from 143,000 in 1990 to 267,000 in 1995 to 335,000 in 2000" (p.2). Moreover, research by Majors and Billson (1992) as cited in Ross (p.2), found that only a few studies explored "the lives of successful African American men who live complex, middle class or professional lives" (p.106) with extended involvement in family, community, and nationally" (p.106). Ross pointed out not only have there been few studies of "mature, successful black males, but there is also a paucity (scantiness) of research wherein young black males narrate their own life stories" (p.2).

For instance, Edwards and Polite (1992) in their book *Children of the Dream: The Psychology of Black Success,* a focus on success stories among African Americans born between 1954 and 1968, revealed how Blacks in a variety of occupations have successfully negotiated the early racialized gendered complex, sulky, and stress producing circumstance of post *Brown* and civil rights era societal integration. Their stories, in part, suggested the saliency and relevancy of developing, cultivating, and maintaining a sense of cultural anchoring that drew upon the resourceful, inspiring, and dauntless social-cultural and psychohistorical experiences of Black African American peoples, in structuring a response to social reality relative to who they were and were working to become.

Said further, there is an absence of more extensive literature speaking to educational success among Black males and the working strategies and habitus that gets them there. Very importantly, there are Black males who have been working side by side with their brethren so to speak, who are struggling and disengaged, who can stand witness giving direct and indirect nuanced perspective. However, I would suggest that a complex site of inquiry that needs formulating, although developmental in nature, is not just the absence in the literature regarding successful Black males, but exploration of the role of Black masculinity and manhood, in the pursuit of learning, academic achievement, and living as seamlessly connected with the enactment and basis for their existence.

To further explain, what appears to be absent from inquiry in a substantive way is recognizing that the development of Black masculine/gender identity characteristics, frames of reference, psychological and cultural orientation, do not stand aside during participation in one's schooling and education, *but are a presence all along* perhaps, as, borrowing from Ellison (1990), as the "invisible man" inside us.

Woodson, in his historical work *The Miseducation of the Negro (1933)*, presented a thesis arguing the danger and contradiction of absenting the Negro from his own education, via gaining an education outside of the self in cultural trade-off or ethnic group cultural non necessity. Shujaa (1994) argued that, "Cultural orientation makes a difference in the way one critiques society" (p.28). I assert that the same thing should apply to the critique of self, in group and society. The connection suggested here is that Black masculinity and manhood are not simply representative of an acquired or ascribed social science named status but conceptually representative of the social-psychological fabric of one's sexuality, spiritual, cognitive, and personality characteristics, and as such need to be critiqued.

We need a more cultural-sexually adaptive - responsive approach to investigating, analyzing-studying the construction and response to society reality in a multiculturally complex U.S. society. For instance, Price (2000) in a study regarding the meaning making of a high school diploma, class-room experiences, and their relationships with family and peers among six young African American males, sought in part to examine the ways in which these six males were "privileged or penalized through systems of race, class, and gender" (p. 118). Thereby gaining more informed under-standing specific to "how race, class, and gender played out in their lives" (p.118).

Study aims and designs such as Price's contribute to building and de-veloping analytically informed conservation regarding the role of the pres-ence of Black masculinity, manhood, sexuality, among Black African American, bi-multi-cultural males in educational space, and how they should be considered, discussed, and cultivated. **Question**: *If a merger is not waged where learning and education are not perceived and practiced as the fabric of one's identity/existence (i.e., cultural masculinity, manhood, gender orientation), does this contribute to lost opportunities as in academ-ic underachievement, school dropout, college drop in without completion, and a loss of opportunities to engage in deeper more intimate approaches to learning and education among Black males? Is there a connection between masculine development and attitudes towards a desire to become learned?*

Ford (2011) conducted a qualitative study and analysis of 29 Black American college students attending a large research university. The aim of the study was to explore "how Black masculinity was physically, behav-iorally, and materialistically constructed from idealized images resulting in a contextually adaptive sense of self" (p.38). Study results, viewed from a social constructivist framework, suggested that Black masculinity, particu-larly the "thug image, was symbolically affirmed and denied" (p. 38) through exacting a "type of raced, gendered, classed, and sexualized dis-course within the Black public of social spaces" (p.38). However, the con-cept of manhood was found to have thoughtfully captured and evoked more "genuine interactions, regardless of the social location" (p.38).

Perhaps these findings among participants' differentiating sexual characteristics between masculinity and manhood suggested that they perceived masculinity as a raw physical part of sexuality to be supported by social-linguistic and non-verbal symbolic posturing and actions that were responsive to a detached "thugged out style." Whereby, manhood was perceived as the more cognitively reflective, civil, and respectful part of their sexual sense of being.

Conceivably, from the above perspective of masculinity, emphasis was placed upon *talking with one's body* (as one the study respondent's in this book acutely stated). Ford coined the phrase "doing masculinity" (p. 38) as representative and more reliant upon a raw physically symbolic style of being.

Note that masculinity or masculine is generally believed among people in society as being natural to biological apparatus at birth that subconsciously and/or consciously alerts one to an implicit link to biological determinism regarding construction and response to social reality; there is the que for externally sanctioned heterogeneous socializing, but where are you the person in all this. Then to there are the demands of fitting-in acceptance, and in what ways you/person experiences/perceives this. To wit, there is an automatic cultural assumption of difference based upon biology thereby destined for ascribed social construction via references to the dichotomizing of female or male, feminine or masculine.

For example, Walker, Butland, and Connell (2000), broaching the subject social-gender linguistics, claimed the presence of implicit biologically gendered determinism in taken-for-granted categories of female and male and/or woman and man socially conditioned references, which was believed to be natural among participants in their study. A cohort of multiethnic European and Southeast Asian participants responded to questions regarding their beliefs as to *why among men and boys there was a greater chance of experiencing road causality in injury or death.* The researchers found that the presence of implicit biological determinism was often signaled among participants through their use of the terms "man" and "female" rather than "man" and "woman" (p. 1). Spanier (1995) discussed how the *fallacy* in biological determinism was used to support thesis arguments that homosexuality was innate, by one's genetics, which represented a throw-back to 19th century biological determinism theories aimed at legitimizing race and sexuality inequalities among people of color and women.

Finally, under biological determinism, traditional notions of heterogeneity are still argued from the value perspective that man is, for instance, the bread-winner or lead in a relationship. Put another way, the Black masculine self in Ford's study was found to involve the symbolic scripting of the body that can be described as "doing Black masculinity" as in physical-social hyper sexuality, that involved negative sexist and bullying connotations that engendered false ways of being a man. I would argue that it is like giving one's self a *placebo* sense of ethnic-cultured-racialized male-ness and manhood.

Martin and Harris II (2006) conducted a study from a social construc-tivist perspective that considered the creation and enactment of masculin-ity among African American male student athletes who are "academically driven" (p. 359). Some of their background discussion and presentation of study findings revealed the following:

- Given the doggedness of racism and issues related to social aliena-tion among African American males, they "often typically rely on alternative modes of masculine expression" within and outside of the ways of masculine expression via "mainstream and traditional ideals of accumulating wealth and material possession and by gaining social power and position of influence" according to Oliver, 1989 cited by Martin and Harris III (p. 363).[5]

- Study participants (student-athletes) "equated masculinity with having integrity and courage to do what is right" (p. 367).

- Unlike many among their teammates study participants did not define their masculinity relative to the acquisition of material pos-sessions and the acquiring of athletic status, they considered mas-culinity as a "call for accountability, making unpopular decisions, and setting positive examples for others to follow" (p. 368).

The study authors found that contrary to research by Gilbert and Gil-bert (1998), which stated that there is incongruence between academic achievement and developing masculine identity, that, "being a good stu-dent does not equate to being a man" (p. 369), *their* findings showed that study participants placed a high value on academic success.

---

[5] Martin and Harris II stated that Oliver identified several primary orientations among Black males through the expression of masculinity, "the tough guy and the player of women" (p. 364). I suggest that both of these warrant careful culturally contextual discussion given the propensity among people within the U.S. society at large regarding the stereotyping of African American males, relative to stereotype vulnerability thesis. This concurred with my perspective garnered from my review of Oliver (2006) in his works that presented an analysis of streets as a site of alterna-tive socialization among Black African American males, and from my autobiograph-ical essay on the subject of young Black males and urban socializing experiences relative to masculinity in their view and construction of social reality.

In sum, Black masculinity and manhood in its' continuously emerging bi-multi-racially culturally U.S. society, should not be consciously and unconsciously experienced and/or overtly or covertly presented as a paradoxical competing choice, nor simply something that is perceived as too controversial to realize outside of certain social arenas. Arguably, what joins Black masculinity and manhood in educational context, is that educational subject matter in a historically dominant Eurocentrically influenced society, (Shujaa 1994); Spivey (1978) is expected to be learned and acted upon in the presence of self that is not to be developed, understood, and lived, as the fabric of self in acculturation context. Such a project, for example, culturally responsive teaching and classroom management, is still very wanting and being challenged by conservative thinking educators, critics, and citizens among society at large. Among whom there are those political pundits, educational leaders, practitioners, and parents who are opposed to multicultural/social justice approaches to learning and education throughout this country's educational systems, private and public. Argumentatively, I contend that such approaches could provide a more cognitive-intellectual, attitudinally lucid, and transculturally equitable framework with which to investigate and study the idea of such as seamless merger, within the borders of U.S. society.

F. Bi-Multi-Racial Masculinity and Manhood

- Racial tension and division exist on most college campuses today. When Blacks and Whites are polarized, where does this leave the biracial student?

- Many monoracial college students view biracial persons' dating choices as indicative of their racial identity. In turn, biracial college students find who they date to be a litmus test of their racial self-definition.

- Biracial persons must deal with the fact that there is not official "biracial" racial classification.

- Many monoracial persons maintain that a biracial person cannot have a true racial identity (Korgen, 1998, p.5).

Unlike other categories of ethnic-cultural masculinity, it appears that the literature specific to *bi-multi-racial masculinity and manhood construction, meaning, and enactment* is scant in the literature. I purport that it is liked to a hidden voice among those who are bi-multi-ethnic-cultural-

racial male specific to their perception, identification, meaning, and enactment of their masculine self and manhood, and their racialized gendered self. There is more pronounced contribution in the literature relative to hyphenated ethnic-cultural (ethnic-national identity) masculinity
and manhood, (i.e., Native-American, Chinese-American, Mexican-
American.....), but not in reference to bi-multi ethnic-racial.   Kilson
(2000), in discussing racial identity development, said that issues related
to <u>self-identity</u> perception and construction are more prominently situated in the literature regarding bi-multi racial persons.

Then too there are discussions reflecting racially presumptive, inquisitive, and ambiguous attitudes, views, perceptions, among peers and
members of the society at large directed toward bi-multi racial persons
that come to their social-cultural - perceptual attention that is detrimental
to their well-being-ness (Breland, Steward, Robbie, Neil, Minami, Chan,
Owens, Collins, & Spearman (1999); Fusco & Wallis, 2003).   For example,
Sinyangwe (2012) conducted a coherent empirical study in consideration
of a "tri-racial hierarchy" (p. 87), regarding cross-racial perceptions of
President Barack Obama given his racial-ethnic-heritage, as it concerned
favorability of him. Among the findings were that participants who embraced bi-multi-racial identity also embraced a "mixed race President" (p.
91); the dominant White population privileged the President's mixed racial
background, while "minority Black population" stigmatized it (p. 91). Furthermore, "while mixed-race individuals generally supported [President]
Obama's identity (those who self-identified as Black) responded most fa-
vorably towards him" (p. 91).

Simone (1989) in his work entitled *About Face: Race in Postmodern
America*, (1989), discussed, for instance, the presence of inter-racial sexual
interaction as a possible source of racial *ambiguity* and *anxiety* in society
at large. In his chapter entitled, "Fearing the Imagination" he stated that,
"Sexuality continues to be a vehicle through which the intense and often
passions regarding race are expressed" (p. 49).

Root pointed out that there was a "biracial baby boom" (p. 3) initiated
in the US "around the time the last laws against miscegenation (race mixing) were repealed in 1967" (p.3). According to Root (1992), a segregated,
integrated, and still racialized society has created an identity vacuum filled
with stigma and polarized choice regarding a quest to fit-in and define
who they are among bi-multi-racial individuals. Subsequently, Root asserted that in a "phenotypically heterogeneous society" the existence of
racially mixed persons blurs dichotomous intra and inter- ethnic-cultural

identity boundaries, as well as presumptive and proscriptive boundaries set in motion by phenotypical racialized markers.

Korgen (1998) discussed what was termed as the biracial "transformation" among Blacks, noting self and societal identification of mixed racial-ethnic-cultural heritage; the author pointed to an institutional shift involving redefining of racial-ethnic-cultural categorizing that has occurred. Very saliently, Korgen asserted bi-multi-mixed racial persons must be attentive to avoid and/or address the internalization of negative image of themselves, "that have historically evolved to suppress multiple heritage identification," and that "have largely benefited White society" relative to the "rule of hypo descent" (p. 5), which solicited "simplistic dichotomous rules of classification (e.g. White versus non-White)" (p.5).

Miller (1992) stated, "As multiracial and multiethnic people become more prevalent in society, the need for theory that can describe their experiences becomes increasingly important" (p.25). Yet, it appears that research investigation focused on racialized gender identity construction and development interest and issues is still wanting, specifically as it concerns the ethnic-cultural identity and heritage, relative to the development, definition, and enactment of masculinity, manhood, and sexuality. I propose that it is within investigative findings and discussion regarding self and societal induced identity choices and experiences in, for example, narrative autobiographical context and the politics of gender identity, that presently one must dig into to extrapolate and construct, in this case, racial-ethnic-gender paradigmatic conceptualizations that speak to bi-multi-racial masculinity and manhood constructions, and relative to learning and academic achievement.

R. Hall (1997) in his article entitled: "*Human development across the lifespan as an identity model for biracial males,*" purported that the use of a lifespan approach to the social construction of identity avoids the bipolar dichotomy of historical "Black/White" (either/or) ethnic-cultural racialized paradigm, used in identity recognition and development in U.S. society. Hall asserted that the biracial heritage man (person) must be prepared to address the perceptional, inquisitive, and often time ridiculing disquieting remarks regarding bi-racial-ness, which can and does become more socially and psychologically complex among multi-racial men/persons, such as two of the participants from the study that this work was based upon.

Curiosity and judgmental-ness among societal members regarding phenotypical racialized features such as skin tone, hair texture, body shape, socio-linguistic style and tone, as they intersect with racialized-gender, ethnicity, class, and sexuality, are all factors detrimental to identity development, health, well-being-ness, and empowerment. For instance, if one achieves educationally how does one associate the achievement, for example, ethnic culturally speaking? Given the historical-contemporary overt and subtle social adversities in U. S. society, regarding racialized gender, it stands to reason that bi-multi-racial individuals (the historical mulatto) must engage in an ongoing and unique developmental path to establishing and maintaining who they are and choose to be represented/defined as. As Hall said,

> *in the interest of mental and emotional health, males who perceive themselves as biracial must counter-define the social and political universe. In the face of two powerful barriers—racism and psychological domination—it characterizes the viability of their existence. (p. 74)*

Hall further argued that the across lifespan as a human development model, where one chooses how and what is relevant to optimize, is more amenable to successful adaptation and compensation strategies across time that avoids putting the self, in this case, biracial and I would add multi-racial stagnation. In other words, the across lifespan development approach is based upon the notion that identity like culture is fluid and adaptable particularly when one views learning and the accumulation of knowledge as a life span pursuit; hence, enhanced opportunities for self-optimization via self-epistemology, identity development and responsiveness to social reality.

Finally, according to Hall the "lifespan human development model serves as a powerful alternative to the pathologizing influences of the black/white dichotomy and to the approaches emphasizing racial characteristics to the exclusion of others" (p.77). Moreover, the lifespan development model involves a set of personal-social concerns "that one's race and/or skin color is not wholly definitive" (p.77). What is strategic here to is that Hall is contributing to the development self-literacy regarding the nature of personal preferences and holding them in worth "in spite of the existence within a stigmatizing social universe" (p.77). I would add that being cognitively aware and interrogative of one's bi-multi-racial habitus relative to masculinity and manhood development, defining, and enacting, has a critical place in this development approach.

Conclusion

In summary, *habitus refers to transportable temporal dispositions and inclinations that are a part of the individual self-identity and self-actualizing styles, strategies, and ways of being, which include racialized gender and sexuality.* The development and enactment of Black masculinity and manhood is subject to *negotiating* the interculturally-racialized social landscape of a dominant White Collective (Wise, 2011), in view of a post-civil rights era multicultural society. Black and bi-multi-racial males are exposed to the socializing, challenging, and sometimes contradictory scripted demands and expectations relative to attempting to construct and enact masculinity and manhood within regard to mainstream European American standards of masculinity. Then to, that of their ascribed ethnic-cultural group and community concurrently; which has experienced social-economic-class, political, and intra-group cultural disintegration (Robinson, 2010).

According to Robinson "Black America" consists of four intra-group segments, they are, "mainstream middle class majority," a large impoverished low income minority, "a small transcendent elite, and finally, "two emergent groups --- individuals of mixed heritages, and communities of recent Black immigrants" (p. 92).

In his courageously compelling works on the complexity and the "burden of racial performance," Young (2007) confessed out loud that

> *To embrace my blackness, my heritage, my manliness, I identify with men who represent the ghetto. I no longer deny my class background or the racial experience associated with it. I identify to belong. I disidentify to escape racism, to avoid the structures that oppress black men. But I also disidentify to retaliate against black men—to punish them for what I perceive as their efforts to disown me. This ambivalence provokes me to imitate and just as often disassociate from the black men I envy. Both efforts fail. Neither alleviates my racial anxiety. Instead, they heighten*

*the angst I experience. As a result I am hyperaware of
how masculine I am (not) or black I (don't) act. (p.65)*

*Was Ashanti Young questioning an ascribed necessity of being and per-
forming Black identity in order to be manly or the burden of both; the burden of being stereotypically defined or imagined by others as being violent,
hyper sexed, disproportionately incarcerated, undereducated, underem-
ployed or embarrassed? Guinier (2010) introduced the works with the provocative lead in title:" Twelve Angry Men" true testimonies from law-
abiding Black men who were profiled leading to detainment, arrest, stop
and frisk, and so on. Is Ashanti Young the 13th angry man, who is of Black
African American descent?*

In the literature on Black males specific to the subject of this review
on masculinity and manhood, it is said that the body was scripted (Brown,
2011) not just for the construction of image in viewing and imaging, but in
its construction "it draws upon racialized, politicized," (p.152), and commodification of Black bodies, in ways that promote and sustain acceptable
stereotypical meaning, this being under-realized in the imagination
among multicultural U.S. and global societies. Brown stated, "in short,
scripting is the process of an individual placing his or her own worldview
onto another—a worldview that perpetuates negative assumption, characteristics, and behaviors of African Americans" (p.153).

Drawing from Jackson, I make the analogy, it is like texting as in having
a conversation that engraves your worldview onto the body of another
which "often requires dislocating the original text [the social-cultural reality and historical circumstance of the person's body being inscribed up-
on] and redefining the newly affected or mirrored text as counter-
positional or oppositional" (p.153).

From the literature, it is argued and/or implied that to be learned, civil,
progressive, and of just-citizenship, as it occurs within the preview of a
racialized gendered society, relative to social-perception, imagination, and
decision making, that these afore-going characteristics/efforts are not
readily recognized nor accepted as being detrimental to the development,
defining, and enactment of Black African American, bi-multi-racial masculinity, manhood, and sexuality. This lack of recognition and acceptance
exists among citizens of a multi-cultural nation state in areas of human
activities such as education, law, psychology, medicine, business, and government, despite the episode of a:

500-year-old process of domination involving the use
of language (white racial knowledge production)
around black bodies inscribed in law, politics, educa-
tion, medicine, and every other major institution in
society through a collective human suffering, violence,
psychological mayhem and the exploitation of labor
and land theft.
President Obama must work within the established
and contemporary racial order or risk the perception
of him as a public danger in the White House because
his race is a "liability" the elephant in the room that
no one wants to talk about it. (Darron, 2012)

It is not surprising and should have been expected that in the after-math of the 1st presidential debate, none of the European American or commentators of color from established mainstream owned broadcasting, paper trail, or social media outlets included in their critiques any consideration of the presence of racialized gender consciously or subconsciously on the cognitive plate of President Obama and the First Lady relevant to the content, style, and engagement in this debate. That the event of the first presidential debate of 2012 was in fact interpersonal intercultural to a multicultural listening, hearing, and/or seeing audience, and was buried, denied, or dismissed as we are clammily in a "post-racial" era in America with his election. Does this mean that Black males in the defining, constructing, and enacting of their masculinity, manhood, sexuality, in cultural context, can expect a non-racial profiling societal citizenry that could more comfortably recognize and handle their social nuances (linguistic, behavioral, culturally imbrued ideology and talk, for instance) in major areas of human activities, such as education, law, politics, business, religion, activities, that are outside of entertainment, athletic, social-sexual-passing interaction, and the military?

In a video-taped speech at the Commonwealth Club of California, Dyson (2009) said that, "post-racial is an obscure, undefined, unexamined, and capriciously biased claim that we now live in a race free America." He most learnedly stated, "I don't think that we should be post-racial but I think we should be post-racist." Most importantly, he made his comments to this artificial post-racial societal assumption with this caveat: *Post-racial most certainty does not mean or include meaning "post-white."* He asserted that "European Americans have never thought of themselves as a specific ethnic formation in the broader context of American ethnicity or race, Blackness has been a disturbing formidable presence of a negative that cannot be totally eradicated."

The subject point implicated is that what is touted as being a nation-state of merged ethnicities into "just-American" (presumed as a universal template for identity and interpersonal interaction) has been tainted via the presence of, for example, Black-African American, Mexican American, Latina/no, Samoan, Native American, Filipino, and so on ethnic-culture representative of what Fusco called otherness, as an "inconvenient truth." This reminded me of what Franklin (1993) so pointedly called "America's False Start," the creation and perpetuation of "America's colorline" (pp.5-6). Franklin had commented that it was Du Bois who concluded that White Americans in the 18th century failed to "take a stand for human freedom at the time that they were fighting for political independence, [which] gave a clear indication of their values and priorities" (p.5). White Americans, and assimilated people of color (borrowing a concept from Lemelle, 1995) continue to engage their "Temporal refusal" to truly and most actively recognize and address this, which holds implications among Black African American and bi-multi-racial males regarding the shaping, defining, enacting of their masculinity, manhood, and sexuality. Perhaps the belief in the existence of "double-standards" among people of color and women, in a touted meritocratic society, stands in temporal refusal as well.

In the literature there were scholars and critics that studied and discussed the politics of language and group cultural efforts towards redefinition and transformation,

> *All of which is to say that Black Arts rhetoric, whose ostensible objective is to promote racial solidarity, actually engenders a division among blacks that is paradoxically necessary to the nationalist project—a division that, furthermore, is predicated on a profoundly problematic masculinist ethic. (Harper, 1996, p. 53)*

Harper revealed sources of contradiction and exclusion regarding defining, structuring, and enacting masculinity and manhood in the political and social context of declaring what is Black or African American culture, in transition *from* being called and self-identifying with the name-cultural construct of Negro American. In his treatise he insightfully argued, for instance, that to be a gay Black male and a fighter for social justice for the

Black community, is a contradiction and an insult to masculinity and manhood. A major reason is because it does not meet the gender condition, that is, criteria of conventional heterogeneous masculinity, manhood, and sexuality, for example, not manly enough or a contradiction to so-called manliness. There is the lingering question of what constitutes the defining cultural ingredients of Black or African American culture, in view of the historical-contemporary circumstance and conditions. I can comfortably say, that among Black African American, bi-multi-racial males, there must be a mustering of cognitive-intellectual wherewithal on a daily basis to carve out social-psychologically safe places just to take a breather. (Interestingly, one of the bi-racial participants in the study this work is formed from, quizzed out loud, upon hearing reference to the concept of Black masculinity and manhood, but doesn't that contain feminine too")?

The literature and media sources in particular are silver-tongued and primed to find and develop stories regarding negative disproportionality numbers among Black males but not so much *success* in ethnic-cultural context; and it's interesting to note, while generally ignoring and running away from the demonstrated evidence regarding the presence of disavowing or imponderable attitudes vis-à-vis the historical and contemporary impact of racialized gender in U.S. society. Mirza (1999) observed that Black masculinity was not something intentionally talked about in academic study.

The literature points more to collective and forming fragments of the self as in, for instance, forming the "academic self" in relationship with gender and academic study and learning, or pedagogy relative to gender and approaches to teaching, but not the merging of Black masculinity and manhood roles with academic participation, study, and success. [6]

Despite the focus on negative disproportionality statistics among Black African American males, there exists real and perceived contradictory and contentious historical circumstance and issues involved among Black African American males who are achieving concerning the defining, development, and enactment of their masculinity and manhood in the face of racialized gender. As Dyson (1996) so provocatively stated, "trapped between statistics and stereotypes, however, the brittle textures and uncomfortable truths of Black male life are too often smoothed over

---

[6] Edwin Nichols (1988) stated that the axiological value systems general applicable to European Americans thinking is parts-to-whole.

to fit easily into a pat explanation of either their prosperity or failure" (p. 68).

Most certainly among the large numbers of Black, African American, bi-multi-racial males who are hard-working, law abiding, and have experienced social-economic health in U.S. society, there are those that would agree that their lives do not neatly fit into the dichotomous trappings of "prosperity or failure." For example, Alexander (2004) informed us about the critical event of depression among gay African American males who face racial identity conflicts and the homophobic obstinate attitudes within the Black African American community and general society at large. Head (2004) called depression a silent epidemic among Black males because, for instance, there are those among them that literally believe that they can "ride out their illness, allowing it to run its course" (p.4). Then of course, there is the self-medicating involving drugs and alcohol, *like yours truly, frederick* (with a small f.).

The habitus of emotional stress, is socially and culturally informed via the conventional ways of defining and enacting masculinity and manhood, and the negative undertone, taboo, and ridicule around mental illness, are still present in the Black, African American community, and general society. Head too cited a report entitled *"Mental Health: Culture, Race, and Ethnicity,"* which was a supplement to the 2001 *"Report on Mental Health"* by the U.S. Surgeon General that stated, "racial and ethnic minorities collectively experience a greater disability burden from mental illness than do Whites" (p.2).

Mutua (2006) stated that,

- Black men have the lowest life expectancy rate of any group within the United States.

- Black male suicide rates doubled between 1980 and 1995, constituting the third leading cause of death among black men.

- Black men have the highest rate of diabetes among all men. Cardiovascular ailments prematurely kill four of every ten black men.

The point is that among Black, African American, bi-multi-racial males who are law-abiding, productive citizens, there are real and perceived concerns related to facing the potential of racial profiling, microaggression, stereotypical expectations, and imagination, that can and do result, in borrowing from Mutua, "psychological injure and constrain, that dismisses and lowers expectations of their humanity" (p.19). Root (1992) and

Mutua argued in the literature that the ideal of American masculinity is informed by binary Western thinking that dichotomizes categories of good-evil, male-female, heterosexual-homosexual, that have constraining working implications for the forming and shaping of masculinity and manhood among Black males.

Mutua (2006) asserted that "ideal masculinity is defined in opposition not only to women but also to homosexuality" and that "A real man cannot be either feminine or gay" (p. 13), and finally, "the ideal is also racialized and classed" (p.13), in other words, *we are opposition ally defined and socialized by race, ethnicity, assimilation, assigned sexual identity, political orientation, competition, and so on.*

Mutua also discussed how hegemony is at work in the forming of racialized gender, heterogeneous social and sexual roles among men and women. Here Mutua stated that "the ideal man is currently an elite heterosexual male" and the measure of man is "how close he comes to this ideal" (p.13). Both hooks (2003) and Mutua argued that there is need for the defining, structuring, and enacting of "progressive Black masculinities."

In this regard, Carbado (1999) contended that:

> *Heterosexual privilege is one of the few privileges that straight Black men know they have---not being a "sissy, punk, faggot." This is not to say, of course, that Black male heterosexuality has the normative standing of White male heterosexuality. It does not: straight Black men continue to be perceived as heterosexually deviant (potential rapists of White women and heterosexually irresponsible (jobless fathers of children born out of wedlock) Still, Black heterosexuality is closer to White male heterosexuality normalcy and normativity than is Black gay sexuality. (p. 431)*

Moreover, he stated that, among straight (or closeted) Black men there are many who would want to avoid even the suspicion of homosexuality, because it carries with it the "Black Gay [Male] ...triple suspicion to which Marlon Riggs referred too. Challenging heterosexual privilege creates (homo)sexual identity suspicion" (p. 431); heterosexuality cannot occupy the same space as any kind of identity accused of being representative of less than a man, which joins the historical complexity of the racialized gendered status of being Black African American and male, inside-out of the so-called American mainstream.

The paradox of Carbado's is held to an historical complexity, because of racialized gendered forms of institutional-societal racism, the impact of White supremacy via slavery, Jim Crow, and the residue of post-civil rights era blow-back. Further, there is promotion of socialized rigid standards of behavior, attitudinal, and cognitive distinctions of heterosexuality, of which hegemonic characteristics are a central part of. Such standards have been strongly endorsed and accepted in the African American community for the purpose of reaching for mainstream claims of heterogeneous normalcy.

hooks (2003) in her critical discussion the social, cultural, and racialized sexuality aspects of Black masculinity and manhood, correctly argued that *"Rejecting the seductive privileges offered by prevailing ideas about masculinity constitutes a complex project for African American men"* (p. 92); it would involve renouncing the subordination of other Black men via "sexual dominance," unconsciously and consciously advanced as a misperceived lack of manly-ness. As hooks advocated, there is an essential need to learn the difference between strength and dominance, in the relationship with other males, women, and children, with in the diverse range of our sexuality and orientation. In essence, this would represent a cultural – intercultural transformation of masculinity, manhood, and sexuality.

Namely, progressive Black masculinities need to be established as an on-going project in the forming of gender sexuality that is *anti*-racist, sexist, homophobic, and formulates strategies that aim to empower a "black humanity in all its variety as part of the diverse and multicultural humanity of others in the global family" (Mutua, 2006, p.7).

"I thought of myself as "African American or African Irish." Growing up I thought of myself as mixed.....I probably would have said "Black" or I would have said "Well, my mom's White and my dad's Black" (Kilson, 2009, p.91). "Which one are you?" (Miller, 1992, p. 24). Where does the hybridity of self – identity stand given the persistence of the color line (Kawash, 1997), for bi-multi-racial males, regarding self-identity, concept, development, enactment, management, relative to their masculinity, manhood, sexuality?

Root and others, in her edited works told us that the stigmatic and dogmatic historical effects of miscegenation in a bipolar (Black or White, this or that) press and demand that "we as a nation ask ourselves questions about our identity, Who are we? How do we see ourselves? Who are we in relation to one another?" (p.3). Heterogeneous dichotomous categorizing is not only inappropriate but unrealistic relative to this nation's bulging multi-ethnic cultural society. Miller stated that Eurocentric models are not only clearly inadequate to describe biracial identity, but "perpetuate an oppressive psychology" (p.34). Miller pointed out, "as multiracial and multiethnic people become more prevalent in society, the need for theory that can describe their experiences becomes increasingly important" (p.25). Yet, the literature is scarce and leaves us deficient regarding the interests and issues concerning the development, enactment, and management of bi-multi-racial masculinity and manhood experience among this diverse group of individuals.

My friend and colleague, who is a clinical psychologist, stated in therapeutic conversational discussion that societal racialized hybridity, that is, bi-multi-racial ethnicity, in the formation of masculinity and manhood can be a contributor to depression related issues relative to perceiving the self in interstitial society social space (Personal communication with Benjamin Rhodes, September 2012). Borrowing from Franklin (1999) racialized gendered hybridity has the potential of promoting the "invisibility syndrome" among bi-multi-racial males as it concerns how they experience, how they are being perceived during intra-interpersonal ethnic-cultural group interactions, and in defining and psychologically establishing who they are in private thought, public sphere.

Chapter Three
Declarations and Confessions of Multicolored Men

Interlude

> *Missing from contemporary debates are studies that explicitly ask African American males to articulate what manhood means for them. (Hammond and Mattis, p. 114, 2005)*

"Here's a chance to dance our way out of our constriction," is George Clinton's lyrical line embedded in the title, "P—Funks Black Masculinity and the Performance of Imaginative Freedom" by Royster (2011). Royster adeptly stated, "Most significantly, P-Funk's music explores black experience, particularly bodily, sexual and sensual experience at points of ambiguity, vulnerability, pain, desire, and laughter" (p.1). Abrams, Anderson-Nathe, and Aguilar (2007), stated that, the contextualized understanding adopted as a belief by masculinity theorists implied that there is "no universal essential masculine identity. Rather, "throughout the course of their lives, men adopt a range of gendered responses to their social environments" (p.24). Very saliently, these authors stated that "masculinity as a personal practice can be best understood only within the historical context of societal institutions, such as the state, schooling, the workplace, and the family" (p.24). What needs to be out front in the discussions on masculinity and manhood is the role and impact of patriarchal racialized masculinity on the shaping, defining, imaging, and enacting of sexuality and other social-cultural gender related role expectations.

Tyree, Byerly, and Hamilton (2011) in discussing a series of *19* stories that appeared in the Washington Post in December 2006 under the title of: *"Being a Black Man: At the Corner of Progress or Peril"* cited Merida (2007, p. viii) as stating, "the series sought to absorb the experiences of Black men and allow them to be seen and heard in uncommon ways – their challenges explained, their complexities examined, their lives reflected upon" (p. 468). Tyree et al. further explained that the series pursued the use of "Black men's narratives to tell their own stories about life, love,

hardships, and triumphs" (p.468). My recording and video taping of interviews were to similar ends, from the testimonial response of interviewees I
was able to garner their knowledge about self-views and experiences in
relationships with others, joined in with their perspective regarding social-
cultural events, conditions, circumstance, and their valuation of them.

In analyzing interviewees conversation I was able to compare and contrast their perspectives, observations, and descriptions of life experiences
with the emerging literary text and media struggling with perplexing with
interests, issues, and questions, regarding the conditions and circumstances of defining and enacting masculinity and manhood, among Black
African American, bi-multi-racial males. In other words, I was able to locate their perspectives via engaging in synthesis work with the literature.
Works such as *Masculinity in the Black Imagination: Politics of Communi-
cating Race and Manhood* (Jackson II & Hopson, 2011), *Black Men and
Depression: Saving Our Lives, Healing Our Families and Friends* (2004),
Hung: A Meditation on the Measure of Black Men in America(Poulson-
Bryant 2005), *Twelve Angry Men: True Stories of Being a Black Man in
America Today,* (Parks & Hughey, 2010),   *Black Masculinity in the U.S.
South from Uncle Tom to Gangsta* (Richardson, 2007), *Progressive Black
Masculinities,* Mutua, (2006), *Are we Not Men? Masculine Anxiety and the
Problem of African-American Identity,* (Harper, 1996), *We Real Cool: Black
Men and Masculinity,* (bell hooks, 2004), *Black Male Deviance,* (Lemelle,
Jr.,1995), *Fatheralong: A Meditation of Fathers and Sons, Race and Society,*
(Wideman, 1994), all examined the materialistic and ecological circum-
stance, condition, and psychohistorical experiences that contribute to
producing the persistence of racialized gendered patriarchal and class
antagonisms, while contributing also, for instance, to the occurrence of
"racial microaggressions" (Sue, 2010) in public sphere.

Along the same line as racial microaggressions, Calmore (2006), in his
chapter entitled: "Reasonable and Unreasonable Suspects: The Cultural
Construction of the Anonymous Black Man in Public Space (Here be
Dragons)" argued that, African American citizens were socially-culturally
constructed as unwanted traffic based upon Supreme Court's 1981 City of
Memphis v. Greene decision, in which the court endorsed and legitimated
a street closing that blocked traffic from a Black neighborhood through a
White one" (pp. 137-138).

In further reference to this, he said "that from the court's legitimation
society more generally has viewed Blacks, particularly Males, *as unwanted
traffic*" (p. 138). Calmore most lucidly purported that,

> *The particular cultural construction of the anony-*
> *mous black man in public space prompts an ambiva-*
> *lent societal gaze toward him, a gaze that may reflect*
> *both reasonable and unreasonable suspicion. As a re-*
> *sult, people tend to despise, to fear, and to avoid him.*
> *As arrest, inmate, and probationer records indicate,*
> *moreover, the black man as unwanted traffic often*
> *translates more precisely into the criminal element*
> *that must be apprehended, prosecuted, and sent*
> *away. (p. 138)*

In keeping with Calmore, he attested that the social-psychological weight that the *anonymous Black man in public space* must carry involves having to work cognitively and behaviorally, hard or harder to prove civility, decent law abidingness, as the burden of proof lies with this person, in view of historical-contemporary racialized gendered stereotypes, the threat of racial microaggression, and the complexity of historical social and institutionalized racism and White supremacy. In part, Calmore's thesis rests with noting the stigma of skin color, age, racial- gendered appearance and positionality, (issues relating to them are often times psychologically buried within the sub-conscious mind, and kept down by social declaration amounting to denial in the form of manly Western individualism rationale, regarding the fear of admitting vulnerability), where it is a general style of self-presentation that social-culturally marks the anonymous Black man in the public sphere relevant to the threat of becoming *unwanted traffic*.

It seems that the threat of the anonymous Black man as unwanted traffic is applicable to integrated public space, thereby donating his relegation to the racial-social-economic spaces that are marked by residential-community segregation.

In sum, an underlying issue is that the stereotype of the anonymous Black man can simply rise up and appear in the imagination and perception among European Americans, conservative and liberal alike, assimilated people of color, when the bi-polar archetype of the Good Black male that distances himself from Blackness, does not show up during interpersonal cultural interactions, as a part of his construction and response to social reality.

I concur with Jackson II and Hopson (2011) that Black masculinity has become a focus of a more widely all-encompassing lens. That is, "masculinities have become the focus on a daily basis from a variety of cultural, social, political, and economic standpoints" (p.3). Issues related to Mexican, Latino masculinity, manhood, sexual, and social conditions join that among Black African American, bi-multi-racial males.

Vasquez (2010), relative to the issue of *racialized gender*, called attention to the social-psychological and cultural issues (and I would add the raw anti-immigration attitudes and policy challenges) faced by Mexican Americans in U.S. society specific to intergenerational assimilation and identity public-societal expectations. The author discussed, in this case, third generation middle class Mexican Americans. He purported, "third-generation Mexican Americans living in California, had their identity experiences shaped by two-poles called a racialization process continuum" (p.46). Vasquez named a concept called *"flexible ethnicity"* as representative of what occurred along the racialization process continuum. Flexible ethnicity is defined by the author as the "ability to deftly and effectively navigate different racial terrains and be considered an insider" in more than one racial or ethnic group" (p. 47). Moreover, the author felt it was relevant to indicate that flexible ethnicity was different from *"situational ethnicity"* having to do with a performance of ethnic attitudinal, linguistic, and behavioral adjustment relevant to the situation concerned, which was not as being different from "strategic ethnicity" (p.86). Situational and strategic ethnicity are is analogous to code switching or what I call cultural commuting, which really embodies the named situational and strategic ethnicity.

In the author's differentiation between the terms *situational ethnicity* and *strategic ethnicity* he cited Stanczak (2006, p. 186), in pointing out that *strategic ethnicity* represented strategic movement "toward a purpose goal" (pp. 46-47). Importantly, Vasquez cited Golash-Boza and Darity (2008, p. 901) in saying that, "As supporters of racialized assimilation assert, Latinos can be racialized as non-Hispanic white, Hispanic/Latino, or non-Hispanic black" (p.46).

Recall from Chapter 1 that I discussed the concept of "cultural commuting" in referring to cognitive, attitudinal, linguistic, and behavioral techniques or styles among Black African Americans in movement back and forth between critical mass of European Americans and Black African Americans; skin color, racialized physical features, intergroup power relations, legally sanctioned law enforcement threat power tactics, and social-economic status are among markers that alert to needed shifts, which can and does become unconsciously and consciously habitual. Specific to the role of cultural commuting there is the role of transactional communication and its', for example, informants (Alcorn, In-press).

From Vasquez's discussion I suggest that among Mexican Americans/Latina/Latinos there are those who work to culturally commute as they attempt to negotiate issues related to racialized assimilation and attempts at categorizing them in the fluency and more routine situations in their response to social realty.

In the study this work is based upon, the original structured interviews were designed to last a maximum of 60 minutes, however, the average interview lasted 75 minutes expanding to a semi-structured format. Because each participant engaged in a process whereby he reiterated and provided addenda to previous responses, the 60 minute's time expired. The results of the analysis represent 450 minutes of transcribed video and audio-taped structured interview responses. However, because the questions were open-ended what became apparent was that the participants continued referencing back to previously answered questions in making connections and reiterations with the present question they were responding to. Thus, a cyclical pattern emerged during each interview, as opposed to a linear patterned response from one question to the next.

This cyclical pattern revealed the application of synthesis thinking in the form of deeper reflection as each participant called attention to what he previously said in an attempt to merge and enrich the present question being responded to. It became obvious that as these same six participants moved through their respective interview session, there was an attempt to assimilate their responses with other observations and thoughts on life experiences. In other words, they became retrospective and discerning as they moved through the questions. As a result of my hearing and observing the looping back on previously responded to questions and prompts, a decision was made not to direct the participants back to a more linear patterned response that had a neat convenient beginning and end. I chose to honor the authentic emergence of participant voice in an attempt to capture the depth and breadth of their worldview. As Kearney (1984) stated, "analyses of ways that people think about themselves, about the environments" entails a study of worldview (p.1).

Added to the open-ended question process was the subject content of the questions. All the participants except one, who was Nigerian, appeared to be somewhat puzzled and intrigued when asked to consider, for example, what the social construct terms, manhood, gender, masculinity, and maleness meant to them in relationship with education and learning experiences, or in association with feelings, beliefs, and habits regarding these social construct terms. Most, it seemed, were unaccustomed to consciously thinking and speaking aloud about these terms in relationship to something. Some of this I suspect had to do with unfamiliarity with the terms. For example, there were notable pauses accompanied by searching expressions on five of the six participants' faces before they responded, except the Nigerian participant. Recall, as previously discussed in Chapter 1, Definition of Selected Cultural Terms, worldview means how any person perceives and experiences the world in relationship with self and other people around and beyond one (Sue, 1987). Insightfully, Sue's approach to worldview is in part based on an examination of internal-external locus of control theory and its implications for people of color who have systemically survived in a racialized patriarchal-dominant society. The shaping of one's or a group's worldview is also strongly influenced by social political agents such as culture, race, gender identity, ethnicity(s), the social-economic ecology of the neighborhood they grew up in, and socializing. Connected with this are a person's perceptions and experiences with sources and opportunities to access power relative to empowerment, given the presence of social agents such as race, ethnicity, culture, gender, and class. Furthermore, as it concerns power and empowerment, the questions one may ask are: *who has it, who does not, and why is it like this way in the world?*

What also emerged from their dialogue was that they were discussing conditions and circumstances that formed their survival thrust, and that of other Black American and bi-multi-racial males. Recall listed in Chapter 1 Definition of Cultural Terms, is the construct "Survival Thrust" (Baldwin, 1986). Baldwin extensively studied the "cultural-survival condition" (p.235) of Black African American people. According to Baldwin, survival thrust is defined as a reaction and response to a Eurocentric dominant social cultural reality that does not include or sufficiently consider its impact on the social reality and "self-consciousness" (p. 236) of Black African Americans. Therefore, fundamentally, worldview and survival thrust equates to how one approaches daily existence given one's perceptions, interpretations, and experiences of social-reality. The reason that I reiterate these two constructs is because of the participants' efforts to elaborate on what appeared to be their attempt to describe the social reality that they and others liked to them worked to negotiate, resist, or react/response to daily reality; very salient, to advance themselves as they are acted upon and as they themselves act upon the world.

(Please know that react-respond are differentiated but can be overlapping. Some would say that react is more off the top of the head knee-jerk action – i.e., jump to it without pause being more, perhaps at times, emotionally laden. Whereby, response is pause and/or strategic thinking and management of self, as appropriate to the situation concerned. However, there is the issue-driven expectations and habits present relative to racialized gendered, and so on, experiences and views on self-empowerment, save-face or put differently, *in-your-face* options).

Although participant responses, except one, did not reveal a direct conscious association between masculinity, manhood, education, schooling, and academic success, results did show participant awareness of gender identity in racial context as Black African American and bi-multi-racial males relative to institutional and life experiences. In other words, their manly dispositions and tendencies were a part of their interpreting and experiencing life as Black African American, bi-multi-racial males.

Declarations and Confessions

"The social world constructs the body as a sexually defined reality as a depository of sexually defining principles of vision and division" (Bourdieu, 2001, p. 11).

Perception and Response to Social Reality was the overarching theme that was developed as a result of my effort to capture the tenor and content of participant perspective that merged in a way based upon their self-epistemology (self-knowledge), views about life experiences, autobiographical reflection, and worldview/survival thrust. More, their responses suggested consideration of risk assessment relative to their view of social reality. Finucane, Slovic, Mertz, Flynn & Satterfield (2010) conducted a study regarding perceived risk on the subject of gender, race, and the "White male effect" (p. 159). The results suggested consideration of sociopolitical factors and circumstance rather than "biological factors" (p. 159). Moreover, in consideration of the sociopolitical factors and circumstance among White males, that showed their distinction regarding risk perceptions, world view attitudes and trust and "risk-related stigma," (p. 159) from others. Further investigation was recommended because of the complexity revealed via analysis of empirical data showing gender and race differences in risk perceptions. Some of the complexity involved taking into consideration the possession of dominant group cultural power among White males in relationship to others in U.S. society, and consideration of the locus of control attitudes regarding race, gender, and discrimination as part of world views among non-Whites and women.

The authors stated that:

> *We speculate that the world seems safer and hazardous activities seem more beneficial to White males than to other groups. For people who place less weight on the importance of individual achievement, and more weight on distributing wealth equitably and endorsing community based decision regulation, many hazardous technologies and activities are viewed as posing great risk. Compared with White males, many females and nonwhite males tend to be in position of less power and control, benefit less from many technologies and institutions, are more vulnerable to discrimination, and therefore see the world as more dangerous. (170)*

My review of the literature, along with conversations with expert witness practitioners in social psychology, who engage in interculturally responsive practices, and my professional work, educational, and life experiences as a Black African American male interacted with inductive reasoning that arrived at the overarching theme. In on to attempt capture and reveal the eclectically culturally rich content of participant responses in structuring this chapter, I formulated a combination of bulleted summaries and narrative discussions. [7] The final summary/narrative pertains to unexpected findings.

Six Participants *were* named for anonymous purposes: Computer-Artist (**CA**) Culturally In-Tune (**CT**); Multi Defined Artistic Man (**MA**); Administrator Community Outreach (**AO**); I will not be defined (**ID**); and Community Centered-Giving Back (**CC**). They all live in the Puget Sound region of Washington State. All have post-secondary experience, with

---

[7] Berger and Luckmann (2011) in their analysis regarding the social construction of reality that involved its interaction with the sociology of knowledge, discussed how reality is socially constructed as a result of one's perception, interpretation, learning, interpersonal intercultural interactions with people, and the natural and material world, resulting in the accumulation of knowledge, as to what reality is, and therefore social construction.

three possessing bachelor degrees. Of the three degreed interviewees two hold master degrees, geography and education respectively, with the third steadily moving toward his degree in psychology, in progress, at the time of the interviews. One of the interviewees who holds his masters is working on his doctorate degree, and now has served a term of duty as a Commissioner on the Washington State Commission on African American Affairs. All interviewees were working, and very connected with family and friends. Among the interviewees who are still pursuing their bachelor degree, one has studied Japanese in Tokyo, Japan, and works for Microsoft, Redmond, Washington, as a program writer for technicians who work on programs. Among the two youngest interviewees, one is studying music as a gifted singer, while another was contemplating majoring in physics at a major state university. Interviewee responses are structured based upon their accumulated self-epistemology.

Cultural Self-Identity as a Response to Social Reality

All participants believed that they needed to "manage" the viewing of cultural self- identity; how they were being perceived and responded to and who they were becoming in their development, was central to their lives in general. As astutely stated by one of the bi-multi-racial participants:

> *Culture is how society looks at you, masculinity is different for every culture; race is a part of who you are not necessarily defining you, but it changes how people look at you, and this can affect you; definitely affecting your own points of view, something you could get a lot of strength from, but also gives you a lot of hardships.*

All participants acknowledged and discussed their views that among Black males there was a societal and self-imposed need of having to "perform" their manhood daily, although this did not necessarily reflect views about themselves. Here participants talked about the over-simplifying views about Black and biracial males that exist in society, as thugs, athletes, entertainers, and hypersexual performers, and suave communicators.

All participants believed and expressed concerns regarding the impact of stereotypical views and expectations associated with their racial pheno-types, such as skin complexion, hair, and facial features, and one partici-pant talked about penis size and sexual performance expectations, in rela-tionship with his perceived ascribed as he put it, "ethnic-cultural herit-age." All participants were concerned about how they were looked at and expected to behave given their racial-gender and ethnic-cultural heritage.

All participants expressed an awareness and recognition of their eth-nic-cultural heritage and that of their families and communities in con-sideration of their life experiences. They recognized the socializing influ-ences and views of parents and significant extended family members re-garding manhood, learning and education, the ism's present in society based upon race, sex, and class, their ethnic-cultural identity(s), and group experiences.

The entire group of participants associated respect and responsibility with manhood as being salient to their ethnic-culture(s). (This had to do with civility and respect for elders and avoidance of public embarrass-ment, i.e., not losing one's cool in public). They understood masculinity generally as manhood role – responsibilities; as one interviewee succinctly put it, "the act of living out the virtues of being a male."

Results revealed that all the participants believed that their identity as males was racialized and tied to their ethnic-cultural group membership. Then to participants as a group were more familiar with the terms man and manhood in association with gender and sexuality, than masculinity. They were particularly familiar with the social construct of race in associa-tion with man and manhood. One participant saw masculinity as charac-ter; another participant saw race and ethnicity as "in your blood," a third participant said that "race determines who you are," he saw identity as being an African American male." He also stated, "I grew up very Africen-tric with my mother and father."(His meaning of Africentric had to do with pride of being an African American male, and studying about the history of African American people). Then again, a fourth participant described gender "as the act of living out the virtues of being male, depending on playing your role like a father, being courageous, [inaudible] with God." While a fifth participant viewed masculinity "as strength and different for every culture," while seeing "race as a part of who you are, not necessarily defining you." Interestingly, a sixth participant viewed masculinity as "complicated" and manhood as "strength."

Performance as a Response to Social Reality

While no one per se discussed how they themselves "acted Black," or Mexican, Cuban, or Nigerian, participants did talk about what they believed that Black, African-American, Chicano, or Nigerian masculinity and manhood performance was relative to their self-perception, knowledge, and social-behavioral styles of communicating and interacting. All of the participants agreed that there was an unspoken requirement for Black males to perform who they were in their community, out in public in general, in work and school settings.

(A sudden heighten sense of awareness is likened to the song lyric, *me, myself, and I,* in a group or public setting. As an undergraduate at a small private university, I was attending a special topic seminar featuring a local guest celebrity. Suddenly, I realized that I was the only person of color there, as the speaker talked and I worked to concentrate on the discussion, I felt myself looking out from within me and suddenly experienced surges of panic).

Five of the participants talked about that among their Black American and bi-multi-racial friends and peers in community, work, and school settings, they had observed those who engaged in "socially down" (cool pose/reserved demeanor) attitudes and behaviors, demising that there existed an uncertainty as to whether or not academic activities were relevant to *who they are were* and was this worth their time, perhaps doubting relevancy or there was something distracting going on in their life that demanded or pleasured them more; schooling was just not fitting-in. Participants talked about socially-down attitudes and behaviors among Black and bi-multi-racial males as a dilemma, that is, a quandary, a tight spot, a "catch-22" (Heller, 1955). However, they made it clear that acting socially down per se should not be looked at as a cool pose attitude and behavior that one engages in to demonstrate, in this case, a rejection of or resistance to school and academics.

Finally, participants described a dilemma for some among their peers as to whether or not one could be a man, own his time, and "be academic" *all in one.* In other words, the silent (unspoken) question perhaps was – *what does this (schooling) have to be with me as a male, and my social time, my real time?* According to Billson (1996), social-psychological strategic styles among adolescence Black males, can involve consideration of interpersonal power relations, culturally symbolic ways of interaction and expression, in collaboration with identity development as a response their social reality; very importantly there is the social-economic experience that are an outside looking in and around in regards to self in relationship and comparison with others. Here the youth concerned seeks empowerment as to maintain face, i.e., dignity in reaching for maleness.

These six participants pursued the point that there seems be this conflict of interest among some Black males between "being this down brother" and liking school at the same time. As one participant put it, there were Black male friends and peers that he knew were smart but felt that they had to hide this in the community and in school, as it made them appear that they were not this "down brother." Consequently, among the participants, the idea of how one represented the masculine, manhood, sexual persona self-daily relative to activities of learning and education, was a "catch 22" situation. In other words, there was this undeclared boycotting of school participation and learning had consequences, but one may be of the mindset that there was this unrecognizable attempt at preventing the trading-off of masculinity, more colloquially discussed as manhood or "manning up."

CT spoke extensively about African American male friends he observed in high school who he knew that were "really smart and struggling about who they were." He very pointedly summarized the self-conflict he observed in a self-referenced dialogue:

> *I was really smart, I was in an advanced program but when I go home I can't walk around being that same person because I'd be square, it's funny and challenging at the same time. This is really related to something I said earlier, if you can comes to terms with your identity it doesn't really matter whoever can't accept the fact that I have chosen in my life to think about my future, I had learning habits that were a part of me that I wasn't cutting loose.*

All participants made it clear that learning habits were a part of their lives that they were not cutting loose; and that coming to terms with their identity was important in their life. One of these six participants talked about how he believed that "acting down" was relative to "acting Black," and that for some this was a defensive response. For example, CA stated, "acting down was a response to not be bullied." Participants talked about how they encountered societal and peer expectations in social, work, and/or academic settings, regarding how others saw and/or made conversation as to what was perceived as "Black culture." Further, among all participants there were candid remarks made regarding how they had encountered social situations where it was expected of them to show behavioral styles or attitudes that represented "Black culture."

Stereotypes as a Response to Social Reality

All participants were very clear about the fact that they were working to ensure that they were not a part of ethnic-cultural stereotypes and performance expectations in defining who they were and working to become. As ID stated, "I define my own self-concept with maybe a little outside forcing, but mostly internal." Along these same lines, participants discussed how they recognized themselves ethnic-culturally, while being fully aware of their racial physical looks. Moreover, it appeared to be central for them to express management and control of and responsibility for their own attitudes and behaviors, while clearly recognizing group and societal issues relative to race and masculinity. For example, CT and CC spoke adamantly regarding their concerns about "racial profiling," and what both described as racism related issues in society.

(Please discern that these were not arbitrary remarks regarding perceived racism in the public domains of our society. It is salient to come to know and weight that racism is an applied pseudo anthropological – social psychological construct, has been embedded in U.S. social and political consciousness with implications for all areas of human activities relative equality of life opportunities and we in nature).

CC, who is Nigerian, became very animated in discussing his views about Black male performance when elaborating about racial profiling, stating that,

> One of the things I have experienced from the time that I have been here, is that, Black males always have to prove what they are because they are automatically categorized, viewed as being this person that society perceives. You are automatically stigmatized, and so when you get in that environment you have to prove to them that no, I am not this person.

Furthermore, CC provided candid remarks regarding his experiences walking in the downtown area by the university he attended, and into his classes, "folks see me and they walk on the other side of the street. Then alternatively, when you walk in an environment [classroom] where people are already sitting down, and you can see that look." He stated that, "We [Black African American males] have to physically work on getting the system to accept you." Here he talked about a concept he had learned in his psychology graduate studies called "masking," which he explained involved a change in "persona" (hiding yourself in plain sight), regarding how he felt that he had to pretend to be someone different in order to get society to "accept" him. In revealing this, he stated, "so I had to go beyond my own cultural beliefs and values in order to really engage into whatever dialogue or conversation was happening."

It is striking to note that there were many times throughout the interview that CC reflected upon his experience from his cultural orientation as a Nigerian, even when he was offering observations and views regarding the status and views on Black males in U. S. society. Further, it appeared throughout his interview that he was acting in undeclared associated-solidarity with Black African American males and the interest and issues facing them; it was as if *he was participant and observer at the same time.*

AO explained how he felt about performing as a Black male in the community in combating stereotypes: "I represent myself first of all as a conscious Black man, a father, husband, a citizen just like any other, and I always check myself to listen and always seek knowledge." As a "conscious Black man," he discussed how he had to maintain a sensitivity and awareness regarding how he was being looked at as a Black male, particularly as it concerned being in various community-education-work settings. Examples he provided were, his role as a community college administrator, a member of a State Commission, and as a father being attentive to his son's education, learning experience, and academic performance. In addition, he discussed how he worked to keep abreast and informed by a broad range of literature and networking interactions specific to Black Americans and multicultural interests and issues. Very specifically, he reiterated a number of times during the interview regarding the socializing lessons and guidance he received from his "Grandmama" specific to his role and responsibility as a Black male and the importance of education. Likewise, all of the participants discussed and reiterated these cultural socializing kinds of talks and conversations that they experienced in growing up and still receive from time to time from parents, elder relatives, and friends of the family regarding masculinity and manhood self-awareness as Black and/or bi-multi- racial males. They related to these types of personally intimate kinds of talks and experiences throughout the interview process as they reflected on events, attitudes, and habits related to their academic and work experiences, and social interactions.

Five of the participants talked about issues concerning limited academic expectations and learning attitudes toward education among Black African American, bi-multi-racial males that joined in with public and peer stereotypical perceptions, ideas, and reactions. For instance, AO discussed at length throughout his interview about his work with middle school African American males, particularly the athletes who he said "acted out" in learning situations in ways that were not positively responsive to their education. In other words, AO pointed out that he encountered Black males who misbehaved in stereotypical ways, as he put it, like "bad boys," that matched societal expectations that many of these young men believed that were expected of them despite being told differently. Again, although there was not this preconceived thought among participants regarding academic achievement efforts and accomplishment being directly associated with gender identity development or status, all participants were clearly aware and knowledgeable about whom they were as Black African American, bi-multi-racial males. For instance, one participant stated, "I never really thought about academically achieving because I am a "Black male." Similarly, another participant said, "I don't think about myself that way as a bi-racial male" in discussing his desires to learn and achieve, but *neither* denied that gender identity affiliation was absent from being relevant to their education and learning.

One participant expressed concern that "Black maleness" was connected to stereotypes." MAM stated that "there are a lot of stereotypes out there these days because people believe that African American males are not going to college, and expanding their education, having babies, doing this and doing that you know." He pointed out that it was because of a "talk given by an African American male faculty member teacher at a local post-secondary art school about the absence of African American males in higher education and unspoken expectations about graduating," that assisted him in trying harder to "gain an education." He declared that he wanted to not only prove them wrong, but also prove that he "can academically achieve." Two participants, CA and ID who had both identified themselves as being "ethnically mixed" revealed how they had encountered societal expectations relative to their racial-physical features and names, regarding attitudinal and behavioral expectations.

Again, CA stated that he was "Black and Mexican," while ID stated that he was "African American, Cuban and Mexican." CA said that, "what set his experience apart regarding manhood was that "people would be always trying to figure out which side you are really on." This included high school and university experiences among some peers, teachers, and professors. He discussed how behavioral expectations were attached to his physical looks – "You know it's like um whenever they look at you and they want you to be Black or Mexican, and if you don't fall into that category they look at you like it's weird or something." He spoke about how there seems to be this need for you to "be a Black man" and how if you did not meet certain expectations that "you know, you're not really a Black man." He went on to talk about how these kinds of expectations were not only among members of the African American community but said that "it is from anybody."

CA revealed how in several high school and college settings he heard "comments from other Black people, mostly from Black women" exclaiming how "mixed race is wrong you know. And people shouldn't have those kinds of kids." I imaged that this disturbed him given the very low tone and slowness that occurred when he was discussing this. He pointed out that what was even stranger to him was that a number of times these kinds of remarks would occur during discussions or conversations "where they are trying to complain about racism and then they say something like that."

CA discussed another instance where he experienced a preconceived projection regarding his ethnic-cultural affiliation. A "Filipina teacher" saw his name and associated him with being a Filipino and tried to recruit him for "a Filipino student group," he said laughingly. Moreover, he commented on how the existence of certain perceptions in society regarding Black males around aggression made him think that when going into situations when he was around "new people," that he had to "tread lightly" because "there is just an idea that people are looking at you in that way so you feel like you gotta be careful." However, he went on to state that many of the friends, he has now, do not generally have a "tendency" to think in stereotypical ways.

ID, who is 5 years younger than CA, shared some similar views regarding societal perceptions and expectations about bi-multi-racial ethnicity, in astutely stating that:

> *Americans don't expect duality, so if it's like you are*
> *two things, which one are you going to be? People*
> *don't really see things as being able to have it both*
> *ways, you gotta be one or the other. I really tried to ex-*
> *press both sides of who I am, I'm Black, I'm Hispanic,*
> *[Mexican, Cuban, Black African American] I feel that*
> *if I don't bring attention to both sides of myself I'm*
> *leaving apart of myself out, people just want the quick*
> *and dirty, when you have multiple backgrounds.*
> *Sometimes the conversation with whoever appears to*
> *go like this, they all seem to have the same response,*
> *"Oh you're Hispanic, but then you're Black, and that*
> *appears to be easier."*

ID adeptly talked about what he observed about this societal view and response to bi-multi-racial ethnicity saying, "this may sound new or like a novelty, but it is really old news." He pointed out that people do not want "complicated answers," to him this was "not a bad thing." For instance, he candidly remarked about situational perceptions he was involved in re-calling, "People say, oh he's this and this, oh now I'm confused be more specific, you know people want you to be overt about who you are." CA made similar remarks regarding identity-performance expectations among certain of his peers and people in the community at large regard-ing his racial-physical looks stating that, "they think I am Black and look for how they think I should be acting and talking."

Finally, ID referred back to one of his earlier remarks about identity. He commented,

> *As I stated before you conceptualize what you want to*
> *be, how you perceive who you are, bi-multi-racial is*
> *old news to me, in that I guess I am part of the first*
> *generation in America that's really getting mixed now,*
> *some people are kinda weirded out about this.*

Socializing Influences as a Response to Social Reality

Participants discussed the influences of their parents and elders on the formation of their ethnic cultural identity, what was involved in manhood, and issues regarding racism, sexism, and classism in society. Generally, it appeared that they all believed that the socializing and cultivating experiences occurring earlier in their lives played a significant role in how they perceived and personally identified with the family, ethnic-culture or cultures in their lives.   For example, AO talked about the degree of significance that "cultural roots" plays in his life. He expressed his concern regarding what he perceived as the lack of cultural roots in the lives of the young Black males he comes in contact with through his educational outreach work. He insightfully observed that "culturally speaking," Black males represented themselves *"talking through their bodies in communicating to one another what each other is about more through physical attributes rather than through mental ones."* He felt that the young Black males in the middle and high school who he saw in his outreach work, were more about being *"something about something with their body, and not about their tongue,"* as in giving voice to who they were and where education was in their lives.

AO said,

> *Black males in the schools I visit talk well with their bodies and but have problems and issues talking with their mouths, many are just about or try to be about the social and sports, which too many [sic] as the sole source of who they are or want to be.*

AO also pointed out that the Black males he worked with demonstrated what he called *"an attitude of fear."* He explained that *"an attitude of fear"* meant not knowing what to expect within them if positive change was to occur, given that they seemed to act out knowing stereotypically what was expected of them to misbehave. In other words, AO discussed how among a number of Black males there are those young men who are so comfortable with knowing what is negatively stated or portrayed that they had manly tendencies to believe and expect this. There was fear within them regarding how they could "turn a negative into a positive."

CC spoke strongly about the socializing influences of his father in the Nigerian community where he grew up. CT, MAM, CA, and ID spoke very reflectively about the informative and influential conversations, encouragement, and advisement they received from their parents about, for instance, their extended families regarding ethnic-cultural heritage, the role and importance of education, the importance of family, and the relevancy of respectful attitude/behavior. For instance, CA stated that his parents said to him a number of times, "you have the best of two worlds," regarding his having parents from two different ethnic-cultural backgrounds; while ID spoke about the socializing influences from parents involving multiple ethnic-cultural backgrounds, whereby he experienced more critically adamant comments and observations from his father regarding his education, character, and behavior, but observed that the experience with his mother, a renowned artist, was more affirming, attentive, cultivating, and in-depth.

ID pointed out that his mother, who was biracial, was a strong advocate for social justice and deeply anchored in her cultures, and conveyed this to him consistently. Both bi-multi-racial males revealed that their parents and among certain of their extended family members and peers, exposed them to issues related to social justice, demonstrated social justice advocacy and education, expressed the relevancy of group ethnic-culture empowerment, and the empowerment and non-subjugation of women/women of color.

Attitudinal and Behavioral Switching as a Response to Social Reality

MAM discussed how he had to "code switch" his behavioral and communicating style when he was socializing or was in an educational situation, sometimes when interacting with predominantly European Americans, while other participants alluded to a tendency to do this in majority setting of European Americans. He stated, "I would really have to work on speaking correctly for them to speak to me "straight up" without them imitating and trying to come at me like I'm this down Black man they are trying to communicate with." He felt that "Black males should act as they normally [sic], but I do believe that there is a time and place for everything so it depends upon where you are at." Contrary to this, he felt that being around "minorities" he could be who he wanted to be. He further explained that when anyone among his peers found out that he was majoring in music, there was always the assumption that he was into "hip hop." Thus, when he sang, MAM stated he would receive comments like "oh you sing so soulfully, you have a church voice, and that sort of thing." It appeared that he did not want to feel that he was seen as being racially typed-casted, as he was engaged in the study of musical genres such as classical, jazz, and R&B.

CA recalled experiences in high school class when he was around Black males, "you probably would not be thinking about being a Black male, but in a situation that given you were the only one, you may feel that you have to perform as a Black male." CA pointed out that there was a difference in social settings of a "regular class than going to those advanced classes, in terms of feeling that you had to perform being down." In those advanced classes, he perceived that you really had to "ignore a lot of stuff to stay out of trouble." Depending upon the situation, the subject of Black and bi-multi-racial male performance, seemed to depend, among all the participants, on what they were involved in, and who was present.

In this regard ID stated,

> *I do think that a lot is expected of them because Americans expect that things can't operate in duality so if you're like two things, which one are you going to be, one or the other, and people don't see things as being able to have it both ways.*

ID also talked about how it was not realistic for him to leave any part of his self out in any situation, learning or otherwise saying, "I don't want to *choose, disregard* any part of who I am."

What was very keen among participants was that they all felt acutely aware and thus paid attention to how they acted in public-private situations, relative to their racial features and ethnic-cultural background(s), and so on. For example, CG, CT, and AO expressed an importance and awareness of their racial-physical looks. CT was tall, sculptured and dark in complexion, (as was his Mama who was an expert witness and authored educator, and brother. They were a tight family), while CG was also dark in complexion with a Nigerian bi-lingual speaking accent. AO was also dark complexioned, and spoke with an articulate urban accentuated style. CA spoke in low most-times very hard to hear tones during his interview, which seemed to be connected with his discussion regarding his felt need to be quietly observant to his surroundings subject to race, ethnic-cultural, social makeup of people he was around and/or interacting with, which his father discussed with him. However, in general, he was very composed, prudent, and non-judgmental in his affairs with people, as well as contemplative. (He is a gentle spirit of thoughtful-ness). CT discussed at length fears about racial profiling by police, others in society and the community, to apparently hyper perceived attention at work from "White co-workers" when he happened to cross paths with the two other African American male colleagues of his from other departments in a physically visual area. (He discussed how it made him feel self-conscious (but not ashamed) about his racialized phenotypical features, and concerned about the type of car he would buy). In fact, all interviewees discussed insights, and real time attention to self-consciousness regarding their presence in public-private situation, and in public sphere. He, CT, stated that in those work situations, they (his Black African American male colleagues) played their feelings off by joking about what their presence together might have meant to others around them in office space.

Finally, ID, CA, AO, and CT participants expressed their concerns about negative mis-perceptions and views relative to hip-hop culture within the society being connected with being Black, African American, and bi-racial males in the public space, as stated by CA:

> Once people have a negative idea about something like the thing that all Black people in the hood are thugs, they get stuck with that idea. The only time they notice a Black person is when they see a thug or what they think is one. They carry that over to when they see normal ones and it doesn't even register with them, to them it is just another example of hip-hop culture. There are all kinds of positives in Black culture and in the media, but they use hip-hop as an excuse when they want to say something negative.

Conflict and Anger Management as a Response to Social Reality

> *"I can talk myself through a lot of challenges by telling myself that I have gone through worse" (CT).*

Summative Note: In the face of challenges in work, academic, and life at large settings, participants expressed the importance of working to maintain a calm demeanor outside and within in order to assess the challenge at hand or condition. Moreover, it seemed important to participants to look for what processes were available to them when facing issues and challenges prior to taking action. Participants either alluded to or directly spoke about the consideration of/or presence of race-gender-ethnic identity, or other aspects of positionality, when describing and discussing challenges and how they approached them.

Participants explained how their self-talk and questions contributed to how they behaved in situations where they faced issues or challenges. Included in their discussions was how they approached and addressed the situation concerned, and their awareness of the racial, ethnic-cultural connections to their masculinity. Primarily, participants pointed out challenges they faced in academic and work situations, and some both. Moreover, much of what they revealed connected with what was discussed in the previous section, that is, the expectations and perceptions they felt were present among certain of their peers, and others in the community at large to include educational and work settings, regarding who they were as Black African American, Nigerian, or bi-multi-racial males. For instance, four out of six of the participants talked about the concerns and frustrations regarding the racial profiling of males of African American descent, again, one interviewee to the point of even being concerned about the type of car he had purchased.

CC spoke very directly about being in challenging situations, like that of interviewing for the Masters in Psychology program at an urban university. He felt that on that occasion as in others because he was *African* (and he believed this true for African American males in general) you had to be "perfect." Very disturbingly, he talked to me about an incident where he was working at a large warehouse type store clerking when an older middle-age European American woman without provocation, spit in his face and declared why didn't he "go home!"

(CC explained this event in a quiet slow very deliberate tone of voice and delivery. It was as if he wanted ensure that I fully understand and pictured this belligerent slandered racist act, but at the same time saying he was not allowing himself to be stigmatized by this act in public).

CT spoke very ardently consistently throughout his interview, regarding his sensitivities about being an African American male; who was tall and dark complexioned with concerns about racial profiling and his striking appearance in general among his peers, out in public, and school and work settings. To him, being clearly aware of his "cultural self" was central to facing and addressing challenges and issues in his life. CC discussed how self-reflection allowed him to "look deeper like Jung talked about into the subconscious, so you can look deeper into the questions." He discussed how self-reflection allowed him to question "self."

What appeared to be a common thread among participant response was maintaining "one's cool," apparently this demonstrated state of mind assisted them in remaining able to look at the situation and/or challenge at hand, and "work on negotiating it." Maintaining one's cool was important to participants even if it meant in some cases not directly and/or immediately experiencing the outcome sought. Moreover, this was not perceived by any of the participants as compromising one's manhood or one's ethnic-cultural identity. For example, CA, Black African-American-Mexican American, bi-racial, talked about his experience of being a "minority" in a Japanese culture and language course of study he was taking in Tokyo, Japan. Here he was the only student of Black African and Mexican American descent, among a minority presence of Korean students. CA discussed how he believed that the Japanese teachers in Japan were "getting pressured because of their performance." Apparently, there was a point during his course of study whereby the teacher did not think he was studying hard enough. According to CA, "this is something that would happen to a lot of American students, but not towards the Korean students." CA went on to discuss how the Korean students were always punctual and attentive, whereas the "American students were seasoned, already in the workforce, and had a different attitude towards studying." Furthermore, apparently U.S. students felt that since it was their money paying for the course of study that whatever happened grade wise, "it was on them, and they did not want to be treated like high school students."

CA discussed how he had been asked to stay after class, and was lectured to regarding his performance toward studying, which amounted to being repeatedly told that he needed to "study more." He stated how irritated he got about this, particularly after he had at first tried to explain his process for studying and doing homework, and that there were others who he directly knew among his Korean and European American friends, that approached studying and doing homework in a similar vein. His rationale in regards to such situations was, "our money, our fault." In the situation he described, the teacher told him to stay and make up the work, which for him was "weird because this is something that doesn't happen in college," and he "didn't think it happened there." What he pointed out was, despite this challenge, "I never lost my head in this matter."

MAM faced a similar situation relative to an academic situation when he was a student at a local performing arts college. As previously noted, at the art college he enrolled in right after high school, he came to realize that he was among a very limited number of Black male students and faculty members. MAM discussed how he experienced a difficult academic situation as a result of his having to make an emergency room visit regarding an acute healthcare issue. This visit required him to miss class time. Upon his return to school, the professor concerned would not allow him to make up an assignment, which would negatively affect his course grade and overall GPA. He stated that this professor made this decision despite his having the documentation available regarding his emergency room visit for the acute health episode. (The faculty member did not clarify whether or not this was course policy: however, it was usually up to the instructor or professor concerned to develop reasonable policy regarding course attendance and assignment-examination make-up). In facing this issue, he recalled a private conversation he had with an African American teacher when he first arrived at the arts college. The teacher had said to him, "look around and you don't see many of us." MAM felt that this faculty member was reminding him to be aware of whom he was, and the need to "work my studies and my crafts." MAM went on to explain that it was his general rule, when faced with challenging situations regarding procedural issues, to ensure that he put things in writing, locate an appeals process, and look to "work things out that way." He described how he never lost his composure despite the fact that he was upset about this particular situation, which in this case worked out after bringing it to the attention of the academic dean. MAM explained how his mother had taught him the importance of paying attention to processes that were available to him, to go through when dealing with issues. MAM said that "even now I consult with my mother when things like this come up in school, or where-ever."

For AO, part of his strategy for meeting challenging situations involved being well prepared and knowing who he was, as it concerns, Black culture, his temperament, and being aware of preconceived notions, such as "we are easily perceived by others as being apt to be seen as too aggressive or too emotional, are words used to describe Black males." He talked about how his self-awareness allowed him to be more "tactful" in facing challenging situations in certain places where he has worked and in college academic situations where material and subject matter of a racial-cultural nature was being discussed about people of color. In these instances, he described how he was able to, for instance, challenge things during class situations in which material from authors of color was absent or discussed in a way he felt that he needed to offer up a different perspective.

What became apparent was that although all the participants, accept CC, did not make statements or comments that directly associated the attitudes, motivation, and behaviors regarding academic achievement performance as being synonymous with Black masculinity or manhood, they did express an awareness and connection with their ethnic-cultural identity or shared identities as males specific to challenging situations in the public sphere. In general, all of the participants expressed a sense of pride in self-accomplishment and a connection to their respective ethnic-cultural community or communities via learning and achievement, and being persistent in furthering their knowledge regarding subject matter or a professional career related area of expertise. In other words, learning and achieving was personal and community related, community having to do with their ethnic-cultural communities.

ID discussed what he termed as "power dynamics" when facing challenges in university course educational situations. According to ID,

> *When it comes to power dynamics and you have less power I think that for the most part people try to understand – what you gotta do is try to talk to them and work things out and if that doesn't work then you go to their higher up; I know that's easier said than done, particularly since they are the ones marking you [sic] down for the course.*

ID talked about how he felt that the "oppression of minority people" was the main problem to overcome, as it concerns "these pre-conceived notions of a certain race, those are the type of things that you have to overcome, so from my bi-multi-racial background and features I get a little clashing occasionally." In this he ardently talked about how he received his strength to overcome such challenges from his "own ethnicity" and "sense of self to plow through these problems." He concluded by discussing how his ethnicity was not the only thing that helped him "get through it." Like AO and CT he talked about how reading a book from an author of color such as Isabel Allende or *Things Fall Apart* by Chinua Achebe, helped him looked at "things about race," or he would look at some art from Peru, or looking at some art by Van Gogh. According to him, "whatever that could definitely help."

Similarly, CT spoke very movingly regarding self-reflection in addressing challenging situations. He pointed out how self-talk aided him in facing "harder situations" than the one he was currently facing. He too talked about how he had turned to readings such as Booker T. Washington's *Up from Slavery*. Moreover, he also looked to his mother, and how she addressed challenges, and drew lessons from her experiences in the Jim Crow South, as a single parent of African American descent. Of note, CT talked about how it took him a long time to differentiate the term coward from being afraid about something he associated "being afraid with being a coward." This perception included his not responding to situations in public where, for example, while in a store even his friends who were not African American believed that he was getting harassed and experiencing subtle racial epithets. This perception was generated from his belief that if you were afraid of anything you were a coward; he talked about how he "struggled to define his courage," finally realizing that they (being afraid of something and being a coward) were really two different things.

CT revealed that aside from time and counseling, what eventually helped him to overcome this belief was engaging in a physical confrontation in coming to the aid of one of his friends during his adolescence in his community. He discussed his realization that being a coward was not the same as being afraid, explaining that to him it was something that had to do with lacking in courage, while being afraid involved being fearful of something. He talked about how being afraid of something does not necessarily lead to carrying out an act of cowardice. AO was pointing out how, as a Black male, he came to understand that because he was fearful of something did not mean he was a coward; to him at that earlier point in his life as a teenager this meant possible involvement in verbal or physical street confrontations and academic related learning situations. It took looking back at this incident year later to realize that though he had experienced fear and uncertainty when he acted in coming to the aid of his friend, he realized and affirmed, that it had nothing to do with cowardice.

From experiences such as the preceding, he gained encouragement from which he established within himself the confidence that he could handle and learn from the challenges and any mistakes in his decision making that may have put him there, as he had previously perceived making mistakes as a side of weakness in his character. It is relevant to note again that CT is a tall, dark-complexioned African American male that grew up with a degree of self-consciousness regarding this, his dark complexion and racial facial features, and his height (he was much taller than his peers in elementary and middle school). For him, this added to his concern about police racial profiling, which he stated, "is well-documented."

Awareness of Societal Perceptions, Racialized Physical Features, as a Response to Social Reality

- All participants discussed their awareness of their racial physical features regarding internal and societal stereotypical attitudinal and behavioral beliefs and responses to Black males in public domain.

For instance, participants talked at length about perceptions, self-consciousness of self, regarding physical and social-cultural presence, within the context of being to varying degrees racialized. These entailed descriptive discussions about, for example, pertaining to physical presence concerning height, skin complexion, clothing attire and how worn, and attitudes, that made them stand out and be subject to societal and peer questions about who they were ethnically. AO talked at length about why he surrounded himself, as an "African American male" with "positive people," in a response to helping him to ward off the effects of negative stereotyping and other racialized gender issues. In talking about racial physical features that made Black African American males stand out in public, he ardently discussed his concern regarding a lack of communication among Black males in public places. His rationale was that since they physically stand out in a crowd where there "were fewer of us," it seemed to him that it would really be important to recognize one another given such circumstance. He lamented, "I think it is a concern I have in being a Black male about how we treat each other, we don't communicate with one another enough. It's even getting tougher on college campuses." He aptly pointed out that there is communication among us at "important things like meetings," but outside of these kinds of settings, he talked about a lack of communication between Black males. For him it was a matter of treatment of each other among Black males. Recognizing one another in public via respectful communication appeared to be salient to

AO on the subject of racial physical features, ethnic-culture membership and affiliation, and societal perceptions of them.

ID, CT, and CA made direct references to racial physical features, and/or skin's color tone experiences regarding peers' perception/feeling of being gazed upon in the public at large. Recall in the section on Cultural Identity that CA made reference to challenging remarks that he was Black and not bi-racial. His remarks were based upon expectations regarding the assumption about his racial physical features and ethnic-cultural group membership. It was this felt assumption that he was expected to or the expectation was there in which he might engage in cool pose - thugged out attitude, behavior, and communicative style, but nothing that could be associated with any educational and learned redeeming value. ID called attention to the fact that he is the son of "bi-racial parents" making him "mixed." To this, he felt that he was "uniquely physically made," further saying that, "I don't look like anyone else so that makes me different from a lot of people."

CT spoke slowly and deliberately in saying that,

> *Over time it is the life of the body that changes about you. I came to be okay about me, I came to the point that I am what God gave me. Growing up we're all shades and that - I was pointed out, and my brother is even darker than I am. The funny thing was I got more harassment from African Americans than from White kids, and it might have been the fact that I was around them more.*

CA, MAM, ID, CT, and CC all talked in very descriptive terms about how Black males and males of color received racial-stereotypical preconceived attention out in public areas such as downtown and community urban areas, in stores, university and college classrooms, at clubs. CA carried on a composed thoughtful dialogue about his perception of Black males in a downtown area of where he lives. He stated,

> *I mean it's like somebody thinks you are a drug dealer, if you look at a newspaper you see people's comments about being downtown and they don't say much about their experiences, they just see Black males and*

> *they call them gang members without having any*
> *idea of what they are doing. I am pretty much aware*
> *that people have that stereotype. (CA has since moved*
> *away from the downtown urban center in the state of*
> *Washington).*

CA went on to talk about how he was aware at school and downtown of drug dealing.

He stated that "They looked like regular folks." He concluded by pointing out that "downtown everywhere you go" one can come across a "White guy in baggy sweats jogging" and they aren't profiled.

Similar to CA, CC stated very candidly that,

> *There are preconceived notions that can really be det-*
> *rimental and damaging to one's esteem and confi-*
> *dence, for me you had to have this perseverance, resil-*
> *ience, and consistency. Because if you have already*
> *been preconceived to be this person by some people*
> *automatically, who respond to you like that or treat*
> *you like that, you have to work harder to face the re-*
> *sistance, like the condescending looks from your pro-*
> *fessor when you go to discuss your paper.*

Finally, MAM discussed how he felt isolated when he was at a predominantly European American student campus at a local college near an urban center, which was in a predominantly European American neighborhood. He discussed how he felt "alone" even though he was this "openminded person with a crazy wild side." He talked about how "being left out or someone looking at you like you are trying to be the prize" made him think about what people perhaps thought about him. After a short stay, he transferred to a nearby local private university where he viewed the student population and faculty as being more diverse (which is the site where his interview was held). MAM had come from a small urban public school district where students of color were close to being the majority.

What Achievement Means as a Response to Social Reality

> *I know that when I get a task and struggle you can*
> *pick yourself up, either try harder or you don't. I can*
> *come to terms with that, so when I do fail I'll know*
> *this is not because who I am. (CT)*
> *My racial physical looks don't prevent me from*
> *achieving, it most influences who you are* when you
> get in those situations, like if you go to start a new
> job or something. (CA)

All the participants discussed their views and perspectives regarding the meaning of achievement in their lives in consideration of their ethnic-cultural background and experiences. Five of the participants expressed their belief in the importance of self-knowledge, as associated with the desire to learn. They believed that the acquisition of knowledge played a role in their development and responsibilities as males as a part of ethnic-cultural group membership(s). There were overarching references made by all the participants concerning their desire to learn and gain knowledge throughout the interview, even in responding to questions not directly asking about maleness and academic achievement. All participants believed that wanting to learn was a central part of their lives, and achievement was an outcome of this, wanted-ness, i.e., desire.

For example, AO stated that,

> *I believe that achievement is very important, its boosts*
> *morale and I think that it is equally important for you*
> *to understand your culture your Blackness and your*
> *heritage. It builds confidence, it builds confidence in*
> *knowing that you can speak about who you are, and*
> *then you perform at a higher level. So that when you*
> *achieve as it concerns knowledge about self you start*
> *achieving in other things that are connected to that.*

Responses here represent a tone of profound candidness that was a challenge to summarize. Participants revealed what achieving meant to them given their racialized gender identity. In other words, their responses suggested experiences with achievement under racialized condition and circumstance, given the overall content and tenor of their responses/perspective. For example, AO cogently discussed how reading stimulates you to a point of wanting to dissect and question more once you "start to understand." Here he went on to say, "you start digging into why more and then that starts to give you a high to know what you read and applied to it." However, what followed was the condition and circumstance under which this occurred for him. He paused and discussed the question, "how do you intellectually feel about being a minority in any of the courses that you have taken?" He was referring to his experience at a private university near a small city urban downtown area. He then discussed the term minority stating that, "Psychologically the minority word means less than, so you put yourself in a situation you believe that you are less than, I never believed that about myself. I believed I was more than, I'm not less than nothing." CT forthrightly stated that he believed among Black males that there was this issue to openly engage in learning and education as an on-going pursuit. He had chosen not to sit on the fence regarding this, and a key process to him was in knowing and embracing who he was and wanted to work on becoming.

He talked about how it,

> *Seems to be to this sub-culture of males, brothers, who believe that it's cool not to be smart, so in an academic setting there was this sub-division of those who decided not to go academic and then there are those who were inherently academic, but are kinda strugglin' with being on both sides of the fence, trying to fit-in with the sub-culture and the popular culture, trying to be very Black. I got lucky in that although I was surrounded with a lot of friends who didn't take the route of going to college they still respected the fact that instead of running the streets I tried to better myself by going to school to better my future. I really got lucky because they were going off on another tangent.*

AO discussed his experience of being an African American male undergraduate student with an English minor at a university with predominantly European American student population, administration, and academic faculty. Apparently, there was an absence of culturally diverse readings in this program of study he was enrolled in. He described and emphasized how it was important for him to "really assert" himself in order to experience growth under circumstances where the readings were "not appealing" to him. In one such class he astutely noted that his being there and challenging things from his perspective as an African American male reading "Hawthorne" seemed to have made an impact. Here he raised the question during a classroom session, "Why not Frederick Douglass, Harriet Tubman and the Underground Railroad, why are we not also learning about them?" He felt that "they [the students] would not have gotten a lot out of that course" without him expressing himself. AO further noted that when he raised this question his professor said, "why don't you read and write about that." The feeling for him was that he had "stepped up." AO stated that when you, and add I see this as being very acute, "step up and feel the achievement then you feel that you must continue."

All participants discussed how they were raised to believe that achievement was important but not just for the sake of achieving, learning appeared to be the source of what achievement meant to them, self-epistemology. One participant, CT, emphasized the importance of learning how to encounter failure in school and life experiences. For instance, he solemnly talked about the importance of how his "mom" providing him with "these building blocks to gain an education." He talked about how he was raised to understand that if you fail at learning something that you don't have to give up, "it doesn't mean that you can't achieve." He stated, "I was taught that when you do fail you will be able to say that you tried as hard as you could at that time, and when you say that, it is almost like you can reduce the guilt." One of his major life lessons regarding failing and achieving was his becoming a young father. CT talked about how he struggled with the guilt of thinking that he had failed. He pointed, out though, that the "failure and accomplishment built into the structure of growing up really helped." Very importantly, he revealed how overcoming guilt assisted him in not just sitting still but moving forward with what he needed to do to be a supportive and loving father, while continuing with learning, education, and career pursuits. He recognized that struggle and challenge did not push him to give up, even when his daughter's mother moved with his daughter out of state.

All of the participants related achievement in education or at work to "giving back to the community." For instance, CC talked about how his becoming the first to go college in his village community would provide an opportunity to "bring college education" to them, while CA stated that "when I do achieve something at work that was difficult it surprises me and it feels like I am giving back to the Black community." According to ID, achieving is doing "the best that you can do." Interestingly, he believed that "the achievement thing is like a common thing for Black males." In talking about the pressures of achievement he concluded by stating, "I think it's different for White people under pressure than it is for Blacks, I mean for the minority communities to do better it is about build the race."

Unexpected Results

The following findings were surprising in that they were garnered from the breadth of participant discussion as they were engaging in a kind of annotating of previous responses to interview questions they had already responded to during the present question they were being asked.

Although participants except one did not directly associate their academic performance with their masculinity, manhood, or ethnic cultural heritage, they did believe that it was salient for them to perform well given their ethnic-culture(s) as a part of their manhood.

1. Five participants expressed an increased curiosity and awareness in their perception about learning and achieving as an expression and development of their masculinity and manhood, as the result of participating in the study.

2. The only participant, who was of Nigerian descent, directly associated his masculinity and manhood with education, schooling, and learning.

3. All participants valued the relationships, socializing influences and knowledge of their parent(s), and extended family members in their lives as being salient and interconnected to their development and perception of self.

In contrast to all the other participants, as previously stated, CC, who was Nigerian, clearly believed that his education and achievement was directly a part of his masculinity and manhood. He very acutely explained how in his culture, "education is believed to be only for males, females are excluded," although he indicated that this was changing. CC had grown up in the physical geographic location and cultural context of his Nigerian community, coming to the United States as an adult. His belief was consistent with the patriarchal ways of his culture. He described the historical and traditional rootedness of his cultural socialization.

Most central in his life, as it concerns masculinity and manhood development, was his father. His father taught, demonstrated, and socialized him in the patriarch ways, which instilled in him that this was the fabric of Nigerian cultural anchoring into masculinity, manhood, and sexuality development and enactment, physically, cognitively, spiritually, and for self-empowerment.

Thus, all human cultural categorical activities, such as knowledge, education, law, spirituality, morality, the duality between males and females, contributed to his masculinity, temperament, and characteristics related to it.

In his culture, manhood, masculinity, and maleness, was community-culturally-centric. For him then education, learning, and academic achievement was part of the fabric that made him a man "the act of becoming," (personal communication, Benjamin Rhodes, April 30, 1989). But for the other participants, learning, achieving, and being educated were not consciously thought of as a part of their masculinity, manhood, and sexuality. This doesn't mean that it was absent from their felt existence as males, that is, that they were not socially culturally conscious aware of it as the drapery of constructing and experiencing their masculine, manhood, and sexual existence. But, perhaps, it was there but masked.

Relative to this study, it appears that what brought masculinity, maleness, and manhood into focus for them in the interview was as stated previously, race, ethnic-culture, career and work, a love of learning, or wanting to engage in a particular field of study.

Conclusion

> *Now everyday that I wake up I know that there are all the facets of institutionalized racism are built into society. You don't even have to leave your house, you can pretty much turn on any form of media and it's all so hard to remember all of this because each day its going to be rough (CT).*

What was abundantly strong among participants was the view that managing their cultural identity, how they were being perceived and responded to, how they represented themselves, and finally who they were becoming, *was* central to their lives in general. Participants believed that Black males had to perform who they were on a daily basis, although this did not necessarily reflect their beliefs about themselves. They alluded to or directly discussed their concerns regarding the presence of "institutionalized racism" in society. Participants revealed that there were stereotypical views and expectations that were associated with their ethnic-cultural heritage, racial physical appearance, and attitudes toward learning and education. It appeared to be prominent to participants, in the context of racialized gender, to remain vigilant about these views and expectations, which they believed existed in the society. For example, CT felt that much of the portrayal of Black males in the media and studies as expressing improper ways of behaving and showing attitudes was tainted with racial "profiling." He pointed out that "shows like *Cops* can influence you in popular culture to stereotype as you see Blacks and Latinos as criminals, particularly when a number of Black and Latinos are disproportionately incarcerated." (Thrill seeking, plays on what a violent society we live in holds implications for feeding into our gun toting mentality). Pointedly, he talked about how "a lot of people straddled the fence between trying to be cool, commit a crime, and studying in school, you know the cool is portrayed in hip-hop culture." Moreover, CT astutely discussed how people have heard about hip-hop artists currently on a fast ride admitting talking to media sources about how they were once into crime, and he believed that influenced some people to try and "reach both sides." In other words, people who had academic potential felt that they needed to "have this risky behavior just to show that "I'm cool." He asserted that there is "some misrepresentation in what the majority of African American males are doing, because the things that *"don't get exposed are accomplishments that African Americans males are bringing into modern day living."*

Although participant responses revealed that they had not directly thought about their masculinity and ethnic cultural heritage as being directly associated with their academic performance, they did believe that it was important for them to perform *academically well* given their ethnic-cultural background as associated with who they were as men. One participant, the youngest MAM, felt that there was a lack of positive references to the accomplishments of African American males, and alluded to the pressure he felt because of this. The two bi- multi-racial participants felt that they experienced preconceived assumptions identifying them as African American males, based upon their racial physical appearance.

Moreover, they experienced social situations among peers who expected them to engage in "Black culture."

Chapter Four
Critical Reflection

Too Black, Too Strong, Bring the Noise are powerful warning/declarative rap lyrics from Public Enemy, (2005) which brought to mind that there are Black African American, bi-multi-racial males among us who are silently adept and disquieted, and/or more overtly averse and controversial in their construction of social reality/self in relationship with mainstream dominate society. Historically, and contemporarily in real-time it has been a crafting exposé among Black African American, bi-multi-racial male in evolving of identities of resistance and adaptation, aiming, and struggling to avoid compromise, that has multiple physical-psychological-spiritual health implications.

Results showed participant perspective in light of their ethnic-cultural and gender-racialized, education and learning, sensibilities, awareness, and construal of interview questions that represented their response to social reality and worldview. To reiterate, and further explain, the term concept of *habitus* is formed out of social-economic conditions, experiences with societal institutions, and the social-economic, ecology of community, that results in the forming of attitudes and behavioral strategies that are routine to one's experiences and living conditions.

They discussed their felt and experienced masculinity, manhood maturity, and sexuality relative to neighborhood community experiences and broader geographic regions of state and country via direct and indirect interactions and sources of medium. Cross and Naidoo (2012) said that "habitus arises from one's history and the physical spaces one occupies or the field---and that in turn shapes the field" (p.233); for example, growing up in suburban or urban places (say row houses), relative to social-economic experiences. Put another way, habitus is what attempts to *synchronize* the individual with the new or different settings as the result of past experiences, attitudes, behaviors, ways of communicating, reasoning, and accumulated knowledge, and worldview. However, if there is a mismatch between habitus and the new setting then conflict can occur if adjustments are not made, or the negotiation of the setting concerned is perceived as too much of a compromise, threat, or one-sided cultural trade-off, or then to simply not relevant and time consuming to existence.

Ethnic-cultural-gendered identity and experiences assist in shaping communication styles and choices during social interaction and during introspective reflection before and during interactions, that is, I am suggesting that habitus is communicated, behaved, and can be a part of one's intuitive-ness in cultural context; habitus is mentality, in the form of attitudes interacting with intellectual wherewithal.

From the perspective of Cross and Naidoo (2012) individual-group habitus emerges among people of color, relative to interpersonal-cultural relations within a diverse multicultural society such as ours, within institutionally dominant European American/White group social-economic and political power. In turn, individual-group habitus among groups among people of color, reshapes and influences societal spaces, interpersonal-ethnic-cultural perceptions and experiences, and continues to increasingly impact the dominance of power arrangements, and so on.

Bourdieu (1990) talked about habitus being a "feel for the game" a sense of what is going on during the "social game" of interactions that one accrues that is "turned into a second nature" (p.63). Then too habitus is the cognitive accrual of experiences that can be used in a comparison and contrast sense from situation to situation, across temporal and geographic location. Moreover, Bourdieu said, "The habitus, as a society written into the body, into the biological individual, enables the infinite number of acts of the game" (p. 63).

Maton (2008) said, "Habitus is the link not only between past, present, and future, but also between the social" (p. 53), the individual's agency, that is, ability to act, relative to structural materialistic experiences.

According to Maton (2008),

> *Habitus links the social and the individual because the experiences of one's life course may be unique in their particular contents, but are shared in terms of their structure with other of the same social class, gender, ethnicity, sexuality, occupation, nationality, region, and so forth. For example, members of the same class by definition share structurally similar experiences of social relations, processes, and structure. (p. 53)*

I suggest it seems to follow that the occurrence of, for example, racialized gender, class, sexuality, and associated ism's regarding attitudes, dispositional tendencies, perception, ideology, and behaviors, influences and creates the circumstance under which, in turn, effect the development of individual and individuals in group habitus. Cross & Naidoo stated that "habitus arises from the social spaces or objective realities one lives in as well as from knowledge and cognitive construction one has access to" (p. 234). Participants' perspective in actuality represented their habitus as Black African American bi-multi-racial males, given their self-epistemology, (accumulated self-knowledge), social-cultural socialization, educational achievement, and social experiences; however, it is salient to know that one participant very deftly exclaimed, *"But doesn't masculinity and manhood involve femininity as well?"*

Figure 1 next, represents a conceptualization entitled "Participant Response to Social Reality." This conceptualization depicts the overlapping presence of social constructs of race/racialized gender, relative to masculinity/manhood that are viewed as intersecting within the individual male/person concerned. The overarching listing of social psychology is concerned with the influence of social-cultural attitudes, behaviors, characteristics, temperament, inclinations, and cognitive-mental processes at work, such as, worldview and survival thrust, relative to defining, developing, and enacting of Black African American, bi-multi-racial masculinity and manhood.

The idea is to situate Participant Response to Social Reality within the context of social constructs that intersect with self-identity, sexuality, ethnic-culture affiliations, interpersonal-cultural interactions, and racialized gender experiences as a part of their response to social reality. The listing of social psychology asserts the complexity involved in the social construction of masculinity, manhood, sexuality, involving sensibilities related to ego-integrity, temperament management, interacting/shaping *habitus* that are implicated within the construction of Black African American, bi-multi-racial masculinity and manhood. Put another way, habitus is involved in the how, why, and in what ways they exist and demonstrate their masculinity and manhood as Black African American, bi-multi-racial males. For example, Ford (2006) conducted a study entitled: *Masculinity, Femininity, Appearance Ideals, and the Black Body: Developing a Positive Raced and Gendered Bodily Sense of Self.* The study data suggested that,

> *Black men and women learn to differently present, manage, and negotiate their bodies in accordance with social norms. Reinforced through inter-intra-group peer interactions and the perpetuation of stereotypical images of Black men and women present in the media and mainstream consumer culture, the men learn to physically, materially, and behaviorally do or claim Black masculinity (body work); the women, in contrast, engage Black femininity based primarily out outer appearance and to a lesser extend based on behavioral attributes (beauty work). (p.1)*

Moreover, Ford stated that men whose ascribed or achieved traits failed to live up to "this thug-like masculine image in some way were classified as effeminate or gay, acting White," while women who did not conform were labeled "as emasculating bitches and lesbians" (p.1).

Young, Jr. (2011) authored an essay discussing the intra-intercultural tendencies of social conduct among African American men, that was reflective in the presidential campaign of Barack Obama, a bi-racial male. Say another way, his essay explored how African Americans' efforts to behave in public settings embodied ways that were presumably indicative of making a strong social connection with one another (one that validated each over non-African American standards), or that reflected African Americans' efforts to adhere to presumably "mainstream" behavioral standards. This, whereby "the humanity of black Americans is demonstrated and advanced" (p.206).

Young, in his essay explained how bi-racial-cultural Presidential candidate Obama represented both perspectives during his campaign, revealing the implications "for forwarding new conceptions of Black African American masculinity" (p. 206), contributed to from a bi-racial ways of being. The question is though, *could such new conceptions be considered progressive, healthy, and culturally responsive to defining, developing, and enacting Black African American masculinity, manhood, and sexuality? What I'm referring is are we producing shadow conceptions, i.e., inner-cultural and interculturally restrictive or over-modified-negotiated and actualized representations of self for the sake of making it in "mainstream society," or making mainstream society wealth/cash flow?* You know, like John Edgar Wideman's astutely inventive reference to hood Black masculinity, manhood, and sexuality, MPT, (money, power, things). To me in all instances, we may well be chasing our own shadows someone else's, either that or shadow boxing. I'm just saying. We need a new meaning to the term being culturally down that adheres to progressively self-group culturally studied, non-sexist, non-homophobic, anti-racist and classist ways of becoming on our own terms.. *Ya feel me.*

Then to, when, why, and how did thinking and representing myself as an African American or Black American become so loud in my head that it permeated the fabric of my consciousness and unconsciousness to include dreaming and nightmare scenarios? (I must admit that I dream about meeting and talking with President Obama. This never happened to me before). The fact is there was always the guts of the matter, i.e., the social-political, cultural, sexual, raced, economic, religious, content of living situations, observations, sights, sounds, smells, and experiences and how they applied to myself, parents, elders in my family, my friends and neighbors, and other Black folks in Philly, Coatesville, Pa, Harrisburg, Castle Hayne, North Carolina, Baltimore, Lawton, Oklahoma, Washington, D.C., the Bronx, New York, that were the precursor to my self-declaration and association with others of similar, more reserved-conservative, or opposing mindsets.

In **Figure 2** I present a discussion regarding social-emotional, cognitive perceptual-motivational filters. It suggests that both sections contain sets of constructs and perspectives that overlap, shape, and influence participant perspective as a response to social reality, as being interwoven with their social construction and habitus of their masculinity, manhood, and sexuality. Deonna (2006) argued that in actuality the gap between emotions and responses to a situation or condition and perception does not present that significant of a gap. The implication here is that social-emotional (tempered and non-tempered or managed feelings in social settings) are a character actor, that is, a source of energy in the expression of masculinity, manhood, and sexuality. The overall purpose of this two-figure conceptualization then is to organize the analytical discussion of findings that positions participant perspective with related subject topic and issues within the research literature. Still further, the depiction is an attempt to recognize the complexity involved in structuring, developing, and pursuing a healthy Black African American and bi-multi-racial masculinity and manhood.

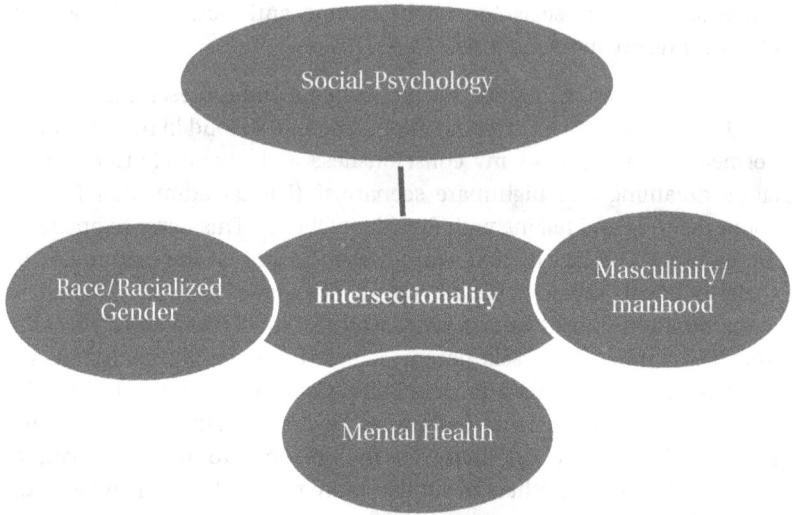

Figure 1. Individual-Group Response to Social Reality

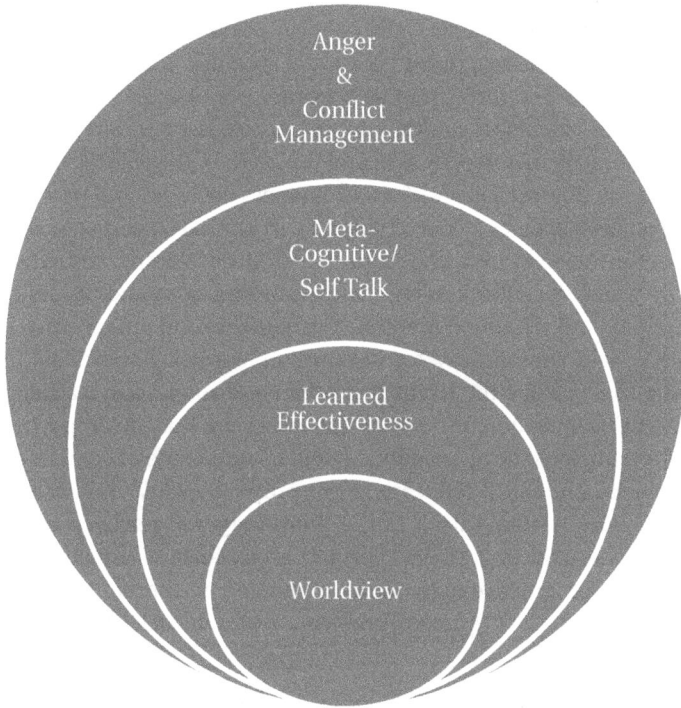

**Figure 2. Individual and in association with Group Response
to Social Reality**

Recollect that in Chapter 4 the point that participants became more acute, discerning, and elaborate in their responses when interview questions and prompts turned to the relationship of race, ethnicity, and culture, relative to masculinity and manhood identity, learning and academic achievement. Participant perspective emerged in contrast to the mindset among U.S. citizens, media, and political pundits that race and related issues have been "*downgraded*" to a social anomaly in a post-civil right era U.S. society, now so-thought of as post-race era, that is "reliant upon the fallacy of, for example, "colorblindness" as discussed by Sue (2008) in his treatise on racial microaggression and the myth of the colorblind society. I would argue that the fallacy of colorblindness attitudes and practices in a still racialized society is not conducive to the advancement of studies promoting the relevancy and importance of developing and cultivating healthy-progressive Black American African American and bi-multi-racial masculinity and manhood identity conceptualization and creative inventiveness. Said another way, for instance, unless being colorblind involve working to recognize the realities of urban and rural decay, racialized urban gentrification and the social displacement that disproportionately impacts poor, low-social-economic people, and people of color, the history of Black criminality, [8]educational disproportionality, then this/it, this position, does not lend itself to the promoting and realizing conditions that are conducive to the relevancy and importance of the need to cultivate healthy-progressive masculinity, manhood, and sexuality, as culturally applicable to Black African American, bi-multi-racial males, on their own terms.

What appears to *need* more prominent attention in mainstream research literature and social-cultural thought in general is the defining role and relevancy of developing and cultivating a healthy progressive Black African American, and bi-multi-racial masculinity, for example, in the fields of education, social psychology and psychiatry, and sociology beyond conventional patriarchal masculinity models that still inform, for instance, parental socializing, and participation in so-called mainstream culture, and various public spheres.

Bear in mind that all participants believed that they needed to manage the viewing of cultural self-identity and concept on their "own terms." or example, participants made candid remarks while expressing their concerns over media sources and research literature containing issues related

---

[8] See *The Condemnation of Blackness, Race, Crime, and the Making of Urban America* by Khalil Girbran Muhammad

to Black males, with regard to mis-educated and misrepresented views of hip-hop culture that encourage stereotyping, racial profiling, and presence of a capacity to learn, achieve, and productively in society. A raw implication that has been worded to me from anecdotal remarks and sited in various commentary and research material that amount to: is worth folk's time in, for instance, teaching, the administration of education and schooling, and where re-in-engagement support funding and programmatic development efforts are needed?

There is an implied critical daily awareness and informed perception regarding interests and issues related to men of color. The fact that participants found it necessary to manage or oversee the development of their cultural self, how they are perceived and responded to, and who they are becoming, points to their observations, experiences, and concerns regarding how Black African American, bi-multi-racial males, are looked at, not only among their peers, but also in greater society. Their perceptions join contemporary provocative views of (Chandler, 2011; Harper, 1996; Petin, 2011; Staples, 1985; Wideman, 1994), regarding about what is and represents Black masculinity and manhood in a heterosexually sanctioned Euro-American dominant racialized society. I would argue that the racialization of historical U.S. society socially, economically, psychologically, and politically, established an ecological template that still un-admittedly informs today's societal citizens.

Findings from an empirical study conducted by Joiner and Walker (2002) revealed that, after controlling for the stress of everyday living, African American males attending a historically Black college reported less acculturative stress than did African American males attending a large state university. Acculturation stress can and is experienced during interpersonal intercultural interactions or general references relative to integration and segregation experiences, within the meaning of who they are relative to group ethnic-cultural racialized-gender belief's, national identity/ethnicity, and the "European American" value of individualism. Moreover, the experiences are associated with the construction and response to social reality and world surrounding the presence of dominant group power relations in areas such as education, law and legal matters, politics, access to healthcare, housing, employment and dominance in social-economics as it concerns control over the distribution of resources, and the availability of jobs, and decision making applied to jobs applications, promotion, workplace intercultural responsiveness.

Philogenne (1999) in the comprehensive study entitled: *From Black to African American: A New Social Representation,* argued the social-psychological complexity of intergenerational acculturation efforts and experiences among U.S. citizens of African descent relative to the impact of historical racialization. This included the distance historical weathering of varying degrees of awareness regarding the social, physical, and psychological quarantine experienced by enslaved Africans from multiple tribal nations/cultures that impacted more contemporary efforts in self-identity and concept socially, among African Americans who emphasize self-cultural-ethnicity as a marker of self-identity, as contrasted to racial-identity. (How are both understood and perceived relative to self-empowerment)? Recall there are stereotypical, and so forth antagonisms to stare down in striving for social-equality as a part of their societal integration.

Please recollect that the recognition by participants of societal and self-induced historical-contemporary negatively type casted stereotypes of Black African American and bi-multi-racial males implied their awareness of the insidious nature of this in a racialized society. Furthermore, when normalized and not realized as such. Bear in mind that, one of the participants knowingly stated that among the young Black males that he encountered in his outreach work there were those who engaged in at-risk stereotypical attitudes and behaviors of misconduct, as if they were responding to a self-fulfilling prophecy of failure, despite being told differently.

The participants discussed how they felt that findings from various studies and in the media coverage often focused on the depiction Black African American males who were portrayed as expressing dangerous, improper ways of behaving, showing attitudes relegated to the angry Black man stereotype, the suave communicator trying to talk his way past or around something in, for instance, social-political discourse, engaged in an educational workshop situation, political office, personal-family business situation and job setting. (Such perspectives hold social-behavioral-linguistic implications relative to dominant-conservative and pseudo liberal views of social reality). One participant in regard to this stated "when you hear things often enough you tend to believe them," this is "absorbing what the media is saying." Another participant stated in his dialogue about hip hop culture and Black males and culture that "once people have a negative idea about something they only notice the negative things about something, that all Black people are thugs and carries that over, so when they see *normal* it doesn't even register." This is another point that seems to have been deftly alluded to or stated outright within writings attended in literature by scholar and cultural critics such as Dyson, 2007; Parks and Hughey, 2010; and Kitwana, 2002.

Participants were keen on pointing out what they viewed and per- ceived as rumors, realities, contradictions, and tendencies among citizens in the society-at-large and peers, regarding how they and/or others who share ethnic-cultural membership(s) were thought and talked about, and acted on, this included the issue of sanctioned racial and general public profiling, which has reached a social saturation point in society so that it has become entertainment and joke material in film media and discussed out of context and haphazardly in social media and anecdotally in social conversation. All participants felt that there is this overrepresentation of Black African American males being depicted as problems, with criminal and pathological mentalities, in relationships with the disproportionate incarceration of Black and Latino males, un/under employment, school drop-out, and the historical conceptualization of black criminality, i.e., "the link between race and crime is as enduring and influence in the twen- ty-first century as it has been in the past" (Muhammad, 2010). In view of this point it was apparent that interviewees worked to be aware of, for ex- ample, historical or contemporary issues, situations, media, or academic literature generated information, and of course generated through the new social media outlets of Twitter and Facebook, where one could find racialized, sexist, and homophobic ill-contrived verbal and written rant- ing.

Thus, it appeared to be notable among participants that they remain vigilant regarding stereotypical race-culture related issues pertinent to Black African American and bi-multi-racial males, and that they too were a part of reconceptualization efforts argued in Philogene's thesis. In this regard then, it is notable to indicate participants in this study are func- tional, civil minded, goal oriented, compassionate, achieving, and con- tributing citizens. Perhaps, this will aid in calling attention to the rich and provocative content of their observations and perspective, despite the limitation of their numbers in this study.

Here too, let me point out that both bi-multi-racial participants en- gaged in discussion on the topic of how they experienced disquieting ob- servations and remarks concerning what Stephan (1992) named "mixed heritage" (p.50). Their reflective responses provided insights into their experiences and observations regarding the gray area that they and others of "mixed heritage" are assigned to; many of whom choose not to occupy the ascribed space.

Participants discussed that among bi-multi-racial and "hyphenated" Black Americans there are those who experience the need to code-switch, involving linguistic-behavioral styles of shifting back and forth between standard and "Black English." Rhodes referred to this gray area, socially psychologically speaking, as "interstitial space." According to Rhodes, interstitial space has to do with the gray (foggy) area of uncertainty that lies between cultures and within cultures relative to identity and where one fits in, (personal communication, Benjamin Rhodes, March 1989). Here to there are implications relative to fitting-in, concerning to the time/space situation events one is presently in, that involve self-empowerment, ego health, and a sense of self-worth and relevancy to the expenditure of energy. What is interesting to draw attention to is that within present "integrated" public space, the gray area seems to be more obscure than in segregated times. Bear in mind that participants formulated their perspective from the recollection of racialized gender related experiences occurring within the context of a multi-culturally diverse society that is heavily reliant rewarding mono-cultural assimilation and individualistic identity development.

Finally, participants viewed masculinity in ways that they were able to set their experiences apart relative to their ethnic-cultural heritage(s) and racial identity.

As noted previously, only one participant of Nigerian descent, who experienced socialization in the *collectivistic patriarchal setting of his village culture*, directly associated his masculine identity **_seamless merger thesis I propose and contend_** with education, schooling, and academic achievement, while the five other participants who grew up in a multicultural society that does not promote collectivist ethnic-cultural socialization were not consciously aware of this association. However, bring back to mind that the interview questions aimed at exploring the association of masculinity relative to condition within and surrounding their education, schooling, and academic achievement perceptions and experiences, prompted considerable pause and curiosity among participants, which resulted in a notable ardency in their response, recollection, and dialogue. All participants did believe that it was important for them to perform academically well given their ethnic-cultural background(s), which is ultimately connected with masculinity and manhood. Mistry and Rogoff (1994) stated that we do remember in "*cultural context,*" and I would assert that this is relevant to consider given the history of racialized gender under separated, segregated, and now under so-called integrated circumstance.

All participants expressed the importance of working to maintain a calm demeanor outside and within when facing and assessing challenges, suggesting the presence and involvement of mega-cognitive reflection, self-talk, and emotional intelligence. Finally, participants presented discussion that demonstrated their acquired knowledge regarding risk associated with their ethnic-cultural masculinity in a racialized society. Risk assessment and association are inherent in one's worldview and survival thrust construction, it becomes a part of one's habitus imbued from individual and group psychohistorical experiences with social reality; hearing news about shooting incidents in public engages risk assessment, which varies between individuals in relationship with one's, for example, racialized gender. Worrying is a prompter of risk assessment.

Section 1

In **Figure 1,** I am suggesting that social psychological complexity was relevant to developing, defining, imaging, enacting, and working to maintain Black African American, and bi-multi-racial masculine self and manhood, among participants. For example, both of the bi-multi racial participants have fathers who were Black American, but also self-identified as Black African American. Their mothers are Mexican and Cubana/Mexican. Both mothers very strongly self-identified as Latina, and believed in and practiced social justice in a Black – Latina concerned feministic context, relative to race-ethnic-cultural-masculine hegemony attitudinal, decision making and behavior issues and socialized habits. One participant's father, who was a Vietnam Era veteran, spoke and explained his military service, *self-designated as a "Blood,"* to his son discussing his recognition and response to what he referred to as "Jim Crow's racist stench." This is pointed out to suggest the social-psychological complexity and the very purposeful self-reflection expressed by bi-multi-racial males, regarding the relationship of their family ethnic-cultures to their masculinity and manhood enactment and representation. Social psychological complexity is noted in part too because of the historical racialized marker on masculinity, manhood, sexuality, and expression, and the aesthetic thoughts and desire relative to one's sexual persona. Historical racialized markers intersect within the rigid walls of heterosexuality masculinity and manhood enactment, that is, what is thought to mean and what it takes to

act like and be a man in a European American dominant patriarchal society. Here, it is relevant to refer to Mutua's (2006) discussion on defining
"progressive black *masculinities.*" Mutua stated that Black males in order
to embrace the structuring of progressive Black masculinities must actively stand against "social structures of domination" (p.7). Although the issue of sexual domination as a construct of social political structures of
domination was not a subject of topic in this study, I am pointing this out
because three of the participants in particular highlighted how their
mothers provided them with ethnic-cultural socializing talks regarding
this. Apparently, these talks involved contemporary-historical information and real-time examples to their development as part of their self-
epistemology, to include exposing their sons to information and conversation regarding social justice and inequality issues and activities, such as,
street organized protests, literature, music, and other artistic genre of
works among people of color, respect for women, sexual assault, the trepi-
dations of heterogeneous expectations/social pressures for men of color
relative masculinity, manhood, and sexuality identity making. And the
centricity of la familia.

The bi-multi-racial participants were ardent in describing/alluding to
the social consciousness and Latina feminism of their mothers. These
conversations also included the saliency of recognizing and working to
understand the presence of privileged attitudes and behaviors involved in
socialized patriarchal masculine empowerment, which promotes and sustains sexism, homophobia, and other acts and attitudes that characterize
male violence at the cost of degrading women. Very importantly, it is relevant to say that one must not be afraid of studying and trying to implant
humanism within the fabric of one's masculine self for fear of being
viewed or thought of as less of a man or person, in the case of this study
less of a Black American African American, or bi-multi-racial male in the
making.

Here too, social-psychological complexity also involves conscious and
subconscious social-racialized attitudes and expectations in contemplation and response to what one looks like in appearance and how one ima-
gines oneself to be. This is to say that ways of interpreting and responding
to social-reality includes: the accumulation and expressions of knowledge,
among Black African American, bi-multi-racial males who wish to construct, critique, and present their masculinity and manhood with a more
ethnic-culturally conscious voice and intellectually informed mind, that is
outside of sports arenas, other areas of entertainment, and other public
venues. Areas and venues, that do not generally serve the desire and

pleasure of comfort zone culture among members of the society at large. Comfort zone culture simply means instances where the phenotypical features, spoken word and behavioral cultural styles, perspective and information interpretative of Black African American and bi-multi-racial males, are consciously or subconsciously perceived to be safe and universal among this country's citizens to experience. What makes this accusation difficult to prove is readily contested/fended off via the pseudo phrases such as "you're just playing the race card" or "your pointing this out is "reverse racism." Such mindsets are socially and scholarly flaunted now that we have entered into a supposed so-called "post-race era," which emerged in national discourse with the election of President Obama. Lum (2009), discussed this in an article entitled "The Obama Era: A Post-Racial Society?" The point is that participant perspective of their lived experiences stands in corroboration with the pursuit of interest and issue satisfaction and resolution regarding the acceptable places and situations where Black, African, and bi-multi-racial males are free to be empowered within the context of a multiculturally integrated society; free of the threat of racial profiling and lessened of other racialized-gender hypertensive circumstance and condition, is far from fruition.

Provocatively, Robinson (2010) has argued that Black America since integration "has undergone a process of disintegration" (p. 91). This process represents complex intra-social-cultural, psychological, and social-economic group fragmentation and incongruence, undergone *within* the African American community. Paradoxically, disintegration has occurred while in interaction with societal integration, economic up-down turns, changes in criminal laws, (War on Drugs), the impact of Reagonics and Bush Sr./Jr. eras raiding and undermining of civil rights and racial equality, anti-affirmative action legislation, and the ultra-modest conservativism social-political-religion attitudes and stands. Robinson's discourse is coherent and lucid in saying that: "instead of one Black America, now there are four."

There is,

- A mainstream middle-class majority with a full ownership stake in American society

- A large, abandoned minority with less hope of escaping poverty and dysfunction than at any time since Reconstruction's crushing end.

- A small transcendent elite with such enormous wealth, power, and influence that even white folks have to genuflect (kneel to).

- Two newly emergent groups –individuals of *mixed-race heritage* and communities of recent black immigrants—that make us wonder what "black" is even supposed to mean (p.92).

Robinson indicated that these four Black Americas are "increasingly distinct, separated by demography, geography, and psychology." Moreover, "they have different profiles, different mind-sets, different hopes, fears, and dreams" (p.92). Hence, the social-psychological complexity of experiencing, socialization, defining, imaging, and enactment of masculinity and manhood among Black African American, bi-multi-racial males, in a society who citizenry has historically operated on the template of European American heterosexual patriarchy that has promoted and rewarded male hegemony.

> *Black men move between majority and minority cultures and must negotiate the racism and discrimination that accompany caste-like minority status. Specially, Black men are expected to conform to dominant gender role expectations (e.g. to be successful, competitive, and aggressive), as well as meeting culturally specific requirements (e.g., cooperation, promotion of group, and survival of group) of the Black community, which often leads to conflict. The negotiation of these varied contexts lend itself to the development of varied and complex conceptions of manhood (Hunter and Davis, 1994, p.22).*

Hunter and Davis commented that the developmental process among Black males required their movement back and forth between the ethnic-cultural developmental needs and demands of their community and themselves, and that of various people, groups, institutions, and their arrangements/policies/requirements within a mainstream social-economic and political dominate society. One among whose citizen have been constantly at odds with our multicultural historical and contemporary moorings, many among whom there are those who are angrily, fearfully, and resentfully bearing witness to continuous demographic diverse grown and shifting population movement.

Participant response suggested social-complexity referring to racial-ized constraints, caution, and ambiance inherent in defining and trying to enact Black masculinity, manhood, sexuality. In an integrated society this complexity implies that Black African American and bi-racial males have to negotiate the challenge of viewing and deciding how to define, repre-sent, and enact their masculinity and manhood through the lens and sen-sibilities of a dominant European American patriarchal society in the face of what *among* males of color see as assimilatory reduction or cultural trade-offs. To these males of color such reduction and cultural trade-off amounts to the dismissal of working to contribute to group cultural self-development and frame of reference. Or put another way, progressive wholeness in ethnic-cultural context. Brown (2005) asserted that,

> *Historically, from this country's settlement, societal pressures to control and dominate Black people have been accomplished by elevating the "race man" who did not pose a threat to the dominant culture's inter-ests and values. The dominant culture has always pit-ted the African American culture against itself by pres-suring blacks to embrace one type of black masculini-ty, while rejecting another. This has occurred repeat-edly throughout history whether it was Washington vs. Dubois, King vs. Malcolm X, Jackson vs. Farra-khan. For African Americans who were already op-pressed politically, socially, and economically, it be-came problematic to accept black masculinities that the dominant culture did not accept (pp.65-66).*

Brown too argued complexity in shaping and enacting masculinity among males of Black African American, and bi-multi-racial whether they are consciously or unconsciously aware of the push-pull of societal social assimilation and acculturation demands; this being very much historically relevant to bi-multi-racial males; who were historically referred to as *mu-latto*. I would argue, in the face of questionable conscious or subconscious awareness and understanding, that assimilation – acculturation demands have historically been a "bone of contention" among Black African Ameri-can bi-multi-racial males, as to whether or not that they are experiencing intentional or unintentional coercion, shame, embarrassment, normalcy, into trading-off or reducing the development and exploration of their eth-

nic-group cultural self in defining and enacting their masculinity, manhood, sexuality.

It is then relevant to note that if there is not purposeful conversation
and exposure to such historical-contemporary interests-issues[9] such as
trade-off or reduction, the possibility of this is just not something that
comes readily to mind to be contemplated. There is so much temporal
space filled with forced and voluntary assimilatory survival and rationalization to work through (Bush, 1999).

Philogene maintained that the American experience taught us that integration was not just mere proximity, but was an active process based
upon joint interpersonal-cultural reciprocated acceptance and the execu-
tion via an equality of equity in our public affairs and private enterprises.
Regarding the particulars of integration in all major areas of human societal activities, mainstream culture is still predominantly shaped by Americans of European origin, that continue to occupy positions of power and
control. This is significant to integration among people of color, relative
the process of assimilation and acculturation points of stress; both of
whom need to be operationally studied and redefined, as there are so
many quiet nuanced subtleties in what is not said but felt, or seen in faces
and eyes, as we pass by one another and/or interact face to face, and indirectly on the phone and through various forms of computer technological
medium.

Philogene argued that, mainstream cultural domination, as what Wise
called the emergence of a White Collective, keeps in existence a process of
cultural hegemony defining an "us versus them context" relative to acceptable ways to meet mainstream standards of participation and recognition that impact all folks across cultures. Finally, as a part of the mainstream cultural dominant group mentality, there stands the self-group
appointed belief that members of the mainstream stand as guardians of
democracy and freedom (and I contend capitalism) based upon the axiological reference to individualism being keepers of the American Dream. [10]
Black African Americans (who/we are not immigrants, Asante, thank you

---

[9] Interest satisfaction as a part of mediation is reached via issue resolution.

[10] White supremacy informed by patriarchal heterogeneous masculinity, and the
Racial Contract maintained by Mills (1997), perpetuated a system of global and
domestic racial domination of people of color that generated subtle and overt demands in the construct and response to social reality, thereby adding social-
psychological complexity to the stress of day-to-day living.

Dr. Claude Anderson, 2015 for emphatically explaining this), and immigrants from diverse ethnic-cultural groups color and religious tribal membership, have had to construct and negotiate their response to social cultural reality by way of being the what I call the *not in good standing* other, or as Fusco argued the term referenced, "otherness."

Study participant response also called attention to being guarded against self-portrayed historical-contemporary stereotypes; their dialogue clearly indicated that they were not willing to frame their masculinity and manhood in one framework of mainstream dominant cultural assimilation but suggested acculturation. Participants were leery of images presented in the media of Black African American males, or being cognizant of obvious or subtle stereotypical remarks made socially or in formal settings during intra-interpersonal communicative group interaction. Again, if there is not a formal or informal effort that heightens the awareness among Black African American, bi-multi-racial males, regarding historical and contemporary stereotypes, counter-productive attitudes and ways, and the social-psychological implications of racialized gender, their cumulative efforts will continue to negatively impact our quality of life existence and that of our community, or as my Aunt Katie would say, "*we'll just fall by the wayside.*"

Bharmal, Kennedy, Jones, Lee-Johnson, Morris, Caldwell, Brown, Houston, Meeks, Vargas, Franco, Razzak & Brown (2011), using a participatory community based research methodology, presented findings among young African American male study participants from Los Angeles County. The study provided them with an opportunity that resulted in their calling attention to "descriptions of institutional racism, unemployment, income inequality, and neighborhood violence" that were implicated in higher rates of conditions that included homicide, HIV/ADIS, stress, and depression (p. 158). Belton (1995), *Speak My Name, Black Men on Masculinity and the American Dream*, presented meditative voices among Black African American male writers who shared their autobiographical experiences, insights, and perspective on masculinity, manhood, and African American culture in U.S. society. The editor's hope was that such anthological works assisted in sparking dialogue and healing among Black African American men.

Results from this study suggested that all the participants possessed varying degrees of self-ethnic-cultural consciousness garnered from home, community, parent, and family socializing experiences, educational institutions, the media, and literature, regarding stereotypical attitudes and behaviors to be aware of, and attention to various reports, formal – informal conversation, significant to the social-health, education, and other life conditions and circumstance among men of color.

Hecht, Collier, and Ribeau (1993) stated that ethnicity as interethnic communication and ethnic identity affiliation, are problematic, retreating, emerging, and situationally responsive, and are significant to individuals as they seek to define and redefine group memberships. I would add not just define or redefine group memberships, but to consciously realize and decide whether or not and how to relate to their ethnicity relative to a number of social-cultural, political, racial, and other variables. Moreover, Hecht et al. cited Bourhis & Giles (1977) who stated that "ethnic identity is more salient when group identity is threatened" (p. 59). What implications does this hold for Black African American and bi-multi-racial males in the shaping and enacting of their masculinity, manhood, sexuality?

Relevant to ethnicity there is the intersection of masculine-feminine dichotomy, sexual orientation, and racialized intergroup power relations differentials, that are consciously and subconsciously, involved in identity making and enactment through intercultural communicative interaction and cognitive appraisal by the individual concerned. Included in cognitive appraisal are considerations regarding the fitting-in to dominant European American mainstream culture (socially-linguistically, how you think and stand on equity and the equality of opportunity, styles of demeanor, temperament during interpersonal cultural interaction, what knowledge base/frame of reference do you work with, it goes on), and the claimed normalcy of heterogeneous masculinity. Hecht et al, stated that for members of nonmainstream groups the process of defining and redefining ethnic-cultural group members often involved consideration of mainstream culture.

As Jackson III & Dangerfield aptly discussed that masculine is a pluralized accounting for "variegations (the introduction or involvement of variety) resulting from culture, class, sexual preference, religion, and other axes of differences" (p. 123). Ethnicity then joins inclinations and tendencies (habitus) involved in demonstrating, feeling, expressing, and simply enacting gender orientation that the individual concerned brings from situation to situation, setting to setting. What I believe is relevant to remember is that before you open your mouth to speak, the body has already spoken, and can be subject to preconceived notions relative to say ethnicity and gender, physical-racial looks, that are already in play, although not necessarily tied to you, but out there and available for consumption, witting and unwitting use. Jackson explained that, "Socially, the body facilitates the perpetuation of ascriptive devises used to assign meaning to in-groups." Furthermore, there is the body as social and politic, and as such gendered and racialized meanings and preconceptions as attached to it among people during intrapersonal - interpersonal interactions.

> *(I hear the words coming out of the mouth of this body and it is interculturally disconcerting, particularly given the controversy of the subject matter occurring, say, within the micro public sphere of a classroom, within the larger public sphere of the university, in view of student, administrator, and faculty ethniccultural and racialized gendered and class demographics).*

Brown also cited Jackson (2006) as stating that since the 17th century mass media has engaged in scripting the Black body which has aided in perpetuating stereotype and negative images of African Americans, continuing to this day. According to Jackson and Hopson (2011), social scripting of Black bodies is the accumulative effect of racialization, commodification, and politicizing of Black bodies over time until negative meaning is normalized and out there in the imagination and social linguistic discourse and presumptions among society's members. Jackson maintained that,

> *The social body facilities the perpetuation of ascriptive devise used to assign meaning to ingroups and outgroups; it also serves to jog the personal memories of cultural interactants, to remind them visually of constitutive discourse that provides form and structure to the social cognitions about racialized bodies* (p. 27).

Such consciousness about race and ethnicity and looks suggested that participants have evolved a perceptional pragmatic lens allowing them to explore and construe historical and real-time experiences and situations in consideration of their manly presence and interactions. hooks (2004) acutely argued that Black males historically have had to work in states of unconscious awareness and in some cases denial in the shadows of a White male patriarchal dominant society. This is relative to shaping and expressing the temperament/character nuances of their manhood styles and sense of being present and interact, while playing dodge ball or my back home street game of childhood dead-block, with stereotypes weighed in on Black males, and among males of color period.

What hooks argued that is pertinent to this study is that Black males generationally were socialized in a society under racially contrived structured cultural arrangements of otherness; or as I said, not-in-good standing. The conceptualization of masculinity, manhood, and sexuality has to be viewed and based upon the existence of mainstream heterogeneous patriarchal expectations, making the viewing and consideration of Black African American, bi-multi-racial masculinity, manhood, and sexual conception in response to social reality, to be viewed abstrusely, if not totally unnecessary.

De jure and *de facto* social-economic, political, educational, integration comes with a cost, (i.e., it should not be taken for granted and for the most part it wasn't), there is the work of integration that many people do not acknowledge, that simply does not cross their conscious minds. I contend too that hooks would argue that Black African American males are free to join in as long as they play by a certain set of White male dominant patriarchal characteristics that many males of European American descent and many males of color say do not exist or are too general to interculturally differentiate, thereby simply perceiving and declaring them generic.

Along the same lines of thought, in this society some argue that Black culture is merely perceived as a variance of European American culture, which is probably more commonly imaged and lies subconsciously among many this country's citizens, as a part of our merged multiple ethnic-cultural pool of so-called *just-American* presumptive culture. The point being, under such societal history it is difficult to connect the dots or imagine there being some semblance of Black African American ethnic group culture, that could produce and bring to visible recognition social conceptualization of tenets of masculinity, manhood, and sexuality, beyond the dominant European American mainstream heterogeneous social-cultural expectations. Hence, this off color reference amused response from a European American physician from a major university in Washington State, during my visit as his patient, "I didn't know that a thing such as Black masculinity existed." [11]

Issues of complexity, regarding the unrecognized constriction of enacting ways to more fully experience progressive masculinities in ethnic-cultural context, also involve the presence of a heightened cultural comfort zone overreliance on the acceptance of Black masculinity and the status of manhood via media projected images of Black men, as previously mentioned, as for instance, "the reigning symbol of aggressive American manliness" (Ross, 1998, p. 599), within sports. In fact, behavioral and attitudinal swagger and dress among of Black males and males of color appears to be historically more acceptable, comfortable, and tolerated in association with the social areas of entertainment, or within the confines of segregated and/or economically poor neighborhoods. This point came out in participant perspective that Black male performance was not readily understood in relationship with education, learning, and academic achievement. In point, remember that one of the study participants made a provocative thesis claim that the young Black males were afraid to assert the ethnic-culture of their masculinity and manhood outside of sports; in this context he was referring to learning and the educated self. Although not directly connected, but relative, over the years Black and Latino male colleagues of mine have discreetly generalized that males of color who attempt to execute a social justice agenda in public or private arena, regarding equality of opportunity interests and issues such as educational equity, general speaking, run the risk of having to work outside of the cultural comfort zone among European Americans and assimilated people of color.

There is too, possessing a recorded status and experience of, for instance, adjudication that makes it more precarious and abstruse in relating to Black masculine and manhood identity that does not carry a thug image in racialized stereotype (Wilson, 1991). Rios (2009) argued that as a result among young black and brown men having experienced contact with law enforcement, juvenile justice system confinement, surveillance, their construct and response to social reality now involves the production of "a hypermasculinity" (p.150), that obstructs cessation and social mobility. I would argue that it increases susceptibility to embracing and engag-

---

[11] During a visit to a healthcare clinic in Federal Way, Washington, my doctor asked me what I taught as an adjunct at a local university, I stated, "The Habitus of Black Masculinity." To this he chuckled and stated, "I didn't know that a thing such as Black masculinity existed."

ing in the ideal of masculine strength as dominance and subordination of others, degree of insubordination in institutional setting such as those for schooling, learning, education as human development, in the construction and response to social reality. This holding further implication for hypersensitive and antagonistic risk assessment (Collins, 2006; Gibbs, 1988).

Although of a different age group, Fordham (1996) in her comprehensive and provocative ethnographic study on representation as otherness and its impact on the academic performance of African American adolescents, attending an urban high school presented two baseless stereotypical notions,

> *(1) African Americans and African American adolescents who look to maintain the Black self as safe cultural space, are weird, radical, and do not want to do well in school or achieve the good American life: and (2) experiencing success is an unproblematic social process fueled only by desire and ability (p.11). (Now that to me is weird in its' simplicity).*

In sum, there appears to be this Catch-22 of Black masculinity and manhood; for instance, that involves an over-reliance upon celebratory acceptance of Black males as athletes, entertainers, and/or acceptance status of service in the Armed Forces, in stereotypical context, (like the celebrity status of former General Collin Powell, not to demean the sacrifice and honor he earned from service to country, and at great sacrifice).

Perplexity exists in the form of negotiating one's racialized gender experiences in U.S. society via the splintered experience based upon one's phenotypical features and how to perform as a male of Black, Mexican, Cuban, or Nigerian, and/or mixed heritage. As Chandler (2011) very candidly queried, "How does one become a Black Man?" What influences this becoming? How does one do Black masculinity as a performance of gender?" (p. 55). Young (2007), noting himself as a "dark-skinned Black man spoke compellingly in the introduction of his works about what he saw in his youth as failed attempts to perform being a Black male, recalling that he spent a good deal of his youth wishing he were White because he "failed miserably at being black" (p. 12). During his visits to an off-university campus Black barbershop he frequented, he meditatively, described a scene where he is observing Black males at this barbershop who had a "lanky dip" (p. 159) in their walk, hip swagger in their social-linguistic nuanced talk, some with sagged wear of their pants, and there was the presence of self-assured tones in their conversation, as they bantered back and forth in a row of topics from sports, to politics, and so on; he confessed that he "wanted to "mimic them" (p. 59). This barbershop was located in the predominantly White populated state of Iowa, where Blacks comprised 25% of the prison population. He explained that somehow this barber scene joined his growing up experiences in a segregated ghetto, where as a Black male he felt that he did not fit. During this time he evaluated and surmised that his gender performance via speech, behavior, attitudes, characteristics, his love to learning, were not adequate to what is now referred to as perhaps being "thugged out" (in the past this was referred to as being hip, cool, hoodlum, or in my 60's jargon, a jitterbug or hardhead). He was an academic achiever, who in his case had distanced himself socially, linguistically, attitudinally, and behaviorally via the social construction and assessment of reality, and how he perceived and felt about his sexuality, from certain of his peers. His dissonance was such that he admitted trying to "be White" because he and "others" had perceived him "to be closer to what a white boy might be" than what he believed "a black boy to be" (p.155). Young to talked about how in his youth his brother called him fag, and directed nasty scoffs toward him like "move his faggot butt" (p. 1019); this was done relative to his intellectual and sexual persona, from a brother who declarative disowned him as his brother when friends observed him playing games designated for girls like hop-scotch and jacks (which I played as a young boy along with playing with my mama's jewelry). Of note here is the threat of perception and reference to masculine performance, attire, linguistic tone and word choice, along with informative response in discourse, and sexual persona that does not embody so-called manliness, as it concerns attentiveness and discipline to self-epistemology.

Young (2007) found that an African American professor colleague of his offered an anecdote regarding a time she felt similarly uncomfortable bi-cultural feelings in a Black barbershop, which she had discussed in her book entitled *The Real Negro: The Question of Authenticity in Twentieth-Century African American Literature* (Eversley, 2004). Young drew upon his colleague's summative example from her book, in which she contrasted experiences for them between the university campus, where they were trained intellectuals and held professorships, and the Black barbershops that both frequented, as being sites where they had both suffered from conflict bought upon them by trying to exist in both places in the same skin. In other words, Eversley, cited in Young (2007) explained, they sought to fit-in at both places, "the (White) campus and in the barber-shop" (p.63). Two varying overlapping orientations trying to occupy the same space, actually at both locations. In these locations Eversley stated that they had "to alter not the color of their skin" (p. 78), but the ways they had to perform race in each location. Eversley further explained that such racial performances were most often carried out through language, "the way we communicate" (p.78).

Recall that one of the participants directly pointed out the dark complexion of his skin along with his tall height that really made him feel his presence in contrast to others, particularly in integrated settings and during interactions, which suggested an experience of hypersensitivity regarding his presence; this could be said of the bi-multi-racial participants as well. This participant stated that his older brother was darker complexioned than he was. He further talked about being in integrated settings where he was socializing with other Black African Americans, and/or bi-multi-racial males or settings where he was the only person of color, and had gathered from the tenor of conversations or nonverbal innuendos in either setting that, as a result of self-conceived notions from his own knowledge and experiences, he was expected or felt he needed to *perform* as a Black African American male. In referencing schooling and community intra-intercultural settings he talked about the social-cultural group expectations and self-imposed urgency and feelings associated with being and enacting Black masculinity and manhood.

What is relevant here is that all of the participants spoke about situational experiences where their racialized gender phenotypical presence was tied to culturally specific performance expectations, such as sexual prowess, and non-verbal-verbal communication styles and characteristics. As a result, my assertion is that social psychological complexity exists among males of color as they attempt to grasp and sustain their masculine self while in view of their racialized gender self in response to social reality in segregated and integrated settings in the public sphere. One's realized/unrealized response to social reality can eventually become habitus.

Then too, I am suggesting racial paradox and ambivalence may be consciously or subconsciously present among Black African American and bi-multi-racial males, in defining and actualizing their masculinity and manhood; and most work at fighting and strategizing their ways through this; but at what cost? Young (2007) professed that his racial ambiguity in his self-reflective analysis while experiencing other Black males in the barbershop he frequented, because he perceived his racial performance was being rated in comparison and contrast to theirs. At stake for Young was recognizing and owning the hard work and accomplishment of his self-epistemology in settings away from the university, in settings that were predominantly European American, in settings back home where he grew up, and in the setting of the barbershop he discussed. He also adeptly raised the point that expectations for racialized gender performance in masculine space, was even more perplexing "for those who are gay or taken to be gay" like he sometime was, because they were often alienated in those spaces in the public sphere, implicating private thought about self and fitting or not fitting in (p. 92). (Why was he taken to be gay, was it because of an academic demeanor)? As a consequence, Young recognized feelings that were not only about his "racial performance" being judged but he was also cognizant that his "gender performance" (racialized gender) was being judged simultaneously (p. 92); There was psychological push and pull with physiological implication, like constantly experiencing uncertainty eventually marked with stress-related symptoms.

Chandler (2011), in her study of Black masculinity performance, stated that African American "masculinities are particular kinds of gender performances influenced by the intersection of race and ethnicity" (p. 59). For Chandler, ethnicity as performance was necessary to integrate into the investigation of African American masculinities and "as a performance of gender" (p.59). Specifically, for the purpose of her study Chandler designated race and Blackness as separate categories of ethnic performance, because of how race is used and situated among broader audiences within the society at large and within the diversity of African American communities differs. Interestingly, as pointed out by Philogene, the designation of *Black represents* more of an association with race, whereby the designation of *African American* has to do with reconceptualization efforts related to the social construction of culture. Chandler stated,

> *What race is to the broader society cannot be defined in the same way it would be within the confines of a particular cultural group. How one negotiates race within one's native culture and outside of that culture differs. Thus, it is the varied dimensions of ethnic performance that influence how one performs gender. (p.59)*

Hence, for instance, I point out the lead in phrase that is part of the title in her exploratory works, "*How to Become a Black Man*" (p.55), as contested, disquieted, and social-culturally complex ground to walk and work
on.

Much of what is implied in participant response was their desired will
to manage their cultural identity in light of their views and experiences
with racialized gender performance. This perhaps suggests a higher astute
awareness, not simply related to or implied as being over sensitive, regarding how they were being perceived in the public sphere, given their ethnicity and racialized gendered presence in relationship and interactions with
others. Given the presence of this astute and informed awareness, it is
further implied that their tendencies/inclinations of behaving like a
"man" are embedded in their response to their construction and response
to social reality that surrounds them, and in which they participate while
being cognizant of the phenotypical features. That is, their regional and
ethnic cultural influences, speech tones, mannerisms, and so on. Several
participants suggested that once one opens his mouth there is the subconscious awareness of interacting in ways regarding how he wants to
represent the self, be perceived and understood. This becomes difficult in
situational settings, such as school if the person concerned does not perceive that he is are a part of or can relate to, for example, the institution of
education in which he is enrolled. I argue that there are instances where
one bargains as to whether or not to own one's ethnic-cultural, gender,
racialized, self, and if so how.

Jackson III & Dangerfield (1997) comprehensively argued that there is a
need to define Black masculinity "as cultural property" that cannot afford
to be accepted, approved, and adopted using the same cultural, social,
and political agendas as "traditional White masculinist scholarship," and
as such they conceptualized a "Black Masculine Identities" paradigm calling for the negotiating of Black masculine identities (pp. 120, 125). In
concert with this, I contend that there are racialized gendered psychohistorical and social circumstance and conditions, relative to the forming of
habitus among Black African American, bi-multi-racial males, that war-
rants the consideration and study regarding their social construction of
reality, interpretation, and response.

Overall, **Figures 1 and 2** attempted to suggest the dualism of complexity and constriction issues representative of participant response and perspective in the broader context of their working to develop, manage, and
maintain a healthy Black, African American, and bi-racial masculine and

manhood self-identity and concept, in a dominant heterogeneous patriarchal society that is racialized (Murji & Solomos, 2005). Participants' response joins what Whiting and Lewis (2008) stated as the uncertain situation of Black masculinity as being "laden with racial tensions" (p.1). In this regard, I suggest that there is a natural tendency to move away from things that make one uncomfortable or believe do not add to the quality of necessity in a person's life. It is suggested that the participants in this study have worked to ethnically culturally anchor themselves within their groups, and are consciously aware of the social –political challenges of their racial phenotype and social linguistic styles of presenting themselves. Then too, findings suggested they were acutely aware and engaged in risk assessment in their response to daily social realities in the presence of historical controversies surrounding their existence, relative to their ascribed ethnic-cultural groups regarding who they are. Moreover, this does not make them uncomfortable, but it adds to the complexity of who they desire to become. The following provides a summative discussion of components that make up the theoretical construct that conceptualizes the *self (Figure 1) in response to social reality (Figure 2)*.

Intersectionality

In Figure I "intersectionality" is listed as an approach to use in reviewing study results. In other words, it is suggested that participant perspective should be viewed in consideration of race, ethnic-cultural background, class, sexuality, and the racialized politics of schooling and education, as they all intersect in their lived experiences. Smith (1982) in her discussion regarding what it meant to be radical, was cited in Collins (2000) stating that it felt "radical to be dealing with race and sex and class and sexual identity all at one time" (pp. 232-233).

Crenshaw (1989) evoked the term intersectionality in arguing the intersection race and gender as essential in the analysis of Black women's subordination, as opposed to add on approaches in the examination of social inequity and oppressive issues. Collins (2000) within the context of Black feminist thought, formulated and argued intersectionality conceptualized as a *matrix of domination* that embodied the intersecting of race, gender, class, and sexuality, in the oppression of Black women.

Argumentatively, in the individual-group social history among Black African American, bi-multi-racial males, there is a need and opportunity to examine how such social constructs act relative to their efforts to realize, define, and enact their masculinity and manhood in a patriarchal-dominant racialized society. Put another way, intersectionality would provide the opportunity to explore how and the degree to which relationships involve social-biological, and political constructs such as race, gender, sexuality, class, events of racism, sexism, repression and   oppression, merge within and around the person concerned. For instance, Mutua (2006) stated that among scholars and advocates some argue that Black men "at the intersection of race and gender, are oppressed by race but are privileged by gender, by which they understand Black men to be privileged over women, particularly Black women" (p. 18). Mutua (2006), in her discussion regarding the positioning of Black males in the use of intersectional theory suggested its' utility in application to Black men could point out,

> *that many social structures contribute to the construction of individual and group identity and that to determine what a particular intersectional identity means requires scholars to look to the context. In other words, when applying intersectional theory to the black male experience, one must look to the context of a particular situation to determine whether black males are being privileged or oppressed by gender or any other structure that intersect with it (p. 22).*

Intersectionality relative to this study calls attention to an eclectically emerging portrait displaying how participants saw themselves in experiencing how others perceived them, and how they desired and worked to present themselves in the public sphere, in interrelationship with ethnic-cultural group historical and contemporary events, situations, and conditions.   Recall one of the participants, who was multi-ethnic, very assertively declared how he intended to *not* leave any of himself out regarding his multi-ethnic heritage, that he is conscious of his parents' racialized gendered, social-class, otherness experiences, and their varying degrees of social consciousness regarding the marginalization of people in society. Intersectionality as an applied theory could be used to delve into his multi-ethnic identity, in consideration of shared ethnicity of his mother who is Mexican-Cubana and his father who is Black African American, in further connection with his social construction and response to social reality. I believe then that the role of habitus as a theoretical tool of analysis holds utility in consideration of exploring, identifying, and discussing the established and emerging inclinations and dispositional tendencies in feeling, defining, and enacting masculinity, manhood, sexuality among Black African American, bi-multi-racial males.

Bi-Multi-Racial Masculinity and Manhood

U.S. de jure and de facto racial doctrines included miscegenation laws that were not completely eradicated until "close to 1967" (Root, 1992, p.3). Root instructively called needed attention to the "biracial baby boom" that occurred when the "last laws against miscegenation (race mixing) were repealed" in that year (p.3). Although the literature on bi-racial and multi-racial ethnic-identity has increased, there still appears to be a gap in research literature regarding the structure and development of bi-racial and multi-racial masculinity and manhood identity development and social-cultural experiences. Root's edited work brings attention to the challenges and complexity associated with experiencing bi-multi-racial-ethnicity, in society inherently based upon the socially and politically dichotomous reasoning of *us* as in dominant mainstream culture vs. otherness.

Both bi-multi-racial participants' perspective and observations were adeptly situated in the multiracial human racial ecology on identity development and enactment discussed by Miller (1992). Miller noted a number of significant points regarding multiracial identity development within a dominant Eurocentric society, as follows:

- Individualistic Eurocentric models are clearly inadequate to describe bi-racial identity development.

- Biracial individuals directly highlight the structure of racial dichotomization because they do not belong to either of two mutually exclusive social groups, yet lack a socially legitimated group that describes their biracial origins.

Bi- multi-racial- participants spoke about the contrary perceptions of others in view of, for example, their racial phenotypical features that prompted social-cultural behavioral expectations and ambiguity from others. In some instances, those among their peers observed their Black African American features, automatically assumed the expectation that they should be engaging and relating to nuanced styles, views, and ways of presenting themselves, in accordance with ethnic-cultural ascribed racialized looks. Thus, they were subject to both prying and peculiar questioning regarding who they were and what members say among their African Americans peers wanted them to be connected to.

The participants discussed how they saw this in people's faces, and as such this became part of their worldview and risk assessment. One of the major implications here is the saliency of identity development and support. Bi-multi-racial youth who do not experience support and cultivation from parents/significant others for the merging of who they are, and the enriching sources of ethnic-cultures they are a part of and have access to, could engage in placing themselves in culturally interstitial space, and increased susceptibility to mental health related conditions such as depression-anxiety, that is beyond having to experience everyday stressors. Take into account President Obama has a European American mother and an African father, but there were many within the Black community that claimed him as being Black American (when he is actually of Nigerian and European American descent), while others reject or disfavor his mixed heritages wondering "whose side was he on?" There also existed speculation that since his bi-racial background shared European American ancestry by virtue of being birthed to his mother of European American descent, this perhaps made him more acceptable ethnically and politically in not being an "Affirmative Action" President for the Black community, among a dominant European American voting populace. Not a comparison, but remember how one of the bi-multi-racial participants talked about how a high school teacher continued to approach him for membership in the Filipina/o club, but felt was uncomfortable and that was not necessary for him to self- declare who he was by naming the ethnicity of his parents. Finally, bear in mind that miscegenation laws outlawed "mixed marriages" and thus by birth children of these marriages have been less than socially tolerated if not outright rejected historically in this country. (It is like being by society "convicted in the womb" borrowing that very provocative phrase from Upchurch, (1997) entitled from his work, *Convicted in the Womb: One Man's Journey from Prisoner to Peacemaker*).

Race

Winant (1994) declared that the construct of race is a "key cultural marker, a central signifier, in the production and expression of identity, collectivity, language, and agency itself" (p. 30). Moreover, Winant stated that the construct of race "mediates social space" and "is fair game for racial dilemmas, doubts, fears, and desires" (p.30). Roberts (2011) contended that race is a political and not a natural system in the social grouping of people, but a social-politically, I would add psychologically con-ceived/constructed one, based upon "biological demarcations" (p. 4). Regarding the invention of race Roberts stated that, "Americans are so used to filtering our impressions of people through racial lens that we en-gage in this exercise automatically—as if we were merely putting a label on people to match their innate racial identities" (p. 3). Here too Roberts surmised that the reason we engage in such assigning of racial designation is – "there is enormous social consequences of classifying people in this way" (p. 3). (*Money, Power, Things*).

Omowale (1999) asserted that,

> *Racism is a systemic, societal, institutional, omnipres-ent, and epistemologically embedded phenomenon that pervades every vestige of our reality. For most whites, however, racism is like murder, the concept ex-ists but someone has to commit it in order for it to happen. This limited view of such a multilayered syn-drome cultivates the sinister nature of racism and, in fact, perpetuates racist phenomena rather than eradi-cate them (p. 1).*

Historically, the major construct of race has created artificial bounda-ries and generated named and power arrangements between the individ-uals and groups of people. Participants offered perspective regarding how race as a perceptional social lens was present in their experiences at work, in the pursuit of education, and during direct and indirect interactions in the public domain and private settings. They talked about how others imaged and viewed them relative to the racial physical features, commu-nication styles, political views, sexual partner associations, such as those in cross ethnic-cultural relationships. They provided a very lucid portrayal that connected and alluded to how their experiences via masculinity and manhood have been affected by race, while at the same time being cogni-zant that they must not let it compromise and run their lives, regarding who they are and want to become.

For example, the Nigerian participant was extremely clear that he was part of a larger patriarchal cultural tradition from back home that stood in view of the historical-contemporary experiences of Black American males, to include stereotypes perceived about them that tied him to Black Ameri-can males. For him and several other participants in particular, the larger ethnic-cultural group tradition(s) they felt a part of apparently assisted in culturally anchoring them, as they wanted to talk back and articulate in consideration of these cultural group traditions, interests and issues.

Participant responses appeared to join Davidson (1996) regarding the presentation of ethnographic findings that revealed how schools and curricula are sites for the shifting conceptualization, construction, and degrees of academic engagement in collaboration and conflict with their racial, ethnic-cultural, and gender identities. Simone (1989), in his assertion that European Americans are reluctant to talk about race on the subject of biracial couples, and when such discussion occurred it was only in a "diffuse and abstract ways, argued that cultural ethnographies in a range of media had often,

- Constituted images of Blackness where the Blackness itself becomes such as intense and exclusive object of fascination that the observer never has to think about what is at work to make the image or event powerful;

- Cultivated images and repressions of images concerning interracial coupling where it appears that the image itself is everything, is all-encompassing that all message constructed to address it are inadequate or frivolous;

- Presented images of Blackness that are dessicatory (state of extreme dryness or deficiency) that go right to White anxieties concerning emptiness and hollowness, that assault the desire and capacity to interpret what is viewed or experienced; and,

- Presented Blackness as an unsolvable mystery which no amount of interpretive labor will be able to resolve, where understanding becomes an impossibility. (pp. 55-56)

Finally, it was argued in the literature that race, as sociological and politically loaded term, is misconceived and misused as having social construction and meaning (Gibbs, 1989, Roberts, 2011). The preceding suggested that racialized gender identity and response to social reality plays a crucial role in shaping approaches, attitudes, and habits with implication for health and general outlook (worldview), in consideration of one's ethnic-culture, social-economic experience, gender identity, and sexual orientation.

Racialized Gender

Few (2007) stated, "racialized gender has to do with the simultaneous effects of race and gender processes on individuals, families, and communities" (p.1). According to Eckert and McConnell-Ginet (1995),

> *Gender constructs are embedded in other aspects of social life and in the construction of other socially significant categories such as those involving class, race, or ethnicity. This implies that gender is not a matter of two homogeneous social categories, one associated with being female and the other with being male. (p.2)*

The claim is that racialization simultaneously joins gender which implicated participant experiences. Put more broadly, the historical context of U.S. history is racialized and as such heterogeneously dominant gender identity development and demands for enactment are rooted in all aspects of life. I would argue that such history is embodied of racialized gender oppression and male heterogeneous socialized normativity (not recognized as such, for women rights) serves to absence conscious social-cultural and social justice perceptions and sensibilities among people, scholars, politicians, educators, regarding the persistent presence of race and gender, that are now touted as being nonexistent, abnormal, ended, too burdensome, publicly annoying, and/or too guilt laden/accusatory, to address.

Bringing up race as an issue, particularly in this so-called era of "post racial," can result in one being accused of race-baiting or inciting polarization. However, despite this non or limited visibility or ill relevancy of race it seems to stand in plain sight relative to interests and issues such as electoral politics, educational reform, inter-group power relations nationally and internationally, social-welfare domestic budgeting and spending, government involvement in social-racial justice legal matters, demographic housing patterns, anti-immigrant targeting immigrant populations of color, based upon scapegoat illogical rationalizing.

On an individual-group level, for instance, at some early point in my life I realized I was more broadly known in society as "Negro and male." (Given the ages among participants, their parent-elder, peer, and schooling socializing experiences, the advent of social media, the phenomenon of civil rights, human rights, thought-provoking politicizing via hip-hop (Boyd, 2003, for instance, listen to Run DMC), constructs such as race, ethnic-culture, racism, classism, urban gentrification, as a perceived and real phenomena, along with references to self-group identity, were more readily available for popular consumption). My parents, family and neighborhood elders, or peers, in segregated neighborhoods and integrated public spaces I grew up in, did not literally say to me, "Frederick, you are Negro and male." Was it my nuanced social experiences and observations that brought me to this fruition, through the accumulations of inter-cultural interactions across racialized gendered experiences, for example, with people of authority and expertise? How did this occur? Did I simply concoct a felt perception after reflecting upon social-cultural interaction among different ethnic-cultural groups in various settings?

I can recall the first time that I heard myself referred to as Negro was by a childhood playmate of European American descent's Daddy; during White flight phenomenon days. I had gone down the street I lived on to his house to ask could he come out and play. When he came to the door, I heard his Daddy's voice in the background, "I don't want you playing with that Negro boy anymore." The kid whose name was Billy, turned to me and said through the screen door, "I can't play anymore Franny." (My name is Frederick, and my Mama always held her tongue in cheek any time Billy came by to ask for me, and said what was not my name, despite being corrected. Mama would simply warmly say, "come on in honey"). Not long after that, Billy and his family moved. I wasn't sure what a Negro was, but it bounced around my hurt feelings of losing a play buddy all that day. The next time came across myself referred to as Negro was on my military personnel papers during the Vietnam War. Years later, eventually I thought of myself as Black in view of and immersion in the identity social transformation during the cultural revolution push-back against the social-psychological, economic, human conditions of Jim Crow segregation.

What study findings suggested was that participants engaged in cognitive-intellectual assessment of their racialized gender experiences involving the knowledge and language to articulate it. The study, as noted previously in this chapter, provided participants with an opportunity to astutely reflect on the presence of race and ethnic-culture, within the fabric of their masculine and manhood socially framed and constructed lives. In view of the findings, participants acknowledged and spoke directly to this because of, in part, their use of emotional intelligence – in concert with the self-epistemological knowledge insights in view of the ethnic-cultural background, their parental elder socialization, and integrated with the experi-

ences of positionality. It was evidenced from their responses that awareness of their presence in greater society and globally, had matured beyond
simply raw perceptual understanding. Or was it simply this opportunity to
speak out loud?

I would argue that their perspective and voice joined in the subject aim
of such critical works as those edited by Gibbs (1988) that questioned the
human condition of young African American males as being an "endangered species." Here, very importantly, Gibbs (1999) discussed how the
concept of social construction implied that racial identity, which involved
the interactions between cognitive introspective and interpretation activities, was in response to the physical-materialistic and social cultural environment occupied. In other words, participants discussed how social
construction took place in interaction with contextual factors such as
neighborhood demographics, school, parents, and social networks; this is
particularly pointed when considering youth growing up in racial social-
economically segregated or more multi-culturally demographic neighborhoods, under urban ruin and gentrifying conditions. (One begins to question self-worth and that those others who look like she/him if the only way
neighborhood gets rebuilt is via gentrifications). From this perspective,
the fact that masculinity making (the perceived societal sanctioned condition or state of being a man), just intensifies the challenges and complexity of this intimately personal social-psychological, and should be a more
realized intellectual activity, among males of color.

It is also relevant to point to Madhubuti (1990) who chronicled a series
of poignant social essays on Black masculinity and manhood calling attention to the derogatory and stereotypical ways Black African American
males have been portrayed and imaged self and among others, than athletes and entertainers. (It is extremely salient to note that from my older
cousin's Mr. Emerson Whitted from Castle Hayne, North Carolina, (now a
retired educator and a social activist), description of his educational experiences in segregated schooling down South, the seamless merger of masculinity, manhood, and sexuality with the educated self as one in the same
was simply there as an understatement or better put, a cultural assumption unsaid).

Researchers, such as Cooper (2006), Gibbs (1999), Hammond and
Mattis (2005), Hunter and Davis (1994) Mutua (2006), Pascoe (2003), Ross
(1998), and Woodland (2004) have comprehensively argued the connection of masculine identity construction and the development of manhood,
which overlaps with the social constructs of race, ethnicity, class, gender

and sexuality.   As previously noted, findings from this study suggested that participants, in their deliberation on masculinity and manhood, did so in consideration of racial, ethnic-cultural, group cultural sensibilities. This is not say that racial sensibilities dominantly pervaded their critical reflection and social perceptions, but that they seemed to have demonstrated an astuteness regarding the role and presence of race and racialized gender in their lives.   Racial sensibilities appeared to be in concert with findings that participants perceived the need to manage their cultural identity, in response to how they were being perceived and responded to, how they represented themselves and were becoming.

Section 2

Section 2 Figure 2 has to do a response to social reality in considering the presence and interaction of social-emotional-cognition, that is, intuitive ways of knowing and reasoning as a part of perceiving, noticing the nuances of a situation as a part of considering context in relationship with racialized gendered experiences and positionality. The emotion of anger is not considered in isolation as an instinct or a trigger response or the degree of one's temperament, although relevant and critical, but as a broad *interpretive response to social reality and condition,* as well as personal and group social-cultural and psychohistorical experiences and societal issues as it concerns, but not limited to, race-ethnicity-culture and individual and group social-economic circumstance. I suggest that experiences and societal issues, channeled through one's social-emotional, cognitive, and perceptional filters, aid in shaping attitudes, behavioral actions, and styles that contribute to shaping and forming knowledge and understanding among Black, bi-multi-racial men in the defining and enactment of their masculinity, manhood, and sexuality.

> *(The inventive term social psychological digestive tract comes to mind, and hence the idea of how does one socially-psychologically and knowingly, digest and process experience, such as learning)?*

Further, I assert that racial-gendered experiences serves quietly and loudly as an interpretative filter in the experiencing of the self and the articulation of cumulative knowledge about the self in relationship and in contrast with others in society. Shen and Dumani (2013) contended that it is relevant in the study of margined groups to consider that identities are socially constructed as pertinent to individual and group analysis. Identity characteristics of the self then intersect and separate specific to social situational encounters and circumstance relative to the individual concerned. It is relevant to note again, that U.S. mainstream society is preferred by Eurocentric assimilated belief and accountability in and to individualism. This ideological value belief, reasoning, and socializing practice impacts all major areas of human activities, such as, identity and worldview development; the interpreting, constructing, and response to social reality, the planning, structuring and conduct of education, social-economics, political, law and legal activities, and research practices in fields, such as, psychology, psychiatry, cultural anthropology, and political science. The same authors argued that historical and contemporary exclusionary-conditional practices and circumstance continue to perpetuate those today, for instance, intentional-unintentional discriminatory practices such as racial-sexual harassment, bullying, incivility, social undermining, and ostracism. I would add microaggression relative to gender, race, and cultures (Pierce, 1970) and racial-microaggression (Sue, Capodilupo, Torino, Bucceri, Holder, Nadal, & Esquilin, 2007).

Rhodes discussed, relative to social-psychological case analysis, how anger can be the result of ethnic-cultural identity constraint in the context of social reality, based upon the theory of multiple identities construction. In other words, anger in response to social reality may be in actuality, anger also in response to constraint experienced relative to attempts to socially construct ethnic-cultural identity in the context of masculinity, manhood, sexuality enactment (Personal communication, Benjamin Rhodes, February 16, 2013). This perspective further suggested to me that the development of habitus (i.e., in this case masculine and manly tendencies and inclinations relative to one's sexuality), can be in actuality effected by perceived constraint experienced in the construction of identities in the experience and construction of social reality. To reiterate, habitus is formed in the context of experience in social, political, and materialistic reality, and other antagonisms in society such as the propensity toward gun-toting violence and the continued involvement in war and threat power surplus dependent relationships globally.

> *Perhaps, the most important lesson of 12 Angry Men is*
> *that Americans of all races and ethnicities need to be-*
> *come racially literate, not post-racially blind. Racial*
> *literacy is the capacity, to "read" race, conjugate its*

> *grammar and interpret its meaning in different con-*
> *texts and circumstance (Guinier, 2010, p. xxxix.).*

Guinier, in her introduction to the provocative and instructive series of social-cultural autobiographical essays (events of racial profiling among civic minded, working Black men of prominence), resonates with the dialogue of study participants as they navigated interview questions in very intense, poised, and thoughtful ways. We are to be reminded that in actuality the recounts by the essayists and the participants from this study were derived from self-epistemology and their habitus relative to cognitive perceptions of their racialized gendered masculinity and manly self in public spheres.

I believe that habitus also has to do with learned heightened tendencies that serve as filters for being intuitively literate when present in inter-cultural-personal settings and situations, in response to perceived threats to one's, in this case, racialized and ethnic cultural gender, as a part of one's person. I am also referring to any situation and setting where one, for instance, perceives the ethnic-cultural self in isolation, or suddenly experiences a heightened sense of awareness of one's racial features, accentuated by linguistic language style and dress, in a public setting. One in which perhaps quietness and a lack of distraction, may be apt to bring on self-contemplation accompanied by a heightened sense of self-awareness regarding person-physical-cognitive presence, particularly, where seeing/realizing the presence of others in contrast to you. One can suddenly experience the psychological effect of feeling set a part and isolated, as in an surge of anxiety and disorientation in extremer instances. (I have had such an experience come out of nowhere, and I have to say it is a bit un-nerving). Berger and Luckmann (2011) reminds us that "Everyday reality presents itself as a reality interpreted by men and subjectively meaningful to them as a coherent world" (p. 371); sense-making from through the lens of a man-person.

Bring to mind participants discussed perceived societal and law enforcement agent racial profiling considerations relative to theirs and other males of color phenotypical characteristics, dress, and attitudinal/behavior style in public, work, social, and educational settings. All but one of the participants spoke candidly about being cognizant regarding things such as the brand of car being driven, driving through or simply being present in certain demographic urban areas whether or not an incident had occurred alerting law enforcement. Participants also discussed experiencing looks they perceived or felt when congregating with col-leagues of similar or shared ethnic-cultural background/racial features, and social-linguistic styles of communicating in public places, where the critical mass of people were European American. Again, this is not an in-dictment of anyone, but stated as a perspective regarding perception and construction of social reality. One participant's response suggested how his awareness of disturbing accounts, such as, the ones revealed in the accounts of Parks and Hughey, (2010), *12 Angry Men*, had height-ened/inhabited his perceptual filters in private thought-public interaction relative to the intersection of race and ethnicity in self. In *12 Angry Men* you had accounts of racial profiling experienced by law-abiding men who were Black African Americans of various professional status. The exist-ence of such contradictory behavior by law enforcement officials, not to speak of a history of racialized-gendered stereotypes faced by Black Afri-can American males, stands in the face of the disproportionate occurrence of health care and mental health-related conditions negatively impacting Black African American males, like documented hypertensive related epi-sodes, conditions, and related illnesses not confined to diet.

To me, from a social epidemiological point of reasoning, there is an in-creased susceptibility to hypertensive related conditions that have been historically fed by real and perceived concerns regarding social-cultural, economic, and authoritative uses and abuses of power; private thought. Over a decade ago Poussaint and Alexander (2000) chronicled epidemio-logical social-cultural causes related to increased suicide and mental health issues, (to include the lack of culturally considered approaches to treatment within a eurocentrically dominant mental health system), expe-rienced among Black African American males and women. Their findings can be linked to social-cultural psychohistorical posttraumatic stress re-lated events impacting worldview, survival thrust, frame of references strategies and habits applied to daily living from slavery, Jim Crow, post-civil rights integration, desegregation, forced and voluntary and assimila-tion (Burrell, 2010; Leary, 2005; Lubiano, 1997; Nobles, Goddard, Cavil, & George, 1987; Spivey, 1978, Woodson, 1933).

One of the bi-multi-racial male study participants talked about being stopped by a young adult male European American security guard in a local suburban shopping mall in the city that we resided in, because he was wearing a leather jacket and was suspected of stealing it. (His father had purchased the jacket for him as a Christmas present years prior, the time of year was appropriate to the wearing of such attire).

White & Cones III (1999) researched and authored a comprehensive treatise on the issues with reference to the emerging development of Black masculinity and manhood faced by Black African American males in a racialized society. In their work they were lucid in discussing that in no way racism or living in a racialized state abdicated responsibility among Black African American males to work at and address social-cultural attitudinal, decision making habits and behaviors that comprised their ability to engage in healthy, respectful, and responsible ways of being. But, their analytical discussion considered the history of race, and racialized thinking, imaging, conscious/subconscious awareness, social-cultural communicative interactions, and push-back attitudes and behaviors, in response to pre-post-civil rights democratic discussions, protests, then demands, throughout U.S. society, relative to the development among Black African American males.

From the findings in this study participants were not excuse making regarding the presence of racialized gender issues, but providing a perspective from their point of view and response to interview questions and prompts. I argue that Mills' (1997) analytical work, where he asserted the existence of a "Racial Contract" fueled by European – European conquest of populations of color globally over the last 500 years, should be considered in the history of race. (As to how we treat our history of racialized gender in this country I say; What we have normalized, let go of with lack of purpose examination, study, and reflection, as get used to, make assumptions about, deny, emerge ourselves in the seductiveness of materialism, or simply act-think-perceive in the assimilatory- patriotic sublime).

Cooper (2006) contended that popular representations of bipolar heterogeneous Black masculinity exist "that helps resolve the white mainstream's post-civil rights anxiety" (p. 853). According to Cooper images alternated "between a Bad Black Man, who is crime-prone/hypersexual, and a Good Black Man who distances himself from blackness and associates with white norm" (p.853). He further purported that the existence of the Bad Black Man archetype label provided an "assimilationist incentive award" for heterogeneous Black men "to perform our identities consistent with the Good Black Man image" (p. 853). Please understand that the Good Black Man image does not connote being law abiding or civil, but ensuring that one does nothing to provoke European Americans regarding provocative issues such as race, and the related issues of inequality conditions-claims, or presenting too strong of an ethnic-cultural presence in nuanced style or demeanor (i.e., proper place).

What I am asserting here is that the preceding social-political issues have social-cultural psychological consequence of an accumulative overt and subtle effect over time. This accumulative effect is relative and detrimental to mental health and the impeding on psychological space in daily living that is beyond daily stress, regarding Black African American, bi-multi-racial, masculinity and manhood development, defining, and enactment. Moreover, I argue there is implication that such issues influence the shaping of habitus regarding manly inclinations and predispositions. For instance, although all of the participants in this study were law-abiding, civil minded, achieving persons, their responses indicated that they believed that they were subject to, for example, external racialized-gender stereotype, and positionality perception and experiences, which they had to be mindful of; they too felt a hypersensitivity to their presence as males of color.

Fries-Britt & Griffin (2007) performed a study exploring the academic and social experience of nine Black high achievers attending a large public university. As a result of their findings the authors contended that despite the participation of the nine study participants in the campus's honors these "Black high achievers" (p. 1), were "judged based upon social stereotypes regarding the academic abilities of Black students" (p.1). Further, that the results of prevalent social stereotypical perceptions, caused them to engage in various techniques to resist such stereotypes "with their behaviors both in and outside of the classroom" (p. 1).

Racialized Stereotypical Tag of Anger - Conflict Management

Babyface, Thanks "for the Cool in You?" (Edmond, 1993)

The psychohistorical subject of anger and stress relative to segregated and integrated experiences among Black African American, bi-multi-racial males, is becoming more prominent in epidemiological study, relative to, for example, the disproportionate occurrence of hypertension, intergroup homicide, stereotype threat (Mahalik, & Woodland, 2005). Further, I would argue that one must factor in the psychohistorical stress related experiences among Black African Americans, as a diverse demographic, is the resentful push-back attitudes and behavioral response among predominately European Americans, and conservative assimilated people of color, regarding affirmative action laws, equality of opportunity laws, and work force diversity executive orders and policies at the local, state, and federal levels (Delgado & Stefancic (2001); Winant, 1994). Findings from this study suggest that all the participants subconsciously and consciously were made aware of varying degrees of racial, ethnic-cultural, and class microaggressive/subtle attitudes, and behaviors, via visual and written content from various sources of the media, and during interpersonal-intercultural learning, work, and social experiences.

It is plausible that the racialized-gendered hierarchical era history of this nation-state, tempered ethnic-cultural group social and political experiences in such ways as to hold implications for the daily and accumulative psychological (mental-emotional) development and experiences among Black African American, bi-multi-racial males (Poussaint & Alexander, 2000; Winant, 1994). Such real and perceived experiences hold implication for daily and accumulative living experiences relative to one's well-being, risk factors, and ability to access risk; and thus, physical and mental health.

Hecht et al (1993) in their study of African American communication, discussed the role of power as clout, influence, sway, and so on, involved in interethnic-cultural group power relations and situations as it concerned communication styles and strategies. These authors argued that ethnic-cultural group affiliation, intra-inter-ethnic-cultural group power relations, social experiences, and worldview, were a part of shaping one's communication styles, and came into play during situational communication. Relevant to this study were self-group perceptions and experiences with power and empowerment, as it concerned the development, defining, and enactment of Black African American, bi-multi-racial masculinity and manhood. Analysis of participant response revealed that they alluded to being conscious of intercultural power relations, and source types regarding self-empowerment, relevant to interpersonal intercultural interactions and racialized gendered circumstance.

Since habitus is defined as predisposition and inclinations that moves with an individual from situation to situation, from geographic setting to setting, it followed that anger and conflict management, circumstance of experience with this kind of arousal state, are part that person's habitus, and thus relevant to any needed enhancement efforts such as improving one's health, general well-being, and decision making. For instance, there was a study was conducted by Stephens, Braithwaite, Johnson, Harris, Katkowsky, & Troutman (2008) targeted cardiovascular risk reduction among Black African American males via health empowerment and anger management.

According to the study's authors cardiovascular disease has been recorded as disproportionately impacting African Americans in comparison
with other racial and ethnic groups. Specifically, the authors stated that it
was "recognized that episodes of anger appear to trigger the onset of acute
myocardial infarction" (p. 210). Moreover, it was estimated that "emotional stress has been reported to occur prior to the onset of symptoms of
myocardial infarction in approximately 4-18 percent of cases" (p. 210).
Part of the study's protocol called for participants to take part in an anger
management curriculum component containing specific outcome goals.
Eighteen small group intervention sessions that contained between 10
and 12 participants were conducted lasting 6 weeks; participants met bi-
weekly. Findings from the anger management intervention component
revealed statistically "significant differences on three of the ten behavioral
variables examined" (p. 214). They are as follows: "*I fly off the handle;*"
"African American men in the empowerment group" displayed "*significant behavioral changes related to have a fiery temper;*" and "*it makes me
furious when I am criticized in front of others*" (p. 214).

The authors concluded that "although definitive evidence does not exist regarding the beneficial effects of anger management, it seemed prudent to integrate anger management and lifestyle change approaches with
cardiovascular disease education, prevention, treatment, and rehabilitation" (p.215). Recall from Chapter IV that study participants expressed the
saliency of maintaining a calm demeanor outside and within in order to
assess challenging situations and circumstances. Furthermore, it also
seemed essential to study participants that they avail themselves of what
processes were available to face challenging issues as a precursor to action.

The youngest study participant noted how he had grown from expressing stubborn anger in silence, regarding a frustrating situation during his
middle school days, to feeling the emotion of anger and taking personal
steps to deescalate that anger that allowed assessment of what had taken
place that appeared to be in conflict. He recognized how this kept him in a
strategic position to address conflict while remaining alert and focused.

Booker (2000), in his comprehensive work tracing the social history of
African American males, asserted that frequently throughout American
history there lied the assumption "that African American males have failed
to take full advantage of the opportunities presented them has been made
into an implicit or explicit explanation for the contemporary socioeconomic problems" (p. viii). Booker pointed to the boot-strap argument that

claims if one is more ambitious and capable of character and effort then this person (man) is better able to pull self and families (if applicable) "out of poverty" (p. viii). Booker also pointed out how Frantz Fanon (French-Algerian – African psychiatrist) had written "extensively of *decolonization* and its' social, psychological, and psychiatric consequence" (p. 211). To wit, there were social-psychological implications relative to physical and mental health and well-being among peoples who have been "set free" after assimilatory incarceration status, that must be accounted for in efforts, generationally, regarding working at defining, gaining, then cultivating a quality of life existence.

My argument is that there exists historical and contemporary presence of overt and subtle, social-political, economic, educational, and legal, racialized circumstance, that are real and perceived which can and do have a *cumulative effect* upon the health and welfare, and in the various areas of human activities cited previously in this study, among Black African American, bi-multi-racial males, as a diverse population of men. Works by Booker (2000); Jackson II and Hopson (2011), hooks (2004), Lemelle, Jr. (1995), Poulson-Bryant (2005), Root, (1992); Smith, Hung, and Franklin (2011), Staples (1982), White and Cones III (1999), and Wallace (2002), all provide informed and cogent discussion that speaks to the above noted circumstance under which Black African American, bi-multi-racial males have had to work in developing, defining, enacting, and clarifying their masculinity and manhood. It follows that anger, conflict management, and intra-intercultural communication styles relevant to conflict management, can play a salient role in stress management and reduction in their response to social reality within the broader context of society.

Anger as a social emotional expression in lived experiences, that is tempered by racialized – gender, ethnic-culture, and class identity making and circumstance, is also included in the preceding conceptualization in consideration of social constructionist theory (Nightingale & Cromby, 1999). Thompson and Whearty (2004) in their article on the saliency of masculine ideology relative to the active social participation of older men in the society at large pointed out, that from the social constructionist perspective there is a variation of masculinities within society. Moreover, they stated that the "lived masculinities are negotiated performances that maintain the gender scripts that are out there" (p.1), in culture, institutions, and in relationships that reveal the presence of both dominance and subordination. Moreover, they stated that "The culturally idealized form of masculinity, hegemonic masculinity, may not be the lived form of masculinity at all, but it remains a powerful, perhaps the dominant, script against which self and others are evaluated across the life course" (p.1).

From the preceding, one could surmise that in the social construction and availability of already formulated social-cultural scripts regarding masculine identities, that are formed through exposure to parenting, mentoring, peer socialization, military, athletic activities, (relative to ecologically settings, circumstances, and conditions), the role of anger as an emotion relative to habitus stands essential to learning how to manage and assess this emotion relative to conflict and day-to-day situations. Moreover, circumstance relative to racialized gender and hegemony, in the face of, for instance, perceived threat to one's masculinity, should be considered in response to one's social reality.

Courtenay (2000), in his analytical discussion asserted that a relationship exists between the way men *construct* and live masculine, which influences their health and well-being. He stated that

> In examining construction of masculinity and health within a relational context, this theory proposes that health behaviors are used in daily interactions in the social structuring of gender and power. It further propose that the social practices that undermine men's health are often signifiers of masculinity and instruments that men use in the negotiation of social power and status (p. 1385).

Courtenay also explored how factors such as "ethnicity, economic status, educational level, sexual orientation and social context, influence the kind of masculinity that men construct and contribute to differential health risk among men in the United States" (p. 1385). What's more, Courtenay investigated "how social and institutional structures help to sustain and reproduce men's health risks and the social construction of men as the stronger sex" (p. 1385).

Wilkins (2012) conducted a study regarding the intersection of race, gender, and emotions relative to emotional constraint among Black middle-class men at several predominantly White university campuses, and how they used their emotions "to craft and manage their identities" (p. 34). Some of the findings from the study revealed the social construction of moderate Blackness as part of personality, i.e., holding in check and watchfulness of ethnic-cultural demeanor, and distancing self from the stereotypes of the angry Black man and/or dangerous thug image. Moreover, Wilkins found that the crafting of moderate Blackness involved the narrow defining of the meaning of racism, for example, one of his study participant stated that "I never experienced racism; Racism is deep, like lynching" (p.46).

Wilkins argued that these Black male students astutely developed what she named strategic "moderate blackness" (p.34), that served as the impetus of their emotional restraint in order to engender a positive relationship with European American people in response to the social reality of campus racial politics, resulting in the internal consumption of the anger and agitation.   The author explained that the cost of this strategic intra-interpersonal cultural restraint was engaging in a pseudo perception of self by ignoring racism and/or the presence of racialization.

Provocatively, the author further stated these Black males engaged in the use of protecting othering to push the stereotype of the angry Black male onto Black women as to "shore up their masculinity" (p.34), while leaving women responsible for combating racial inequality. Wilkins pointed out that during the 2008 presidential election Barack Obama was complimented for this absence of "an angry Black man" persona, which engendered the avoidance of anger and "too much talk about race" (p. 35). I argue that rationally ignoring or placating the historical-contemporary issue of institutional inequality regarding the presence of ism's in U.S. society to appease one's disappointment, frustration, dislike, and anger, is unhealthy and thereby dangerous. It can lead to what is called an "angry heart" (title of a documentary on anger and heart attack and illness among Black African American males, 2008), that I use here as a metaphor for the condition of hypertension at the risk of heart attack and stroke. Moreover, such attitude and behavior does nothing to work at the reduction and eradication of ism's.

Gooding (2013) discussed the medical heart risk factors associated with "multi-generational anger among African American males" (p.1). Acutely, Wilkins pointed to the paradoxical dilemma faced by Black males regarding experiencing situational anger at the intersection of race, gender, and class.

Then too Wilkins stated that,

Cultural ideas about masculinity grant dominant men dispensation to display anger. Indeed, White men's situational anger signals and shores up their control, but Black men's anger signals their lack of control. Thus, when Black men display anger, they do not gain power, but instead lose creditability and risk institutional sanctions, including incarceration or terminations from jobs (p. 38).

In concert with Wilkins's thesis of emotional restraint among Black males, is the racialized gender normality awarded to White males as it concerns what allegedly constitutes "normal and ideal gender practices" (p. 73), discussed by Collins (2006). I would argue that from Wilkins's emotional restraint thesis, the racialized complexity and paradox of the historical-contemporary distorted image of "angry Black male" stereotype increases the susceptibility among Black African American, bi-multi-racial men of being implicated in their own social-psychological vulnerability relative to their empowerment, physical and mental healthcare.

Cooper's bipolar Black masculinity thesis discussed previously in Chapter 4, in essence involved running away from cultivating a sense of masculinity and manhood that included ethnic-cultural self-learning, versus running toward mainstream offered awards, for assimilation/individual and group cultural passivity. "The Negro has never been educated. He has merely been informed about other things which he [she] *has not been permitted to do*" (Woodson, 1933, p.144); should we add defining one's self within the throes of assimilation to the accommodation of dominant cultural others in mainstream America, as being relative to crafting the moderate Black masculine self?

Collins (2006) in her discussion on Black masculinities and telling the difference between dominance and strength in the construction of progressive Black masculinities, explained this dilemma,

Using White masculinity as a yardstick grounded in ideas about strength as dominance, African American men become defined as subordinates, deviant, and allegedly weak, and Black men's purported weakness as men is compared to the seeming strength of White men. Despite a complicated reality that structurally subordinates both Black men and Black women to

White men, Black men's subordination nevertheless
becomes ideologically defined as a weakness in rela-
tion to both Black women and White men. (p. 75)

I would say that the culturally racialized gendered stereotype of the angry Black man, in the imagination among societal members, is likened to the situation of protagonist in the fictional novel turned into a film within the genre of satire, regarding the struggle for civil rights in U.S. society during the late 1960s era riots and Black military, "The Spook Who Sat by the Door," (Greenlee, 1969). Here you had a token Black man hired by the Central Intelligence Agency early into the Affirmative Action Era, who resigned, used his agency training to design and conduct Black militancy training of Black males in a mid-west urban center, via agency tactics, shortly after the completion of his tactical training and being given a menial assignment of being placed in charge of the agency's copy machines and conducting tours of the facilities. The term *spook* has to do with the stereotypical racial slur used to refer to Black people, but at the same time *spook* in then intelligence agency terms referred to spying or ghosting.

Moreover, there is relevancy to Du bois' (1903) reference to the double-conscious duality among Black African Americans negotiating the social-political reality of U.S. society. The Black men educated during integrated times, with successful experiences in dominant institutions throughout U.S. society, must restrain from accessing the emotion of anger, as Wilkins (2012) stated, "a social product contained, transformed, given meaning and used strategically" (pp. 36-37), in response (not reaction) to the circumstance of injustice and inequality.

From my conversation with J. Vasquez (personal communication, January, 2013), I understand anger as an instinct and cognitive interpretive response to social environment that is learned and therefore subject to social construction and risk assessment. In view of social construction there is the presence of falsified racial - cultural context that gives rise and opportunity for stereotyping of Black African American, bi-multi-racial males. In 2008 a Fox News headline read, "Obama is an Angry Black Man" Why Should He Go on the O'Reilly Show?" Here you have an erroneous, unsubstantiated, and provocatively racialized headline, said out loud about the President of the United States in the absence of outcry of shame among the vast majority of citizens in this so-called democratic nation-state with mainstream culture controlled media sources. Wilkins (2012) spoke to media tags that stated, "No Drama Obama" that pointed out his interpersonal-cultural personal/political cool, which implies strategic habits of enacting emotional restraint to *not* absence himself from any social-linguistic, well-articulated spoken or written discourse in view of a dominant European American society and constituency.

Racism and racialized gender have been implicated as stress related risk factors in mental health regarding the African American experience, and correlated with anxiety-related symptoms (Williams & Williams-Morris 2000, Bynum, Best, Barnes, & Burton, 2008). How conflict and challenging situations were discussed by participants joins this historical and contemporary context. I suggest that guarded moments in which participants engaged in being wisely observant, during interpersonal-cultural, sexual, racial, and perhaps, power differential situations they were in, involved the realized presence of their racialized gender existence.

I am particularly referencing, for instance, challenging situations that had the potential of provoking the emotion of anger, within integrated settings that had the further potential of igniting racial stereotypes in the imagination of viewers and onlookers. Now this is not to say that a person needs to be repressed of anger because how one possesses, (i.e., experiences) anger as an emotion is detrimental to one's mental and biological health. However, I insist that given the racialized history of masculinity, manhood, and gender identity in this country, angry feelings, responses, and appearances carry a particularly challenging paradoxical reality for Black American, African American, and bi-multi-racial males.

What I am referring to is taking that cognitive moment to move back before reacting or responding to strategically think about ways to maintain calm in the face of challenge. Recall, that African American as an ethnic-culturally diverse group experienced a particular era of history by racial-gendered challenges that impacted the development and design of survival thrust strategies and habits in collaboration with an emerging transformational worldview about what it means to be a man, a person, as to avail self of ethnic-cultural tools in healthy and empowering ways.

As the literature has shown even successful, law-abiding, social justice conscious Black men are at-risk and susceptible to experiences that carry with them social-psychological implications from racial-gendered paradoxical circumstance; that is, racial, gender, sexuality, social-economic class, ism's that are real and suspect trying to occupy the same place at the same time regardless of geographic location (Brown, 2011; Chandler, 2011; Hughey & Parks, 2011; Staples, 2011; Jackson, II & Hopson, 2011; Mutua, 2006, Collins, 2006; Harper, 1996). Said somewhat differently, there are racial-gendered *perceptual traps and pit-falls* within the society at large that have social-psychological consequences detrimental to health and well-being in the defining, expressing, and attempts at empowerment that Black African American, bi-multi-racial males should be leery of.

It is relevant here to point out how participants called attention to parental ethnic cultural socialization, that is, they were adept in pointing out how their parents and extended family elders contributed to their sense and/or understanding of the racial realities of being Black and bi-multi-racial in this country, in this case as it concerns temperament and disposition.

The implied point, is that, socialization involving counsel and support relative to developing an alertness in ethnic-cultural context/perspective, to include psychohistorical circumstance, world view, and the noticing and interpretation of social-cultural nuances in public sphere, is important in assisting Black African American, and bi-multi-racial males in cultivating their temperament and disposition. To wit, in order to cognitively judge how to negotiate challenging situations against the unnoticed and denied background of racial-patriarch dominant embedded circumstances.

Banerjee, Harrell and Johnson (2010) conducted a study looking at "the impact of race/ethnic socialization and parental involvement in education on cognitive ability and achievement in a sample of African American youth" (p. 1). The authors stated that the implications of their study joined an increasing body of research that located the "positive impact of racial/ethnic socialization on academic related outcomes" among Black American children (p. 9). Moreover, they stated that "cultural socialization has been shown to be related to cognitive ability and achievement on a standardized measurement" in their study (p.9). Nobles, Goddard, Cavil, and George (1987) conducted a study that involved a Reconstructionist methodology with a strong emphasis on open-ended questions. This approach provided opportunities for Black families to define themselves from the cultural orientation regarding what it meant to be an African American family. Their findings showed "that the family kinship system provided the support and guidance necessary for individuals to negotiate the realities of their society" (p. 9).

Racialized gender tempered socializing messages and vigilance have historically existed in conversation and practice among Black parent-guardians, single mamas, and extended family elders, for instance, particularly during the '40s, '50s and '60s in segregated urban centers, in the southern regions of the country, and nationally. The fact that study partic- ipants pointed to specific conversations and discussions from their par- ents and extended family members regarding public civility, social man- ners, and directly pointing to or alluding to the importance of being cog- nizant of their surroundings, suggested the continued use of this practice. Of note is that both the bi-multi-racial males who were brought up in combinations of Mexican, Cuban, Black African American, and Irish- American extended family circumstances and experiences had these same kinds of parental-elder socializing lessons. I would suggest that any bi- multi-racial union that resulted in parenting a child or children probably generated some degree of intercultural sensitivity and literacy regarding public perception and perception among other extended family members of both spouses and partners that was used to inform their parenting practices, observations, and the content of their council. Finally, Bush (2004), in an analysis of newly emerging literature regarding the Black mother-son relationships relative to the role women played in the raising of their sons, suggests that,

- Black mothers play a significant role in the healthy development of manhood and masculinity

- Demonstrates how Black mothers participate in healthy develop- ment of manhood and masculinity

- Challenges notions about mothers and fathers, males and females, and masculinity and femininity by blurring traditional lines of sep- aration. (p. 381)

Recall the learnedly compelling argument by Jackson (2006) that the Black body has been historically and contemporarily racially-socially scripted in ways that construct and assign stereotypical and dominant cultural comfort zone connotative meaning and expectation to Black males. The abstruse presence of scripting, relative to the emotions of an- ger in response to social reality, and the angry Black male stereotype, ups the social-psychological ante as it concerns the degree of cognitive astute- ness needed in negotiating racialized gendered phenotypical presence, social-cultural linguistics, and nonverbal communicative styles, emotions, and rationalizing, during interpersonal-cultural interactions, and the pub- lic expression of self-empowerment. This I point out as being particularly relevant to integrated settings where one is isolated, so that too much of an expressive communicative style invoked by an African American male can delegitimize, i.e., marginalized the content of the speaker's discourse

and knowledge in the socially-politically forged association with his racialized gender physical presence. (In others words, there are those folks who
admittedly forge marginalizing the content of the speaker concerned
based upon associated racialized gender ascriptions).

Jackson also asserted in reference to Black people's corporeal (bodily)
zones, given the historical-contemporary presence/influence of European
American dominant sources of power in constructing and assigning
meaning in multiple areas of human activities, that there was no such
thing as *not* seeing. This includes the colorblind thesis in this so-called
post-race era, promoted during the Reagan/Bush Sr. presidential administration, conservative think tank organizations, and via their political
mechanisms that incited instigated assaults on multicultural education.

(During the Reagan/Bush Sr. era's the community based racial conflict
mediation/education outreach units were defunded/dismantled, part of
ushering in the public muggings of short-lived affirmative action programs nationally).

Referring again to the works of (hooks, 1992; Jackson, 2006; Mutua,
2006), Black males run the risk of being implicated in their own stereotyping, that is, racialized deficit perception that can contribute to social-
cultural exclusion and distancing in professional settings of work, educational institutions, and political office.[12] Recall Hurt's (2008) short documentary entitled "*Barack and Curtis, Manhood, Power, and Respect.*"
There is a juxtaposed scenario between President-Elect Barack Obama
and rapper 50 Cent, exploring how they differentiated in their expressed
construction of Black masculinity; as one guest expert witness speaker
said, "Barack equaled Harvard, someone like 50 Cent equaled hood, there
is a bit of 50 and Barrack in every Black man." As Hurt discussed in the
documentary synopsis, both were successful, feared, and admired, and I
would add in various social, community, and political circles detested.
President Obama America's top elected statesperson, and 50 Cent a top-
earning Gangsta-hip-hop rapper with Hollywood movie and entrepreneur
cred. But I contend that both still faced the dilemma of the angry Black
man stereotype, the Black scripted body phenomenon, and negotiating
emotions in the public sphere in the face of institutionalized and social-

---

[12] During a social conversation, I was once told by administrators at a large complex
state department that because of my social-cultural linguistics and non-verbal
communication behaviors and critical thinking style, that I would not last long in
my present position as an administrator.

political racism, inequality and injustice that imbrues anger. This despite the fact that there has been intergenerational shattering of negative myths and stereotypes about Black men, such as President Obama and Ralph Bunche who was an African American political statesperson involved in the planning and administration of the United Nations and winner of the Nobel Peace Prize for his mediation work in Palestine in the late 1940s, *but who knew* or was it simply choosing to ignore or not consider.

I would say that a critical question that must be addressed is, where does this all this anger go when one stows it away? What dissipates it? Does in dissipate? (This includes myself, because I am really feeling it. In fact, I would say that Black folk descendants of slaves and Jim Crow elder segregation, affirmative action blow-back, have been extremely polite given the history and contemporary circumstance in this country and throughout the African diaspora). What I am referring to is, where does such anger go when one's psyche gets *peppered* with racialized unrecognized, real and perceived assaults of various situational circumstance? Or, for instance, consistently hears and puts up with major media sources brazen, erring, belittling rants and accusations, from among ultra-conservative racialized news pundits, congressional, state, and local elected officials, and their organizational, and fund contributing constituency and donors; that or really not different than those longing for some "old-timey," like those of Fox News. (A father from the late time period of the Jim Crow era, is in fear of the welfare and safety of his bi-racial son, and his male friends who are all civil, decent, and law-abiding, but among them have experienced *so-called* routine police stops, to include the father's wife and women of color work colleague, when nothing was obviously in violation).

Of concern here too is consideration of social construction of self-epidemiology in ethnic-cultural/racialized context in relationship with ego, integrity, sexuality, emotions, and emotional intelligence in the development, definition, and enactment of masculinity, manhood, sexual orientation among Black African American, bi-multi-racial males. This consideration stands-in- view of national-state-local healthcare statistics placing them at risk for hypertension and related diseases. Hofer (2008) stated that "*personal* epistemology" has a role in the development of intellect, learning, and perception and beliefs regarding education (p.3). Hofer's review of personal epistemology from multiple paradigms suggested that there are implications for a more culturally informed self-epistemology garnered and cultivated within the ideological construct of "multicultural education" (p.3).

Furthermore, Africentric scholars such as Asante, 1980; Clarke, (1993); Nobles, (1990); and Shujaa, (1994) have structured and advocated for the inclusion African centered educational socialization and learning relative to self-development and epistemology. What joins this concern is the cultivation of risk assessment and decision-making ability and inclinations as it pertains to defining and enactment of masculinity, manhood, and sexuality in ethnic-cultural context, relative to emotional and cognitive anger and conflict management awareness, attitudes, belief's, and practices. I am referring to the daily work involved in negotiating emotional feelings generated by private thoughts during interpersonal-cultural interaction in the public sphere, and the psychological space and energy incurred, particularly, given that anger is also an emotion which carries racial-gendered connotations that, as previously stated, signals a "lack of control" (Wilkins, p. 38) among others, among Black African American, bi-multi-racial males.

To me, the emotion of anger while in contestation or opposed point of view events, bears the quiet challenge as to whether or not to allow a flair of expressive contentiousness become presence in one's voice, such as, in the articulation of a provocative point in a classroom setting, a presentation at the workplace, on televised air, or in a meeting. There is the opening phrase spoken by the character Hamlet, Act III, in Shakespeare's play, *"to be or not to be, that is the question."*

Anger can be looked at as a response to and within one's social – perceptional reality (Personal communication, B. Rhodes, March, 1987). Anger as a response or reaction to social reality is not a standalone action, that is, habits develop and change as a result of conscious repetitive ways of looking at, interrupting, and thinking about things, within the context of a multicultural society. Here to Brown, Carnoy, Currie, Duster, Oppenheimer, Schultz and Wellman (2003) argued, that in the myth of a color-blind society the routine practices in the perpetuation of racial inequality among corporations, law firms, banks, athletic teams, labor unions, the military, and educational institutions tend to be ignored, that is, "are rarely

analyzed" (p. 19).[13] In regards to the social psychological impact of continued racial inequality, Wilkins pointed out that sociologists are increasingly
interested in and arguing that a durable system of inequality generates
"destabilizing feelings of anger, resentment, sympathy, and despair" (p.
35), which requires the development and deployment of cognitive strategies in emotional management in cultural context to weather reoccurring
storms in one's life in society. In other words, anger is not just some isolated motivated or stimulated emotion, but it is also based upon interpretation and accumulated experiences, as one perceives, responds, and/or
reacts to social reality; most certainly the trigger can and is that of a felt
presence of one's masculinity, manhood, sexuality, tied to the social constructs of race, class, and circumstance of have a job and/or out of work
related experiences. For I affirm that experiences such as school successes
or failures, are felt in relationship with one's masculinity, manhood, sexu-
al-self. Failure, lack of progress, and/or perceived relevancy of institutional
sanctioned educational programs, can be seen and thus acted upon as
threats to one's manhood and thereby seen as interfering with one's manly pursuits in relationship with time and location. (There is too the contradictory and/or contrary act of stepping on one's own feet in wrong-
headedness to one's own human development opportunities).

As Wilkins (2012) further asserted, anger is both racialized and gendered, in saying that successful participation in dominant institutions
requires that Black African American men demonstrate "extraordinary
emotional restraint" (p.35). Participant reflective dialogue reminds us of
this. From this perspective, how one's habitus, (i.e., masculinity and manhood tendencies) emerge, and the awareness of inclinations and tenden-

---

[13] What the authors argued was that the conduct of "any analysis of racial inequality
that routinely neglects organizations and practices, intentionally or unintentionally, generate and/or maintain racial inequalities over extended periods of times is
misleading and incomplete" (p. 19). As they discussed, inequalities are cumulative,
as evidenced by a labor market still revealing lack of workforce diversity among
people of color, a healthcare industry showing lack of access to culturally responsive healthcare, and availability of healthcare and mental healthcare practitioners,
of color. These same authors further contended that today the predominant approach to understanding and arguing "racial stratification" in U.S. life assumes that
"social life results chiefly or exclusively from the actions of self-motivated, interest-
seeking persons" (p.15); in other words, the on going Eurocentrically established
axiological belief and assumption of rugged individualism underlies and defines
political, psychological, sociological, and educational, conservative analysis and
dogma.

cies, relative to the individual concerned, is a critical part of overseeing how the emotion of anger is negotiated, directed, and managed in healthy self-actualizing ways. (Perhaps, I am suggesting on-the-spot self-reflective practice techniques).

Interestingly, Stevenson (1997) found, in his study of 208 urban African American adolescent males, that those study participants who held an adaptive or more proactive racial socialization identity tended to demonstrate more prosocial adjustment outcomes. (They consciously owned their racial-gendered identity in proactive negotiating and adaptable ways). Stevenson had used different samples to obtain factors of "spiritual/religious coping, extended family caring, cultural pride reinforcement, and racial awareness" (p.35). These prosocial adjustments represented strategic moves for mitigating anger to provide focus when critically needing it.

Another salient point regarding anger is that managing and not being in a state of habitual anger is detrimental to one's mental and biological state of health; hence, nuanced responsive warnings from my mama in reference to stop frowning: "I taught you to be pleasant." Frowning to my mama was a precursor to not only being angry, but being or just appearing to be angry and a Black male at the same time in plain sight of others. Add the look and running down neighborhood streets, particularly within business corridors, made you susceptible to police attentiveness, stop, and search.

There were times in my youth I recall looking in the mirror with Mama standing behind me and rubbing frown lines off my forehead. The point is that being angry, appearing to be angry, and staying that way as habit carries with it racialized, social-psychological, and other life-threatening implications for and among Black African American, bi-multi-racial males. The earlier this is realized and acted upon, the less susceptible Black African American and bi-multi racial males will be to falling prey to states of attitudes, thinking, and behaviors that jeopardize their opportunities to engage in healthy, alert lifestyles. Just think about Black males in the military during Jim Crow WWII and pseudo Jim Crow Vietnam Era times, and negotiating anger emotions daily in a racialized class gender identity context. I witnessed saw rage in the open particularly from southern-born and raised Black males that was righteous as it was dangerous. (I acted in a raged anger that I had never felt or acted upon before; it was disconcerting, scary, and self-humiliating). Nothing can be more habitually nerve wracking than being in a so-called integrated military or work force where there is a critical mass of personnel of color being commanded and/or supervised predominantly by ethnic-cultural leadership of European American descent, thinking that your eyes are wide open when the danger is that they are really shut to who you have become in conflict with who you are trying to be under such temporal circumstances.

Woodson (1933) discussed this in his time-immemorial work entitled *The Miseducation of the Negro*. Here he argued that Blacks were being cognitively, intra-personally, culturally, and intellectually, Euro-centrically grounded and self-assimilated in opposition to their own ethnic-cultural heritage and community. The result was the construction of group-culturally averse self-perception/projection. The individual-group social-psychological, health, economic, political, and other implications of this have been historically complex and psychologically frustrating from one generation to the next. (Ethnic cultural class group uppity)?

Again, participant perspective brought attention to the need to manage their cultural identity and how they were being perceived in the context of educational, social, and work settings and situations; to me this brings attention to issues relative to Woodson's thesis claim. It further calls attention to the historical – contemporary issues related to group cultural identity development in an educational system that was built to stress dominant cultural assimilation, patriotism, and individualism in the absence of lessons regarding humanism and gender/sexuality development in a racialized nation-state. In sum, participant discussion revealed their insights and sensitivities in the presence of their racialized gendered self, ethnic-cultural backgrounds/socialization, and the dilemma they negotiated among their peers and educators relative to being a student who wanted to learn and achieve, but not in the absence of their cultural self/selves and most certainly not in the absence of their masculine person self.

Here too there is the controversial perspective regarding the unspoken and unrecognized social reality concerning Black male existence – progressive equality of life seeking and striving in an integrated society.

> *Perhaps some black men in that barbershop are also trying to avoid racial and cultural punishment. Instead of negotiating two worlds, maybe they have chosen to live in only one - a microcosm, a subculture of white society that accepts and mandates a certain sociolinguistic performance of masculinity. Because*

*they have chosen and are accepted by a community,
perhaps they have no need to envy me as I do them.
But then what do they lose when they don't try to imitate what I represent? I want to expose the factors that
make black racial identity incompatible with literacy,
especially for males (Young, 2007, Prelude).*

Young, in his first person analysis of African American men, revealed the intersection of racial identity, awareness, social-economic conditions, and masculinity that compellingly pointed to the "racial ambivalence" he experienced regarding his felt need to perform Black masculinity, such as linguistic performance in segregated settings that were predominantly Black. He described this need to experience the Black masculine self while in social settings such as those of a "Black Barbershop." In this setting he critically observed and reflected upon his perceived social-psychological need to act Black relative to masculine performance, in the presence of other Black males, many of whom were not social-economically posi- tioned as he was. Moreover, he explained the need to not act too Black in the presence of a predominately European American audience of people such as those at the university in which he was an assistant professor.

Young sharply pointed how he perceived self as not being *ghetto enough for the ghetto back home*, and that because of his racial phenotypi- cal features and despite his Standard English sociolinguistic style, he was not "white enough for white folks" (Prelude). Participant voice interacted with the experiences and observations that Young reviewed in the Prelude discussion of his works that he literally constructed while visiting the Black Barbershop that he frequented. Participants stated that they be- lieved there was a need for Black males to perform who they were on a daily basis, while several explained the dilemma they believed was faced among Black male peers who were smart and wanted to do the work of learning. In other words, there was explanation presented regarding ra- cial-cultural ambivalence of trying to be Black while not showing their student side among certain of their peers in community and school set- tings, as they may have been perceived as being "White" or not "culturally down." Again, being culturally down has to do with socially and percep- tively identifying with what it means and represents being a Black Ameri- can, *but does this involve or preclude the educated self?* Participant testi- mony here suggested the intra-group culturally perceived racialized decla- ration "acting White" was ambivalent as it was dichotomizing. In this re- gard Young explained,

> *To embrace my blackness, my heritage, my manliness,*
> *I identify with men who represent the ghetto. I no*
> *longer want to deny my class background or racial*
> *expression associated with it. I identify to belong. I*
> *disidentify to escape racism, to avoid the structures*
> *that oppress Black me. But I also disidentify to retali-*
> *ate against Black men—punish them for what I per-*
> *ceive as their efforts to disown me. (Prelude)*

While Young felt the need to imitate being a part of Black culture, he too felt the need to disassociate from Black men he envied. In other words, he envied them because of their Black sociolinguistic style, attitudes, and physical expression, representing in part their culturally centered persona; but this did not represent his class, racial experience, sexual persona, and world-view.

In comparison with this, all the participants clearly recognized and appreciated their Black, Nigerian, Cubana/o, and/or Mexicana/o sources of ethnic-cultural heritage and socializing knowledge in their lives, but were clear that Black culturally nuanced sociolinguistic style, attitudes, physical expression did not represent their overall self in cultural persona, but it was a part of the construction and fabric of their social reality. For instance, the Nigerian participant talked about how there were instances when he was perceived as being Black American, until he spoke and his accent was revealed.

Participants witnessed and acknowledged situational cultural adaptive persona among their male elder family members, peers, and among Black and Latino males in general, what one participant's father termed as "*cultural commuting*" (Alcorn, 1994). Among people of color cultural commuting refers to making social, cognitive, attitudinal shifts in the characteristics of one's ethnic-cultural persona in moving back and forth between the dominant critical presence of European Americans in physical locations of the workplace, school, and other locations in the public domain; within the context and social complexities of a multiculturally diverse society. Cultural commuting also includes the sources of knowledge one chooses to access and use during the commute, and the dispositional characteristics and inclinations as part of one's habitus. I am suggesting that participants engaged in cultural commuting in which they made sociolinguistic and non-verbal switches, to include the "internal-management" of thoughts (Hecht et al, 1993, p. 129) that were situation

ally considerate to the politics, power and social issues, of racialized gender in mainstream and their group cultural communities. Shuter (1982),
in Hecht et al stated that,

> *While effective communicators adapt their style to fit*
> *the situation regardless of their ethnicity, the power*
> *dynamics of U.S. society and the history of African*
> *American oppression imbue this type of switching*
> *with a political meaning. African Americans change*
> *their behavior to fit the racial and gender composition*
> *of the dyad. (p. 91)*

In other words, *among* African Americans cultural commuting is engaged in view of individual and group psychohistorical experiences,
worldview, survival thrust, and intergroup power relations that are subject
of self-group empowerment. Cultural commuting is subject to the degree
of life learned experiences, sophistication, maturity, and so forth. It is relevant to note that this cultural commuting or shifting is historically multi-
generational among Black African Americans, Mexican Americans, and
older immigrant communities of color, and thereby detrimental to their
interests and issues such as mental-biological health, social-gender-
sexuality development and enactment, and education-learning performance.

In therapist conversations with Rhodes (personal communication,
1989) it was discussed that when one experiences frustration and ambivalence there is tendency to move away from those discomforting experiences and association as a reaction aimed at making them a nonissue in
one's life efforts and worldview, a conscious-subconscious intercultural
group counter-measure perhaps of intergenerational existence. It is salient then to ascertain the source and intentions in all their complexity.

Meta-Cognitive/Self-Talk

Goleman's (1994) works on emotional intelligence brings attention to
the relevance of developing and cultivating the capacity for identifying,
tapping into, and managing one's emotions. Bluestein (2001) stressed to
both parents and educators the relevancy and importance of "creating
emotionally safe schools." It would seem to follow that this is reliant upon
student development of emotional intelligence in concert with the intel-

lect, and educator understanding and incorporation into their teaching and administrative pedagogy. Thus, playing an important role in the conceptualization is meta-cognition, and its relationship with the cultivation of emotional intelligence.

Meta-cognition is an ongoing comparison and contrast of knowledge and understanding of people, self, and things in the world and community around us, as it is a form of sense making in a more complex way, which intimately involves personal epistemology in cultural context. Meta-cognition has to do with acquired knowledge and is performed through self-regulating and exploratory self-talk that occurs in experiencing day-to- day situations, circumstances, and social realities (Livingston, 1997).

In the development and maturity of emotional intelligence there is a seamless merger relative to the honing of one's active listening awareness, contemplation, and self-talk, in order to decide what to do in, for example, challenging situations, relative to, for instance, intracultural and intercultural context.

Intimately wedded to these processes is the intersection of social-economic, ethnic-cultural positionality, and racialized gendered orientation experiences. These serve to contextualize and influence the intrapersonal-cultural communication favor of one's self-talk. Possibly wedded with these activities is what I refer to as self-action research. Thus, it would seem that the grooming of meta-cognitive voice is paramount to life activities such as working on keeping one's self *in position* to learn and develop.

I propose that self-action research is a form of self-reflective inquiry that can be used to address, for example, social-education, attitudinal temperament, and behavioral decision making habits. In other words, self-action research conceptualized as self-reflective inquiry can be actualized or realized through self-interrogation or self-analysis in individual problem solving or difficulties (Kemmis and Carr, 1986). The reason for the preceding explanation is that participant testimony suggested their engagement in proactive strategic thinking, acts of emotional intellect engaged by meta-cognitive thought/intrapersonal conversation. In other words, they were self-monitoring and critics of their performance and decision making. I am purporting that these collective activities are a form of in-head posturing, to assist in not placing them into compromising situations that could be confrontationally laden with opportunities for habitual anger arousal. This is not to say that participants were afraid of their anger or timid about it, but it appeared that they worked to be self-aware of mood responses during challenging circumstances and thoughts in public and private situations which could make them susceptible to being confrontational, which to say that as males of color, this can be detrimental to them at a number of levels in their lives. Put another way, inhead posturing activities and being a kind of self-critic can assist in honing prosocial habits in response to their masculinity and ongoing manhood development, in social-cultural context.

What appears to have further aided the cultivation of their emotional intellect and meta-cognitive prosocial habits was the cultural-intercultural context of their socializing experiences among parental-elder and peers; moreover, the role of social-intercultural literary development appears to hold relevance regarding the explanation of tension management habits participants discussed relative to the subject of anger and conflict management; as AO remarked, working on being "literate about multi-cultures was important" to him.

Learned Effectiveness

(While exposed to multiple sources of institutional sanctioned use of authority/power in public sphere.)

According to Hunter and Davis (1994), in their investigation of the meaning, structure, and complexity of manhood among Black males, is that, Black men have to shift back and forth between "majority and minority cultures and negotiate racism and discrimination" relative to masculinity and manhood performance expectations (p. 24); this is analogous to cultural commuting as previously discussed. What this implies is an awareness of perceiving and feeling the effects of differential ethnic – cultural intergroup power relations, fluency and quiet subtle of social situational circumstance. (The exposure to the psychic of inter-group power relations and exercises of several kinds and degrees of sanctioned power is very important here).

Wells (1995) in the author's discussion of "Learned Effectiveness," argued that since the data are clear "that African American males are a risk population" then there is need for a "unifying theory on the *functioning of African American males*" (p.7); despite the predominance of research stating that Black males are at risk. Moreover, Wells asserted, "this theory should not be deficit oriented and should address issues relevant to the success of the endangered African American males" (p.7).

According to Wells, "learned effectiveness" as opposed to "social-efficacy" (p.7), represents a more culturally appropriate construct relative to describing and discussing issues and challenges among African American males that they work and/or need to address. Wells further stated that, learned effectiveness, among African American males, has to do with is an amalgamation of their sense of self involving self-efficacy *and* self-esteem, which includes their degree of orientation to African American culture (for instance, racial identity and worldview). Moreover, this implicates their orientation and response to dominant culture, such as, sense and intuitiveness regarding how they are being perceived, evaluated, and judged in relationship with others; in a multicultural society dependent upon their degree of intercultural personal literacy.

To continue, there is the involvement of assimilation and/or acculturation experiences, and what I refer to as locus of control-management, in forming culturally specific means of coping and seeing the world.

From Wells thesis there are a number of hypothesized primary social-cognitive dimensions. Wells declared that the assumption underlying self-efficacy implies that if one processes the adequate cognitive abilities, i.e., motivation, then the individual concerned is in position to experience "positive self-perceptions for successful outcomes" (pp. 7-8). However, Wells stated that - "no consideration is given to systemic inequalities or cultural differences" (pp. 7-8). Wells' study of learned effectiveness strongly suggested that a framework for self-efficacy and esteem, in the context of cultural differences and issues related inequality, are significant.

Very importantly, in keeping with Well's analysis, the role of group culture, ethnicity, class, sexuality, and race, are relevant to participant perspective in this study. From a participant perspective it appeared that learning occurred regarding how to proficiently work at strategies and habitual ways to look at and be effective in healthy self-actualized ways in light of their ethnic-cultural and racialized gender identities and experiences. Understand please that there are more pronounced and then more vague moments in daily intercultural interaction that one's let pass by, but may momentarily note regarding what occurred as to give one pause. There can be and are an accumulation of such pauses that are worth reflecting upon).

Participant perspective revealed their recognition of the challenges, frustrations, and importance of embracing and studying their various ethnic-cultural heritages and racialized gendered self, in order to work at actualizing their existence via healthy empowering ways, that is, learned effectiveness.

Worldview - Locus of Perceived Control or Management

Recall from Chapter 1 that worldview involves how a person perceives a relationship to the world, nature, institutions and institutional experiences, and other people in general and how things work. Individuals act in and on the world as it is perceived in view of recognized, denied, achieved, and envied sources/degrees of person-institutional power, and ways to wield being empowered, and/or simply struggling to exist, within the contextual framework of our diverse, racial-ethnic-cultural makeup, and positionality. For example, anti-gay attitudes and bashing behaviors and the inability among certain ethnic-cultural groups to accept President Obama because of his bi-ethnic-cultural identity and associated racial phenotypical features, is the representation of worldview.

World view is situated here relevant to Rotter's (1990) internal-external locus of control construct that he conceived several decades ago, as there has been seasoned analytical discussion and application valuation and use, regarding the construct's utility relative to, for instance, teacher, counselor, and psychologist preparation programs. Again, Sue argued that the internal-external locus of control dimension "does not take into consideration different cultural and social experiences of the individual" (p.75).

The measured perception of having an internal locus of control simply means that the individual concerned believes that events and outcomes, such as, learning and achieving are the consequences of one's own actions. In contrast, external locus of control means a person's perception/beliefs regarding events and outcomes are both outside and unrelated to one's behavior and degree of being empowered.

External locus of control is directly associated with chance, fate, luck, and unpredictable psychological orientation. Empirically, internal-external locus were normed and measured as an either/or dichotomy social-psychological construct. It is strongly suggested, if not affirmed, that when a person possesses an internal locus of control stress is better managed, a person is better motivated, intra-interpersonal-interactions are more effective; there is better cognitive processing and decision making is achieved and, for example, a student is more efficacious in studying and learning (Brophy, 1999; Lefcourt, 1982).

Culturally speaking, internal locus of control is prompted and favored as driven by the European American value system of individualism backed by specific research in the literature (Stewart & Bennett, 1991). Sue argued that people of color and persons experiencing low-challenging income availability, who focused on constructing strategies in accordance with external locus, may be motivationally healthy from the perspective of discerning opportunities for success against real systemic barriers and challenges, than simply declaring such belief-based thinking and strategizing as "unpredictable fate" (p.75). In other words, empowerment can be and is enacted and struggled over in view of historical-contemporary race, gender, social-economic and ethnic-cultural group challenges.

Participant responses suggested the presence of what I termed as an internal-external locus of control interaction, in consideration of their world view as perceptual filters. Put another way, their respective views indicated that they recognized the presence of their racialized gender phenotype, institutional racism, group-ethnic-cultural heritage, and self-identity as it concerned interpersonal-cultural interactions, while engaging in thinking, acting, and performing in ways that demonstrated their belief in self-management and empowerment in view of external societal forces around them. Moreover, participant response in this regard suggested an interactive self-conscious and unconscious awareness regarding the real and perceived effect of race as a social-political instrumental construct in historical and human activities, situation, and circumstance.

It is my belief that measuring a person's perceived locus of control orientation, should be done along a continuum of internal - external perceived locus of control orientation (B. Rhodes, personal communication April, 2006). Point being, people don't necessarily fit into a neat either-or/internal versus external locus of control psychological construct. In concert with this perspective, it was contended that there is a need to operationally reframe and/or broaden the definition of external locus beyond just chance, fate, or luck (Sue, 1981). Again, one of the bi-multi-racial participant's dauntless remarks resonated in his declaring of his intention of "not leaving any of his ethnic-cultural self out," a worldview of inclusion in the face of external forces simultaneously.

Finally, Lefcourt (1982) suggested that by defining and acknowledging the realistic limits and boundaries within the "locus of control variable we should experience its greatest utility" (p. 183). Perhaps, by designing instruments broader in scope that give strong consideration to the conditions surrounding and impacting people's lives within the context of a multi-culturally diverse U.S. and global society, opportunities would be presented resulting in the increased generality of the locus of control construct and its applications. This is particularly relevant given our habitual reaction to people we fear, think less of or pity, don't care for, primarily with our emotions, them vs. us reasoning, in view of historical facts, conditions, and circumstance, that we refuse to considerately weigh, declare with by-gone era confidence.

Some theoretical implications

I once asked a group of students attending an alternative high school at an MLK day assembly:

"What is your social-cultural platform for making yourself visible in life?"

In the previous section of this chapter, I used a two-part conceptualization to discuss and summarize findings in relationship with various topics in the research literature. Although the results from the study *cannot be generalized* the following discussion involves possible implications generated in view of study findings and analysis.

In the documentary film by Hurt (2008), discussed previously, on the subject of the shifting paradigm of Black masculinity, manhood, power, and respect, Armah, who is a radio show host and playwright, provocatively stated, "Barack equaled Harvard, while someone like 50 cent equaled hood; hood equaled virility, Harvard equaled impudence." Consider that 50 cent (first name Curtis) despite his entrepreneurial success is still hood associated and stereotyped as a well-dressed, physically muscled thug and is more attractive and perceived as socially culturally accessible among young Black and Brown men. Both experienced different worldviews, social ecology, positionality experiences, but occupy the same historical-contemporary racialized space, and are therefore subject to the same racialized gender specific conscious – subconscious views, stereotypical imagination, thoughts, and mis-educated perspectives about Black and Brown men from the society at large and from within their own communities. Both are caught in dominant cultural commodification inculcated by popular culture, major mainstream sources of the media, and social media for public consumption, within a dominant White male patriarchal society. I know in growing up, hood was in constant competition with working woman and man in the segregated Black neighborhoods I lived in and visited; fortunately, *working woman and man won out; southern core Black culture* won out. But ultimately, it was my exposure to older Black males who were cognitively learned, courageous, and disciplined within the social-context of their Black masculinity, manhood, and sexuality, through interpersonal interactions with them, and by way of the literature, that lead me to the idea of Black masculinity, manhood, and sexuality as being seamless with the educated self and cool.

I've found that I constantly have to work at fighting the stereotype, through hiding my African American urban southern sociolinguistic styles of speaking, cognitive perception, behaving, dressing, that provided me with that "ready for the world I am proud to be a Black man" self-perception/esteem. The fact is in predominately European American settings, and among settings of more reserved and assimilated Black folks in the world of work and politics, despite my being analytically informed, linguistically articulate in presentation and dialogue I may still be subject to contrary and disconcerting remarks like, "he's suave, cocky acting, or his gestures are threatening, or as one White male school administrator stated to me, I didn't understand a word you just said." The rhetorical question is, *what is more accessible, popular, and alluring relative to Black masculinity, manhood, and sexuality to young Black males; Harvard or hood, and what is the difference in the face of inequality?* I need an answer, at least, *"for the cool of it."* (Dam, it really hurts my feelings).

In concert, participant testimony spoke to the somewhat socially mesmerized states of forming and enacting Black masculinity and manhood, relative to certain alluring aspects of athletics and prominent hip-hop cultural lifestyles that are "out-there" in society. For instance, there was the attractiveness of wanting to be culturally down among Black males that did not merge with being Black while simultaneously developing the educated self. Dialogue directly referenced or alluded to the attractive states of Black masculinity and manhood via aspects of hip-hop culture genre of rap and athletics, along with the focus on the "social-economic lifestyles" among certain music artists/entrepreneurs and professional athletes found in the literature. Again, w*here does the life of the international diplomat and United Nations Undersecretary General Ralph Bunche stand relative to forming and enacting Black masculinity and manhood in relationship with the virility of the educated self within the context of the shifting ideology of Black masculinity and manhood?*

Provocatively stated, Being a Black man in America can mean inhabit-
ing the *"border area between possibility and peril "*(Fletcher, 2007, p. 3) In
his introduction to the works of Merida (2007) Fletched stated that, "In
dozens of interviews, black men described their shared existence, of
sometimes wondering whether their accomplishments will be treated as
anomalies, their individuality obscured by narrow images that linger in the
minds of others" (p.3). Fletcher went on to say that despite the positive
and viable visibility among Black men there are those who lament that, "it
sometime seems as if the world doesn't believe they exist" (p.4).

On Friday afternoon December, 14, 2012, I listened to President
Obama's mournful words regarding the tragic killing of 18 kindergarten
and elementary students (the slaughter of innocents) and a number of
school educators, and witnessed once again his raw compassion as he
struggled to hold back a flow of tears in talking to the nation in a non-
political moment, yet maintain his composure as our national leader. I
felt his grief and it took me to the title of one of my unpublished social
essays' about Black manhood entitled, "Is it manly to Cry." Yet in this moment what I simultaneously thought, worried, and wondered about were
those citizens who might think him *less of a man* for his public show of
emotions, less sternness/angryness, particularly those who are rigidly
steeped in the dogmatic framework of heterogeneous masculinity and
manhood. My response was no, so what, I've felt the same and none the
lesser of a person, a man, *there is more room on the outside than in, than to
let grief go bouncing around the walls of one's mind-body seeking a way
out.*

Study participants too are caught in the *border areas between peril and
possibility*, as is the President of the United States, Barack H. Obama, as a
bi-racial male. There are the statistics of negative disproportionality subject to various areas of human activities and circumstance, that are constantly at odds with success as achieved and the possibility of becoming,
*beyond what has been proscribed as a long standing heterogeneous model
of hegemonic standards and expectations for masculinity and manhood
developing, defining, and enactment,* among this nation's diverse populace of Black African American, bi-multi-racial males. Bear in mind, Collins (2006) adeptly argued the relevancy in learning to tell and enact the
difference between *dominance and strength* that is relevant to defining,
developing, and enacting progressive Black masculinities.

Saint-Aubin (2002) lucidly contended from historical analytical reference, that there was an concerted effort to scientifically codify stereotypi-

cal assumptions about the Black body, (18th-century European Western science) aimed at establishing "a grammar of Black masculinity," which was necessary to discriminate, to make sense of, and, ultimately, to control these threatening dark males bodies, via the use of "White supremacist, patriarchal culture" as the Black male body was anxiety producing. Put another way, Saint-Aubin argued how 18th and 19th century Western scientific discourse, distinctly identified as masculine discourse, permeated by White supremacist ideology, constructed regarding Black men, "a grammar" to explain and consequently produce what a Black male body looked like and how Black masculinity behaved and expressed itself (p.1).

I continue, there is a need to conceptualize and develop a social-cultural paradigm that outlines and defines the seamless merger of developing "progressive" Black African American masculine and manly tendencies with the social construction of the *educated self.*

Mutua (2006) theorized that progressive Black masculinities minimally mean,

> *being pro-black and antiracist, as well as profeminist and antisexist. Further, Mutua stated that progressive black masculinities are men who take a stand against all systems of domination and who act personally and in concert with others in activities against racism, sexism, homophobia, class and economic exploitation, imperialism, and other systems of oppression that limit the human potential of the black masculine self and others. (p. 7)*

This is challenging given the normative---ideal of hegemonic---masculinity, and the traditional standards and generally socially presumptively limited views of heterogeneous masculinity historical in place as discussed by Collins, (2006), Harper, (1996), hooks, (2004), and Ransby and Matthews, (1993). Most certainly this includes the sexist misogynistic subordination of Black women infused in the subgenre of gangsta rap music, popular culture.

The paradigm then should outline and emphasize ways to develop sexual expression and temperament that do not predispose Black American, African American, and bi-multi-racial males to, anti-intellectualism, mis and under-education of self in assimilation, thereby warding aimed at introducing and developing mindset to not fall prey to the trapping of manly tendencies that lead to regressive patriarchy and popular culture driven stereotypes towards women and manhood.

Hammond and Mattis (2005) conducted a study investigating the meaning of manhood among 152 African American men residing in five metropolitan areas. The following are thematic study findings:

- *Manhood as an Interconnected State of Being* – Manhood meaning is best constructed and understood as an interconnection between self, family, and others. Participants rarely identified, if at all, that manhood was solely dependent upon the self.

- *Manhood as a Fluid Developmental Process* – Constructed meaning of manhood is both fluid and adaptable.

- *Manhood as a Redemptive Process* – Manhood offers several opportunities for redemption. Authors noted that, redemption in this case referred to rectifying previous behavior and taking back one's humanity through active family and civic involvement.

- *Manhood as a Proactive Process* – Among participants establishing a proactive course of action means anticipating potential barriers or threats to one's identity as well as ensuring its maintenance by initiating a set of proactive life actions.

The authors suggested that findings were not in concert with previous "rigid" universal classifications of masculinity and manhood established among Western ideals of manhood. Moreover, the authors cited that other studies in the literature on masculine and manhood construction and meaning suggested that African American males took into account the impact of "socio-historical, economic, and interpersonal influences on their manhood" (p. 114); that is, involving, but not exclusively, locus of external control. The implication relative to this study has to do with how such things impact persona associated with Black American, African American, and bi-multi-racial masculinity and manhood, as it concerns the development of manly tendencies towards academic achievement and the educated self.

Carby (2000) reminds us that racialized identity conceptualizations and declarations of Black masculinity call attention to the need to consider how African American male phenotypic traits, linguistic - social characteristics, and ethnic cultural affiliations, and engagement in courageous social justice work that social-politically praises and stigmatizes Black males, impacts the development of their persona. Further, acceptance and praise both serve to idealize and stereotype Black African American males musically, athletically, and sexually in societal imagination as among some minds, as undeclared aberrations of White males. (During eras in this country's emergence, it has been said that Black men stood as a standard for European American masculinity and manhood to avoid and measure up against in making progress on their own).

Steele (1997) discussed how he and his colleagues Aronson and Spencer used the theory of stereotype threat along with domain identification to describe extra social psychological pressures that can affect the test performance and academic identities among such groups as African Americans and women in math. They found that the stereotype threat occurs when the individual concerned recognizes that a negative stereotypical threat about the group to which that individual belongs is applicable to oneself in a particular situation; that is, the result of this "is threatening." Steele and colleagues sufficiently reasoned that such threats are detrimental to the motivation and self-esteem among African American students. The intent of his findings he argued included the stereotypical threat of discrimination.

Tough (2009), a reporter, wrote a *New Times* article regarding an experiment conducted by Marx (2009) and colleagues in lieu of the stereotype threat theory. His article entitled "Obama Effect," findings with limitations that revealed immediately after President Obama's speech in Denver (2009), in which he accepted the Democratic nomination for presidential candidacy, the negative effect of stereotype threat was significantly reduced for Black students. However, it was reduced only for those who students who had actually watched the speech. Moreover, immediately following the election, African American students again scored better, however, at a different point during the campaign, there was no quantifiable effect on their scores. Recall that all the participants were mindful and sensitive to situation and circumstance whether it was during intercultural or intra-cultural group interactions, observing and studies written sources from social media and various books, newsprint, and visual media, regarding the perceived presence or subconscious awareness (guardedness) against maintaining racialized gendered stereotypes. I would argue, in keeping with Steele and colleagues, that such perceived and real threats are detrimental to Black African American, bi-multi-racial males in defining, developing, and enacting their masculinity and manhood as they engage in various areas of human activities, in situation, and circumstance.

After reading Harper (1996) let me point out that the promotion of heterogeneous conventional masculinity and manhood is perceived as a
group cultural redemptive virtue, in view of the historical-contemporary
impact of slavery, Jim Crow segregation, civil-rights and post-civil rights
blow-back. That is to say, displaying and proving that one is a "man" in
heterogeneous meaning, is perceived as "normal" and culturally empowering to ward-off the threats of stereotypes, not to speak of the religious
references that are used to rationalize heterogeneity. Debates and claims
over the authenticity of African American identity are really subject to the
status "specifically of African American masculinity" (p. ix), and as such
are anxiety producing, which Harper asserted was the principal argument
of "*Are We Not Men?*" (p. ix). One's sexuality is on continuous display and
a part of many waking thoughts relative to identity, esteem, emotional
desires, and world view (how one perceived and experiences self in relationship with self and others).

There exists a chorus of voices among Black African American males
in, for example, social-psychological, sociology, mental health, humani-
ties, political science, and cultural studies literature, that have engaged in
critical investigative reporting/analysis, discussing, and autobiographical
reflection, regarding the meaning and experiences of being a Black African
American male (Belton, 1995; Brown, 2006;Chandler, 2011; Calmore, 2006;
Harris, 2006; Jackson, II, & Hopson, 2011; Jackson, II, 2006; Head, 2004;
Kitwana, 2002; Poulson-Bryant, 2005; Richardson, 2007;Whiting & Lewis,
2012). Importantly, there exists a comprehensive and critical host of Black
feminist analytical thought, criticism, and support from among women
scholars/practitioners of color regarding Black African American men and
masculinity that calls and articulates the need for the construction of a
progressive non-sexist, non-womanizing bully-free masculinity, manhood, and personhood (Collins, 2006; hooks, 2004; Mutua, 2006, Hopkinson & Moore, 2006).

Meta Cognitive	• Worldview/Survival Thrust • Self-Concept/Identity/Esteem • Sexuality/Intra/Interpersonal Empowerment
Negotiating within a Multicultural Society	• Cultural Anchoring/Group Affirmation • Intercultural Commuting
Effective Decision Making/ Categories of Mediation	• Effective Human Relations: Intra/Intercultural Literacy Development • Self-Empowerment: to be capable and confident that you can achieve • Developing healthy ways to cope and deal with daily challenges, situations, interactions, and contradictions

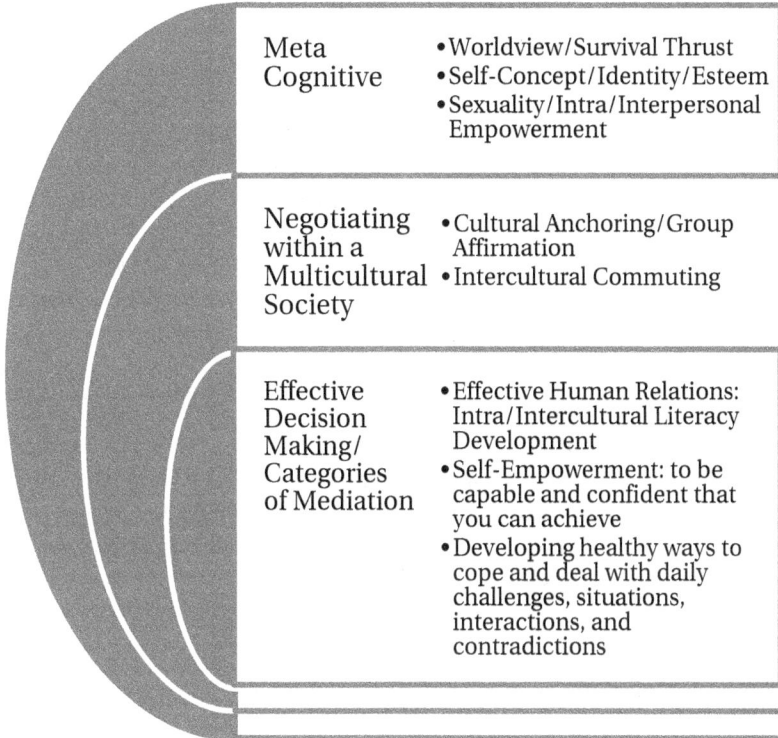

Figure 3. Sample conceptual framework:
The Culture of Effective Cognitive and Behavioral Negotiating
for Black African American, Bi-Multi Racial Males

The Culture of Effective Cognitive and Behavioral Negotiating as it is revealed was done so in consideration of habitus as it has been defined in this study. What I am suggesting that should be calculated is the persistent presence of racialized-gendered experiences in identity formation, socialization, and enactment, as they intersect as a living breathing event daily, requiring spontaneous, sometimes subtle, (light-touch), and other times more assertive critical reflection, to inform decision making to include risk assessment. Included in the contemplation of such a paradigm should be the *agency* among Black African American, bi-multi-racial men to work at engaging in social construction of their masculinity and manhood that accounts for anger and conflict management, civility, risk assessment, respectful relationships with family and extended family, peer and community supports, integrity and empowerment in view of self-ethnic-cultural heritage, and ongoing effort in acquiring self-learnedness. Meyers (1988) wrote that "self-knowledge is the basis of all knowledge (epistemology)" (p.3).

Myers said too that: "all the things we do, we create or construct, concepts, rituals, discourse, enjoyment, and so on" (p.3). I concur, because many times despite what we are constantly looking at, saying, or doing as being external to ourselves we are creating, constructing, and articulating discourse that is coming from within and I contend that it would benefit us more via the work of synthesis; that is, a comparison and contrast of information and intersecting of experiences in order to merge new with old and co-creative new epistemology.

Self-Action research, as defined and discussed earlier, should be of consideration in the design and construction of such a paradigm. Transformative change comes from research turned in on the self in self-interrogation, identifying needed change, adjustments, healing, as one gets to better know the self in various cultural and intercultural situations and circumstance, from an on-going accumulation of epistemology.

For instance, an educator who still un-admittedly struggles with multicultural education as an approach to learning and teaching, who engages in self-action research as a means of self-analysis, should provide self-more of an opportunity to investigate why such a struggle or lack of enthusiasm for multicultural content and discourse exists. This, as opposed to standing on the outside of multicultural content and knowledge with all its diverse complexity, as an observer. In self-action research this teacher-educator would be in a better position to examine and experience, from the inside-out as a more active, (be in closer more intimate social-psychological and cognitive proximity), thereby enhancing opportunities come to the realization that one is a part of the historical and contemporary cultural content, and must take into account the broader implications of one's presence in ethnic-cultural, racialized gendered, and class group and positionality.

The purpose of such a paradigm could be to use as a framework with which to formulate program and project information *across* various disciplines. Also it could for used among professions, such as teachers, mental health counselors, parent-guardian education advocates, social workers and clinical social-psychologist practitioners, post-secondary teaching and research faculty, administrators, managers, and staff engaging in the work of adjudication rehabilitation, intervention, engagement, and reengagement assistance and support work and advocacy.

The function of such a paradigmatic model would not be to engage in another deficit analysis, that underlines so many empirical research studies, stories and commentary in social, local, and national sources of news media, and in popular cultural criticism, but to take into reflective consideration and analysis, historical-contemporary factors and circumstance that impede and demote the pursuit of healthy-empowering ways to define, enact, and experience *progressive* Black African American, bi-multi-racial masculinity, manhood, and sexuality. This kind of a theoretical paradigm should delineate what it means to develop and pursue a healthy bi-multi-racial masculinity, manhood, and sexuality.

It is salient and vital to reiterate that virtually absent or of scant presence among masculinity and manhood research literature are investigative findings and discussion regarding bi-racial and multi-racial masculinity and manhood construction, definition, and enactment. Korgen 1998) asserted that "Throughout U.S. history, the children of black/white interracial couples have faced general degradation; Mixed-race persons have traditionally been portrayed in a negative light" (p.2). Recall among study participants, one is bi-racial African-Mexican American, while another is multi-racial, Cuban, Mexican, and African-American. Both forthrightly described and discussed social interactions and encounters where they received remarks concerning their sexuality and/or racial phenotype features, that is, skin complexion, facial looks, sexuality, and hair textures. In these encounters participants named instances where it was even implied or directly stated that the expectations was for them to "act Black." They noted the ambiguity among others regarding who they were. Think about Blake Griffin, NBA player with the Los Angeles Clippers, who is 9 years younger than one of this study's biracial participants. His ethnicity is listed on a website called "*EthniCelebs*" where "Celebrity Ethnicity" is referenced as being born to African American and European American parents; however, the first thing that most probably comes to mind when viewing him via the photo display, or a media telecast, are his phenotypical features, the texture of his red hair, skin tone, facial features.

Daniel (1992) stated that "biracial Americans of European and African descent have historically faced unique identity issues because of the respectively dominant and subordinate positions of their two ancestry groups in the social hierarchy of races in the United States" (p. 91). According to Perry and Bodenhausen" (2008), the principle *hypo* descent has had "a prominent history in the U.S." (p. 973). The hypo descent principle applied meant that a child of mixed races was a social subordinate, "thus a black-white child would be considered black" (p. 973); the "one drop of blood rule" in racial categorizing.

Miscegenation laws institutionalized and socialized practices contributed to giving a sordid history to equality of opportunity barriers and the burden of social-psychological issues regarding identity development and the pursuit of a quality of life existence. Much has been written in autobiographical testimony among, for example, African Americans, on the survival thrust strategy of "passing for white" and abandoning one's kinship network. It can be considered then that the influence of hypo descent social-racialized perceptions within society may effect and shape masculine and manhood tendencies and identity enactment among bi-multi-racial males.

"Racial hybridity" has and continues to blur the lines the boundary lines imposed by ethnic-cultural racial categories stemmed from various institutional sources and people's social perceptually conditioned expectations looking for the Black or White ethnic-cultural-racial identification during intercultural interactions, hence, the omnipotent question, *what are you?* We continue to be perceptually, attitudinally, and behaviorally plagued by the historical vestiges and contemporary racialized hangover imposed by the dichotomy and the discriminatory boundary setting of the colorline into areas of our human activities, borrowing from Fuller, Jr. (1971) such as education, law, economics, politics, entertainment, labor, war, and religion. Social-cultural and gender racialized interactions are the conduit for all the listed areas of activities.

Implications - Learning and Education

What are some practical implications of knowing more about racialized gender of Black African American and bi-multi-racial masculinity and manhood, as it concerns approaches to school policy and practices, and educational pedagogical and andrological (philosophical basis and consideration for teaching adult learning) belief and practice, and social psychological approaches to assessment and counseling? What is relevant to think about is considering the intersection of masculinity and manhood social structuring and enactment with ethnicity, culture, race, sexuality, and class that occurs within and around the student concerned? Consider working to develop a more informed and assertive understanding regarding how the role of racialized gender of masculinity, manhood identity development, and tendencies in education, learning, and achievement. This would be a personal-professional reflective endeavor that should be aimed at deepening pedagogical/andrological one's beliefs and approaches, within the context of enhancing culturally relevant teaching/facilitation of learning. An integrating merger is needed.

Unfortunately, there are good intentions of applying "color-blind" thesis and perceptions to cultural diversity in consideration of historical and contemporary issues of racialized gender in the conduct of schooling, education, and the social-ecology of communities, are still prominent and perceived as an appropriate response, as it is an inform-lesser response. Controversially, the covenant response and stance of "all children" again ignores the impact of historical and contemporary issues of racialized gender. Such a stance and the pre-post teacher and administrator education that supports it, does not prepare nor encourage educators to engage in study and direct dialogue regarding the realities and politics of "speaking the unpleasant" (Chavez & O'Donnell, 1998) concerning in this case, the dogmatic presence and role of racialized gender in institutional practices.

Taken as a whole, what is suggested is that it is relevant for teacher pedagogy and andragogy to be constructed and engaged in ways that situate the students within the culture of subject content and learning; not simply as observers and/or game show contestants seeking to provide the correct or culturally appropriate and/or comfortable answers. The culture of subject content and learning has to do with the situating of subject content, learning goals, and so on, in consideration of the social-cultural reality that students bring into the school environment within their developmental experiences. A matter of historical-contemporary positionality.

Finally, teacher pedagogy, instructional strategy, and structured learning activities should involve encouraging and cultivating the reasoning activity of meta-cognition. Meta-cognition is a developmental cognitive ability skill that serves analytical work intersection action with emotional intelligence. The undeclared question that may be present in some unarticulated way is where am I in all this? How is this relevant to me? Is this worth my time and effort? Be assured that race, gender, class, ethnicity, culture, and ethnic-cultural group social-ecological community experiences and perceptions in varying degrees to subtly (faintly as in sub-consciously) shape and influence student response and unresponsiveness even if the student concerned is not in a place to articulate it aloud yet.

Implications - Social-Psychology / Mental Health

Nedhari (2009) in his discussion of Black male challenges, as it concerns socially constructing and enacting self-identity, power, and empowerment among Black African American males, contended that one has to consider identities rooted in individual experiences with stress induced psychic embedded trauma via witness, victim, involvement in nation sanctioned violence such as armed conflict, relative to their efforts and strategies in defining and enacting their masculinity, manhood, or sexuality. In other words, there are individual and ethnic-cultural group social-cultural psychohistorical experiences to consider relative to the history of racialized gendered experiences in this country, in various areas of human activities. I am reminded that there is what I called that law of compensation in the perception of self in human affairs. When one's experiences a threat to gendered self in social-cultural context, for instance, in educational space and time that is perceived as a loss of power/empowerment, how does one compensate for this?

Nedhari pointed to the enactment of social-psychological mechanism of defense to ward-off or downplay the threat of their situation or circumstance. He astutely reminded us that historically Black African Americans as a group have occupied socially stigmatized space I would add that this includes the mulatto, according to Wideman (1994), "a word that was imported from Luso-Hispanic culture," (p. xiv), appropriated for use beginning mid-18th century U.S. society connoting miscegenation and laws that were codified around it. However, Rogers (1967) tells us that sex and race copulation has historically created bi-multi-racial ethnicity to include

U.S. society, beyond the miscegenation denoting Black African Americans and European procreation. As Rogers so provocatively declared,

> *The evil of race is also created from scraps---scraps of false philosophies of past centuries; a quotation from this or that prejudiced traveler: lines from this and that semi-ignorant divine of colonial days; excerpts from Gobineau, Thomas Jefferson, Abraham Lincoln, the Bible; passages from this or that badly mixed up ethnologist, all jumbled together with catch-phrases from greedy plantation owners, slave-dealers, and other traffickers in human flesh. (p.1).*

Bi-multi-racial males have not only occupied stigmatized space, but interstitial space because they do not fit into the neat-hyphenated and dichotomized racialized categories.

Bridges (2011) stated that Black African American men face many social-cultural, "academic, and negative stressors" (p. 1) that generate taxing experiences and identity conflict. Such experiences can and do effect intrapersonal-interpersonal relationships, the construction and response to social reality, and real and perceived threat to one's masculinity, manhood, and sexuality.

In the results of the authors' study to identify "what factors helped young African American men at a university succeed academically," (p.1), the use of various coping methods were identified that were put into play by study participants, for instance, interpersonal-cultural distancing from European American students, physically and psychologically. Physical distancing s proved difficult because the university was predominantly European American in student population, thus psychological distancing was often used. The next method was cognitive withdrawal and assertion. Lastly, the author identified several implications that could be derived from the study, including enhanced "self-awareness, self –understanding (self-epistemology)" (p. 164), and an appreciation for the self. The author found that African American males in his study sought "greater opportunities to express their emotion and feelings in a productive way" (p. 164).

Sue (2003) researcher/ psychologist/author of "*Racial micro-aggressions in everyday life and in psychological counseling practices,*" declared that,

The practice of color-blindness is a dangerous and frightening proposal because it will perpetuate and create greater disparities in our society. It will undermine accountability for civil rights violations (hate crimes, discrimination in the workplace and biased profiling), healthcare disparities, and racial/ethnic disease patterns important for medical treatment, educational inequities and so forth. In my research on the causes and effects of racism, I have come to realize that color-blindness uses "Whiteness" as the default key to mimic the norms of fairness, justice and equity by "whiting" out differences and perpetuating the belief in sameness. The denial of power imbalance, unearned privilege and racist domination are couched in the rhetoric of equal treatment and equal opportunity. (p.1)

According to Sue (2003) racial microaggressions are present and of common occurrence in our daily interpersonal-cultural communication whether present intentionally or unintentionally that convey hostile, derogatory, or negative racial approach and insults toward people of color. The point is that there are hidden, overt, consciously ignored, and coped with sources of racialized stressors are present that have the potential to affect healthy gender identity making and defining among Black American, African American, and bi-multi-racial males.

Bernal and Saez-Santiago (2006) presented a thesis argument that although "culturally centered psychological intervention is more considered in treatment, prevention, and mental health service delivery" over the years, the challenge still exists to "develop evidence-based, culturally sensitive interventions" (p. 121). According to the investigators, culturally sensitive interventions have been described as a continuum of the following dimensions:

- Awareness of culture

- Acquisition of knowledge about the cultural aspect (such as norms, customs, language, lifestyle, etc.

- Capacity to distinguish between culture and pathology

- Capacity to integrate the previous three dimensions in the intervention

Very importantly, the investigators noted "cultural sensitivity is a dynamic process that changes across time and in difficult contexts, in which the cultural hypothesis should be constantly tested against alternative ones" (p.122). Finally, these investigators cited that there is evidence suggesting that ethnic minorities in the United States are currently experiencing major health problems, often have lesser access to healthcare, and such care that is available is often of poorer quality than available to the White population.

At length, Wade and Rochlen (2013), in their review of the literature on qualitative and quantitative studies conducted regarding masculine identity related to the health and well-being among African American men, noted that "to date, much of the research has focused on negative outcomes and risk factors. Research on understanding the protective factors contributing to the health and well-being of African American men is needed, particularly with regard to the psychological aspects of masculinity and manhood" (p.3).

Summative Last Words

"The West thinks of itself as masculine – big guns, big industry, big money --- so the East is feminine – weak, delicate, poor" from David L. Eng's Treatise: Racial Castration, Managing Masculinity in Asian America (2001).
I recall seeing two, then Republic of South Vietnam (RVN), soldiers strolling down a beaten road in South Vietnam, on a typical hot day, M16 rifles slang over one-another's shoulder while hugging each other, (I seriously advise you to not get this stereotypically twisted).

I do not claim that the results and suggested implications of this study are patently obvious, nor the condition and circumstance under which Black African American, and bi-multi racial males strive to develop, define, and enact their masculinity and manhood. However, the results are *not* unlikely and unworthy of further research, exploration, and contemplation. The Chapter Four analysis suggested that it is relevant to consider the role of evolving and shifting manly tendencies as *habitus* that intersects with social – political constructs of racial identity, related to ethnic-cultural group background and experiences, expression of sexuality, and other character-temperament dispositions, in response to one's social reality, are not in a vacuum. Very importantly, the study discussed in this book, provided the participants with an opportunity to discuss their Black African American, and bi-racial self-consciousness, awareness, and understanding of their masculinity and manhood from their worldview, knowledge, and life experiences. Moreover, they were able talked about this awareness and understanding relative to their varying degree of ethnic-cultural group cultural orientations. This meant thinking about the sources and styles of expression of their masculine energies and how they, and others like or similar to them, are being perceived in a multicultural society at a time where among certain groups of citizens there are those battling to sustain dominant cultural arrangements and influences, that were more prominently visible in past era's. One has only to look to racialized public overt verbal and visible assaults upon President Obama to real-

ize what has gone hidden in plain sight is now considered to be fashiona-
ble and courageous to declare and act out loud.

Hecht el al (1993) in their study of African American communication,
revealed that African American participant responses to questions related
to communication issues about cultural effectiveness in interpersonal
communication, identified the following thematic issues as being important to achieving interpersonal effectiveness:

- Negative stereotyping – use of inflexible categories that distort individuality (direct and indirect)

- Acceptance – confirming and respecting one another's opinions

- Expressiveness – the expression of thoughts and feelings

- Authenticity – being genuine and open

- Understanding – feeling that meanings are successfully conveyed

- Powerlessness – feeling controlled or manipulated (pp. 127-128).

I suggest that these thematic interest/issues are relevant to interpersonal-cultural situations, given the fact that European American communication has historically been the *in-group* communication standard to
meet, in so-called mainstream America, which is now de jure integrated
space. Put another way, European American patterned speech orientation
(tone-volume-frequency) is the expected standard to meet in formal work
and educational settings. Many work settings in certain arenas or fields of
work are predominantly European American, where African Americans
and other ethnic-cultural people of color find themselves, in many instances, in isolated situations, which is a historical-contemporary part of
their ethnic group's communication experiences. As such they have had
social-psychological, health and well-being, employment, learning, and
educational implications. Then too youth and young adults of color who
are students that find themselves in predominantly European American
settings at public-private k-12 and post-secondary schools and institutions, are subject to intra-interpersonal-cultural experiences of isolation,
to include, the teachers, counselors, instructors, professors, administrative
staff, and administrators of color as well. How does this impact their construction and response to social reality under such circumstances?

Hereto, stand implications concerning the constructional and cultivation of *student-voice* among those students who are from historically-
contemporary marginalized ethnic-cultural groups and communities, that

in educational settings need to be considered and addressed as a part of learning, achievement, human development, attitudes and behavior habits relative to in-fact and potential non-engagement mindsets.

There is the reality regarding the articulation of identities, in consideration of one's ethnic-cultural heritage and individual group social-cultural psychohistorical experiences, to include the accounting for one's racialized physical presence, gender, sexuality, and sexual persona. Jackson (2002) stated that, "identities are the products of collective perceptions and individuated definition of the self," (let me repeat – collective perception and individuated definition of the self), and that we communicate our social-cultural, and so on, gender-sexuality (p. 245). This includes symbolic representation that is part of intra/interpersonal-cultural interaction and articulation of self-concept in private and public spheres; these exist among people's seamless application of beliefs and values.

Of consideration here is "identity negotiation" (Jackson, p. 245) and Mills' Racial Contract thesis (1997), that is, the racialized norming of public space that both quietly-complexly, along with more pronounced undeclared, thought of, denied, and sanctioned ways, establishes restrictions for not only demarcating non-verbal – verbal communication styles and efforts, but also reducing or minimizing one's ethnic-cultural, racialized-gender presence and sexuality. This at the behest of our widely social-political dogma of I'm just-American assimilationism. That I further contend exists within this country's historical-contemporary, interculturally racialized- gendered vendettas.

Mills talked about the "norming of space that was partially done as it concerns the 'racing of space' (p.41) that involved the "depiction of space as dominated by individuals (whether persons or sub persons) of certain race" (pp. 41-42). Identity negotiation involves, but is not limited to, enacting a process whereby one attempts to maintain, retain, or retrieve custody and authority over defining the self despite knowing that one cannot control how the self is social (interculturally) understood. Racialized-gender, sexuality, cultural worldview, and survival thrust orientations are at stake in such situations in public sphere-introspective thoughts. Bear in mind that being in management of their cultural self was a thematic perspective that emerged from the findings, as well as participant perspective regarding the performance of Black masculinity, manhood, and sexuality.

(There is this conscious-subconscious effort-struggle, perhaps battle, if you will, within and without among certain of us in the public domain, and in the privacy of intimate affairs, for self-entitlement rights within the legal and factual make-it-so framework of U.S. democracy).

One of the major underlying interests in this study was the belief that social-construction of Black African American, bi-multi-racial masculinity, manhood, and sexuality should be seamless with the educated self. Put another way, the educated self should be the fabric of self in gendered context. Doss (2008) conducted a case study of young adult African American men investigative of masculinity based on the following research questions:

- What symbolic and cultural resources do African American men with postsecondary education use to define their masculinity?

- What symbolic and cultural resources do African American men without postsecondary education use to define their masculinity?

- What are the main similarities and differences in definitions of masculinity between the two groups? (p. 42)

Among the findings, African American men with post-secondary education perceived *education* as *"characteristic of their manhood,"* while among African-American men who were not pursuing post-secondary education, *"working hard"* was found to be a characteristic of their manhood. Then to, the approaches to resisting stereotypes were different between both groups of study participants. ("Never the twain shall meet")?

According to the researcher, both groups of study participants socially constructed a hybrid masculinity, manhood, and sexuality paradigm that merged hegemonic characteristics from the traditional Western model of masculinity and manhood with an Africentric model. Use of the Africentric model in the social-construction of masculinity, manhood, and sexual identity was involved in advocating for the cultivation of self-epistemology. Use of an Africentric model for frame of reference, was aimed at instilling efforts to become more literate regarding the psychological, social-economic, political, and spiritual history and contemporary status and issues among Black African American peoples, and peoples of the African diaspora (Bush, 1999; Myers, 1988; Woodson, 1933). This includes serving as a countermeasure regarding the over-reliance in personalizing one's construction and response to social reality based upon the dominant cultural Western axiological reference and belief in individualism; particularly, as it concerns being absented from the impact of dominant social, political, and economic systems. The assertion here is that

West axiological (system of value) reference has historically served to sub-optimize an intercultural-collectivistic axiological world view of accultura-tion, as part of individual in group efforts to form and substantiate a Black African American culture; while facing European American *social-political retrenching and push-back.*

(Again, it is significant to realize that Black African American are not an immigrant group voluntary nor non-voluntary. Eliminating non-voluntary may appear to be a contradiction, as it concerns in this case not having any choice of will, but the members from multiple African tribal nations were taken like exported property, numbers among who, were sent to this part of the Americas. They did not have an immigrant status, therefore, voluntary or non-voluntary does not apply).

White and Cones (1999) stated that although European American mas-culinity ideology has many commendable qualities, the "excessive em-phasis on power, dominance, competitiveness, individualism, and control has resulted in the oppression of ethnic minorities and sexism" (p. 115). Put another way, the authors pointed to the European American ideal of masculinity which promoted the following social-psychological drives:

- Being competitors for success, must win

- Being anti-feminine, that is, like womanish in feelings, perceptions

- Being initiators of sexual behaviors and control relative to hetero-sexual interpersonal interaction, which I content can/od increase susceptibility to the objectification of women as they are perceived as objects to be taken-over and shown-off relative to physical beau-ty with little or no substance, I say who's got the finest women syn-drome

- Being defenders of perceived threat against their rights as a man-men

- Being capable of using physical, and non-verbal - verbal commu-nication behaviors as to talk over and to women. I would say among men there are those who perceive that when they are losing an argument the thing is to simply get louder and engage in physi-cal posturing, which is primed to escalate into physical and verbal violence.

(There is too the obstinate *male silence* in a classroom setting in the context of non or refusing to engage; i.e., the angry male silence as a way of asserting power when the perception of winning is not an option (Alcorn, 1994).

Moreover, think about urban territorial gang behavior (Alcorn, 1994), relative to racialized masculine development as a construction and response to social reality. The authors also asserted that it is not socially psychological healthy for Black males to heedlessly follow the excessively controlling, dominating Euro-American ideal of masculinity, which places White males in a paradoxical situation regarding their own health. But, a question is, what happens to the rest of the country (particularly, among women, people of color, gay, lesbian, and transgender people, and those who are economically struggling) when European American males who are politicians, who are high-level empowered administrators at all levels of government, who are wealthy and used to wielding power, who are executives of mega corporations, who are law enforcement officers and officials, who are federal, state, and local judges at all levels of benches among a White male voting populace, *who are used to winning don't get their way, particularly as much as they used to, want and expect to continue?*

It was emphasized that the presence of social constructs, and the lingering and covert presence of institutionalized racism, contributes to the generation of micro-aggressive racial attitudes and behaviors that have and can affect Black African American, and bi-multi racial males' identity development and defining, relative to enacting masculinity and manhood. This is detrimental to physical and mental health and well-being, and that of communities.

(Any time you are in the public domain or public sphere there is this cognitive – social psychological occurrence of exposure. It might not be consciously registering, but there is some work-reaction-response occurring internally in the mind-body. Much of our response overtime becomes governed or taken care of by habitus regarding an accumulation of experiences).

Finally, the complexity and constriction that racialized gender presents challenges/consequences regarding the formation of manly tendencies concerning the role and relevancy that schooling, education, and academic achievement plays in their lives and approaches to well-being.

The results of the analysis suggested the presence of manly tendencies/inclinations were interconnected with the interviewee's awareness of race has in having a real and perceived presence of racialization in society, for instance, in social-cultural intra-interpersonal interactions. Put an-

other way, results purported the presence of participant predisposed masculine attitude, thoughts, and behavioral response to race and ethnic-
cultural membership as a part of a response to social reality.

Social reality is constructed through interpersonal interactions, socialization, situations, perceptions, and thoughts experienced in everyday life
that become expected and habitual ways to behave (Berger & Luckmann,
1966). Bear in mind habitus involves perceptional, attitudinal behavioral
tendencies and pre-dispositions as the result of individual-group cultural,
materialistic, social-ecological experiences in a society. In this regard,
study results suggested that participants revealed in their perspective regarding how racialized-gender, ethnic-culture(s) self-affiliated and societal
views of them, were associated with their masculine and manly predispositions and tendencies.

Guinier (2010) in her introduction to the book entitled *12 Angry Men,*
True Stories of Being a Black Man in America Today, stated that,

> *Racial profiling is reality that we often don't hear*
> *mentioned in the Obama era, because liberal and*
> *conservative pundits alike tell us that we now live in a*
> *post-racial American. Or we are cautioned that to*
> *speak up about race is itself an act of racism is. (p.xii)*

Guinier called attention to the fact that racial profiling is a practice that
is not just subject being narrowly confined to law enforcement,

> *Americans of all colors, including blacks, Latinos,*
> *Asians, and whites, still too readily associate random*
> *images of black people with images of bad people and*
> *pictures of unfamiliar white faces with pictures of*
> *friendly faces and pleasant word (p. xxiii).*

The existence of sanctioned racial profiling and the right to detain citizens hold real and perceived implications regarding the daily social-
cultural outlook and mental health among, Black African American and
bi-multi-racial males, particularly given the fact that law-abiding Black
African American, bi-multi-racial males have and are subject to such tactics. I argue such a contradiction is an ongoing source of cognitive dissonance that has to be mentally negotiated or placed in some degree in of

subconscious or a habitual stress reduction strategy. I further maintain that racial profiling holds covenant with racialized micro-aggressive attitudes, perceptions, and behaviors among law enforcement personnel and among this country's multicultural citizenry. I found argumentative explicit-ness in the statement by Alcoff (2006) that "the reality of identities often comes from the fact that they are *visibly marked on the body itself,* guiding, if not determining, the way we perceive and judge others and are perceived and judged by others" (p.5).

Risk Assessment

Risk assessment is part of a survival thrust activity regarding what one sees as real and perceived threats and challenges on a day-to-day basis, holding implication for racialized gender experiences and circumstance among men of color in U.S. society. Assessing risk to one's actions, integrity, ego, mental and physical social well-being is of daily occurrence. If one perceives risk and challenges directly or indirectly connected with gender identity defining and enactment in affiliation with one's culture, the question is, what toll has this played on the mental and biological health-welfare of self and among historically oppressed ethnic-cultural groups in this country? There is psychological and physical energy exerted in risk perception and assessment, and habitual attitudes, behaviors, and cognitive reasoning as a result of this activity. For example, empirical studies such as the one conducted by Pierre and Mahalik (2005) examined the role of African self-consciousness and Black racial identity "as predictors of psychological distress and self-esteem for Black men" (p.28). In the researchers' pretext to reporting the design and results of their study, they made the following points from the literature:

Research findings had consistently shown that the "racial oppression was a chronic psychosocial stressor that affected the mental and social adjustment of people of color" (p.28),

- Although Black men have positive, rich, and varied cultural experiences, they still continue to experience social-economic hardships, experience marginalization to their families, communities, the labor market, and social institutions.

- The effects of racism on physical health seemed to be "connected to African American men's psychological well-being" (p. 29).

- The accumulative effects of "prejudice and discrimination can generate rage, anger, frustration, bitterness, resentment, grief, despair, or any combination of these emotions" (p. 29).

- Despite adversity that leaves African Americans susceptible to stress-related issues, they "use many effective coping mechanisms that enable them to negotiate adverse conditions" (p.29).

Hence, such real, perceived, denied, and coped with sources of stress and stressors hold relevancy in shaping the overall outlook regarding one's view of the world, a person's place in it, and their ability to pursue a quality of life existence, in relationship with family, friends, and others throughout the society-at-large. Attitudes of denial and/or failure to assess risk may be implicit in one's racialized gender identity, attitude, and behavior that can and have become implicit among young African American males that engage in and assume hypermasculinity, manhood, and sexual identity in their approach to constructing and response to social reality. Such attitudinal and under awareness, would and is to their own detriment, and that of family, friends, and acquaintances. Surely measuring, determining, and holding counsel with, overt and subtle sources of stress and distress that produce/harbor established, denied, and under-realized habitual tendencies relative to the intersection of race, ethnic-cultural, gender, and social-economic experiences, and as social markers among Black African American bi-multi-racial males, is significant to identify, define, and address issues related to their self-identity and development (Franklin, 2008; Poussaint and Alexander, 2000; Courtenay, 2000; Mahalik, Pierre, & Wan).

I maintain that race as a social-political established, and as such the impact of a racialized patriarchal culture on Black African American and bi-multi-racial masculinity, well-being, frame of reference, and world view, is still considered too contentious, abstruse, and nominal to plan, develop, and implement substantive and aggressive research and educational agendas, among European American and conservative people of color, who are: academicians, educational administrators, teaching educators, counselors, in public/private school systems, from various schools of thought, such as, communication studies, education, philosophy, social work, political science, social economics, psychology, sociology, and psychiatry. Very significantly, this group includes those among elected officials and individuals of political office, and high ranking individuals from the private sector.

Functionality

Finally, it is important to consider that the overwhelming majority among Black African American and bi-racial males seek, work to achieve, and maintain functionality in a multicultural society. What has been pointed out is the influential involvement of historical and contemporary societal conditions and psychohistorical circumstance, under which Black African American and bi-multi-racial masculinity and manhood defining, developing, and enacting take place. The conditions under which this kind of critical self-developmental activity must be conducted are still rife with perceived and real issues and challenges that sometimes may and do increase susceptibility of Black African American and bi-multi-racial males to the disproportionate occurrence of certain health related illnesses and medical conditions, and inequality opportunities to learn, grow, gain fruitful employment, and contribute to the cultivation of societal democracy on their own terms. On their own terms as opposed to having to negotiate real and perceives states of otherness, and the social contractual demands of mainstream societal culture.

Under the demands of mainstream culture human-induced social-ecological conditions and circumstance, unrealized stressors occur have and can disproportionately increase susceptibility to, for instance, certain illnesses and medical conditions via social-cultural hyper vigilance contributing to hypertension and related illnesses, thus, lessening opportunities and/or having to construct and engage in more optimal response to social reality among citizenry who wheel a self-will-centric brand of social justice (Courtenay, 2000; Head, 2004; Poussaint & Alexander, 2000; Thompson-Miller & Feagin, 2007; White & Cones III, 1999).

Recall that Head (2004) pointed out that among Black men, admitting mental health related symptoms related to depression, has been a long standing taboo, based upon the perception that it is perceived as weak, (i.e. unmanly). Harper (1996) eruditely argued that gayness in the African American community was promoted as being a contradiction to so-called "authentic" African American identity, and an assault of the heterogeneity of Black masculinity and manhood. There is an increased risk of depression-suicide risk among Black and Latino lesbians, gay and bisexual males (O'Donnell, Meyers, and Schwartz (2011). According to the minority stress model used by the authors, the excess (that is, the surplus) of prejudice, stigma, and discrimination encountered by sexual minority individuals leads to increased mental health problems" (p. 1055), thus resulting in a higher risk for suicide.

I would maintain that there exists a cultural mis-orientation among black and brown males related to rigid dominant cultural expressions and standards of what it means to be a man, that stands in competitiveness, if you will, with the traditional Western paradigm for manhood and masculine hegemony. Such dogmatic ideas that drive socialization and heterogeneous beliefs about manhood, only serve to exacerbate the occurrence and severity of mental health related symptoms and related illnesses, and racialized-gendered stereotypes. As such they limit the social-cultural, psychological, and physical space in which to construct, define, and enact ones' masculinity, manhood, and sexuality. In other words, such beliefs, standards, and practices, are spatially confining and anti-theoretical to the construction of progressive Black African American, bi-multi-racial masculinities.

In part, results bring attention to the research literature concerning the Sociology of masculinity, specifically regarding the subject of Black African American masculinity, (Cooper, 2006; Hunter & Davis; 1994, Ross, 1998; Kiwana, 2002; Laubsher, 2005; Mahalik, Pierre, & Wan, 2006; Mutua, 2006; Spraggins, 1999). Through this study I purported to illustrate the importance of providing opportunity and space for Black African American, and bi-multi-racial males to publicly conceptualize and construct meaning regarding the notion of masculine identity and manhood relative to their response to social reality, as a learned enterprising seamless endeavor.

It is salient to note that the authentic voices of participants bought attention to masculinity, race, ethnic-culture(s), and identity as *intersecting* experiences in the process of schooling and education. Intersection is an analytical tool that is adeptly used in Black feminist literature (Crenshaw, 1989). It is argued in the literature by Crenshaw (1989) and Collins (2000) that recognizing and investigating how the intersection of race, sexuality-gender, social-economic class experiences intersect within individuals, increases the likelihood of transdisciplinary thinking in the study of the individual within groups, particularly as it pertains to the presence, interference, and impact, of social-politically oppressive ideological dogmatic attitudes, behavior, and decision- making practices among certain members of dominant mainstream society, that thwart efforts to eradicate or lessen the presence of social inequality.

James Baldwin (1972) once said,

*Four hundred years in the West had certainly turned
me into a Westerner---there was no way around that.
But four hundred years in the West had also failed to
bleach me---there was no way around that, either (p.
42).*

Postscript

Dear Uncle Charles,

Between 1967 and 1972, the military, the war, my short self-interrupted stay at the traditional Black college, Norfolk State in Virginia, on track scholarship, with its' then two year required ROTC participation, assaulted my senses, my psychic, with realized-realities, and I began facing my-self as a Black male outside of the culturally insulated segregation of Philadelphia's Black neighborhoods. The self that resided within me where-ever I went.

I started writing letters home that turned out to be notes to myself about what I was seeing, feelings, experiencing, nervous about, that served as, well really, periods of self-contemplation; sometimes even calming my nerves. Other times trying on my nerves and confusing. I stuttered at times in trying to fathom our existence and relationships among ourselves and to the world, and how to communicate this to others in Standard English.

As it turned out my writing tried to join my mind in stream of consciousness which is against the grain of good reader acceptable writing. (I'm still working on that one). And so I began down writing phrases and declarations of allegiance to Black folks, and the situations and sometime predicaments that I found myself in. This also came to include our conditions that I saw that were in my face in contrast to how others were being treated and rewarded around me in then so called integrated military settings.

I came out of the service filled with a silent bellowing self-concealed anger, that unbeknown to me was bursting at the seams of my inners. Writing let off-stream, gave me pause, redirected my rage, helped shape my character. Most importantly, it helped me to realize and be thankful for the men elders in my life like you. Black men who kept their anger in tow and did not allow themselves to be held sway to their raced status. This is why I began to write at earnest for whatever it is worth. This is how you arrived in my writings, but were always in my heart.

As a very close and wise friend of mine, who is clinical therapist by profession, once said to me – in introducing yourself relative to your writings you may want to think about; ***what has situated you in the position that you are in, and what historically informs that position?***

Well, what I sense that has generally situated me has been of course: my decision-making, my involvement, my choices, my social-cultural ways of being and becoming; that is, still Frederick and becoming. However, all of these human activities have context, that is, circumstances and conditions in which they took place, laid out clues to discover and study. This is a process necessary to reveal the meaning behind what occurred, how habitual styles of thinking and responding were formed, how I came reveal and hide presence as I do; and how I have come to thank my blessings for this country, my wife, children, grandchildren and great one, *la familia.*'

Indeed; unequivocally, how and why have I come to both honor and fear people's good intentions; and to despise the historical democratic ugliness and open-faced hypocrisy among certain of this country's citizens? (The U.S. has historical doctrines of good intention). Context provides both meaning and simultaneously contributes to the engenderment of what's happening if one mind is lucid, and not dogmatically stuck.

What has lead me to such a paradoxical state of mind and denouncement in multicultural public sphere; is it a lack of past accountability in presence tense? What has driven me to this state of feeling the need to act like the songs says; "I feel like bustin' loose, bustin' loose?" Was it because I found plausibility and credence in what Chester Himes provocatively and with conviction said in his autobiography that; "America hurt me terribly, whether rightly or wrongly is not the point. When I fought back through writing it decided to kill me...When America kills a nigger it expects him to remain dead....The desperate struggle for life informed me that the only place where I was safe was in my skin." Was it because I found an astute connection with Mystikal's lyrical verse-rhyme: "You keep bumpin' me against the wall;" Or perhaps is it because I find disturbing clarity in the words stated by John Edgar Wideman in his book "*Fatheralong*" when I read that,

> *The discovery of people unlike themselves did not spark in Europeans a doctrine of relativity: it produced the invention of race. Of all the weapons devised to conquer and   subjugate the lands beyond Europe, the most effective, pervasive, and enduring, the one that served to coordinate, harmonize, and in-*

> *tensify the effects of all the other weapons, is the con-*
> *cept of race.*

Perhaps is it because I can honestly say that I have been insulted, cussed at, verbally and emotionally hurt out-loud and in writing by people of European American descent, (and just a much in other ways by conservative Black folks). This includes being threatened by a White guy supposedly a grown man, with tire iron in hand downtown Seattle when I mistakenly started to pull into a parking space in a lot. I can straight up say that I did not see him in his car circling around to turn take claim the parking space; my wife and young baby boy were in the car.

On the other hand, is it this constantly on and off thing where I come to think time and time again just my presence, mention of the word-concept culture, *or any of the above and what's coming*, evokes a perception that:

I am just another brother with an attitude of subversiveness, an "affirmative action crybaby," wanta-be citizen lookin' for a free-handout, an ancestral reparation?

You know, I can literally just about name the times when certain White folks said I was acting like Malcolm X and certain Black folks shied away from me. Mama once said to me, "you just love you up on some Black folks." This came out of her mouth with an air of warning and a reminder of what occurred to her when she was offered a promotion at the housekeeping department in the Penna. hospital over a number of Black folks. I'll tell you that nastiness came out of the woodwork like termites on a mission. Mama then finished, "you'd better be careful with that one; besides why are you in that race work anyway. It's too dangerous." Mama knew about the Scottsboro boys in Alabama in her time and location. Mama, and elders like you, I know, Uncle Charles, grew up Jim Crow normal, some starting their schooling out at the "Wrightboro School for Colored Children" located at the very spot where my Aunt Katie Bell Grady's, Mama's older sister's, house stands on Chair Road, Castle Hayne, North Carolina, now a family rental but still the house. (Jim Crow normal is a term I coined in regards to the concept of U. S. political racial exceptionality. In the face of Jim Crow *de facto* and *de jure* practices in our so-called at times democratic U.S. society, Blacks had to develop cognitive, behavioral, and mental health survival thrust strategies, to engender sanity; "that's just the way it is, you'll have to make due)."

Mull over this: I am a man of Black African American descent who gratefully had providing nurturing parents and elders, born in South Philadelphia on a narrow street called Kater which sported row houses with rugged outdoor toilets; right around the corner from a lively South Street, filled with Jewish and other old world vendors. Kater Street was in a largely segregated neighborhood. I loved that neighborhood, I had an Italian woman neighbor, Ricky's Mama, who baby-sat me along with sista Wishy-May's kids (her name was Willamae); tongued that name as best I could.

In 1956, we moved to Frazier Street in the northern part of West Philadelphia, in and around the predominately-Jewish neighborhood, my Mama worked as a young housekeeper and house cleaner. She told me she had to endure poverty wages and once Jewish young-in's at one house, where she was also paid to watch the children, yell racial obscenities at Negro children passing by. Mama said to me, the young-in's they said what they heard, what they thought, and who was their social friend and who was not. I cannot imagine what was going through Mama's head during those times.

The move into the neighborhood was an exciting surreal moment for me as the house and street with steps and a landing were like moving into a giant mansion to my eight-year-old eyes; home is still that house, sold now, but it's starting to evaporate in my mind's eye. (Thank good-ness for Google mapping). In two years' time in that house I lost my Grand mama Agnes and one year later my Daddy had worked himself to death giggin' two-three jobs to make one check, while Mama worked late at night house cleaning at the Penna. Hospital cross town.

In the subsequent years, between 1960 and 1966, I successively lost a string of uncles, aunts, Grand papa John, and my Grand mama Clara. (Who I witnessed in a Kodak moment, running down the steps at the age of about 78 with the fleetness of a 30 year old to my young eyes, as she rushed to the aide of our next door neighbor a nice caring White woman elder whose name was Ms. Purox. Ms. Purox had suffered a stroke in that hot Philly humid heat), from North Philly to Castle Hayne North Carolina from high blood pressure, heart attacks, diabetes, and stokes. Different strokes for different folks and more strokes for brotha's; run for your sanity (I did), walk for your safety don't move too hastily, policia profiles in the makin,' will have you aching and shaking, challenge your wit, make you want to quit...la familia' love, and life ever one is the same?

I came to know something about the Jim Crow nastiness they all have to endure, and the male silence and underlying anger I inherited from my father (who never let it out). Then came the belief and panicky feelings that I was walking dust bait waiting to take a dust nap at any moment. On the day, my father suffered his heart attack our family Dr. Louis A. Chase, had to catch three different kinds of public transportation from South Philadelphia, bustin' his ass to get to our house - beat the ambulance there. Mama withheld that hurtful piece of information from me until I was in my forties, what she'd admittedly declared and knew in her heart; and then it kinda of stumbled out of Mama's mouth over a plate of grits and eggs at our home on Seattle's Beacon Hill, during one of her visits: "that ambulance……" It might as well have been the hearse say's I.

"How does it feel to be inhabited by more than one self?" What one of my homeboy's once said in response to this was: "like there's two people inside playing negro-brother games with White folks, and you're the tennis ball. Some trippin' others ain't."

Now think about this one; I knew Donald Knox my Ms. Helen's son, red hair like Malcolm X aka Malcolm Little, Mama's ace girlfriend, my Neighborhood Mama from South Philly to our block in West Philly. Home-boy was my neighborhood extended family cousin, who left life in 1983 wet like he came into the world "between piss and shit" in the nasty brown - named by Dutch East Indian Trading Company Explorers: "Hidden Creek" - Schuylkill River. I cried "What happened Mama!?" "I don't know Frederick, now don't you go worrin' yourself, won't do any good." "Got to go Mama; Got to go love you." Click… (Lord, I've got to get out to that Seattle see what's going on with that boy).

Why did Donald decide to jump overbroad, like to me, a modern day version of a "Middle Passage suicide?" Brotha Jimmy followed in Lake Washington, notha brotha overboard, cry came over the phone to me: "Jimmy's dead!" Where's Jimmy!? Have you seen Jimmy!? No, last we had a talk downtown Seattle, then he and I walked, gave well wishes in momentarily parting, Donald, I mean Jimmy, no both, are, were the same, Middle Passage made another claim, still causing insanity and pain; I knew Donald and Jimmy, Jimmy-Donald, Donald-Jimmy, both…I… love… u.

I came to know something's about the America's deceitful start in the analyses by two men of African-American descent, and "miseducation" by a third:

Frederick Douglass 19th century and John Hope Franklin 20th century: the inter color-class lines forged by "constitutional contradiction" - that self-imposed catch-22   freedom for all, while sanctioning slavery for many, indentured servitude for others, establishing a system of social-political economic pip wages for the rest.

I came to realize the segregated neighborhoods full of working class Black women and men, of a 1950's – 60's White Flight exodus - Jim Crow response to the passage of Brown in 1954: 60's civil rights laws. After came the 70's take a quick look and see window that so many U.S. folks came to complain about, moreover, most of us never heard about until the 1980's complaining started. *Let's stomp out Affirmative Action – get your own job you fucking bum*; while among others of color folks screamed embarrass-ment and moved socially politically far away as they could get. To wit, the social-economic entrenchment buttressed by1980's Reaganomics helped give segregated neighborhoods continued permanency in an already ra-cialized society, that experienced selective White flight *blow back* gentrifi-cation; the purchase of property in improvised Black, of color, European American (White) neighborhoods by wealthier folks) and helped double clutch propel launch the genre of rap – hip hop culture that took off in the 90's.

All in the spirit of the Horatio Horn blower protagonist from C. S. For-ester's novels, acceptance passport no matter what your ethnic-cultural-racial origins in the mix; *Liar Liar...I set your house, people, cultures on fire; retooled and captured your mind to make you ready for cheap hire*, said the two-dollar bigot in then pseudo integrated times, now called "post-race" times? The dis-spirit of this no different then what was blunted out to me in a Fort Still, Oklahoma barracks in early 1971, while my booted feet heels were locked at attention. "My Mama picked cotton with Negroes in Loui-siana," the fat bellied Louisianan sergeant man said to me. I then quickly retorted, "My Mama didn't pick no cotton," with forehead winkles, that my Mama never wanted me to publicly or private do. But I knew in this instance that I was permissioned to say and do by Mama via her taught-me pat response –" I was then told abruptly told to "get out my sight," with the wave of a fat over-weight nasty lookin' Louisianan finger. Sing ole to Fort Still in Oklahoma territory in state hood status.

Maybe it was the unnerving experience of hearing Mama from our West Philly home over the phone on May 13th 1985 in the afternoon sayin:' "Lord a mercy they burned those mood (MOVE) people up, they bombed them;" What the hell! --row houses burnings on Osage Ave. in West Philly, leaving 11 folks dead including five children, where the po-lice gunned down anyone trying to leave. There were 250 other folks were left homeless as the world watched and nobody raised hell. They just fire-bombed them Black folks just like the Black folks in the Greenwood neighborhood of Tulsa, Oklahoma, 1921 known as the "Black Wall Street." Only difference, on second thought that ain't no difference, Philly's 1st Black Mayor Goode, and his White employee's Fire Commissioner and Police Chief sanctioned this massacre in a racialized segregated West Philly neighborhood. Whereby, the Tulsa White folks race rioted in cognitive dissonance and old some tim-me supremacist thoughts and mentality, while the U.S. Army military ordered the air fire-bombing on Black folks; the only bombing on U.S. soil; that riot massacre left "3,000 African American dead, an over 600 successful businesses" including churches and hospitals destroyed. An event of simply European American rage that was buried to be never contemplated; just seen as some by-gone era shit. Racist "Iceman Theory" like Steven Wonder sang: *"where were you, when I needed you, last summer...?"*

So, Obama me this riddle: *Why is living in America like playing the dead block street game like the one I used to play with others on Frazier Street, in West Philly, for so many multi-colored men?*

Love, your son-nephew Frederick

p.s. Loved your Jim Crow closing down bars story in California from when you were stationed after returning from duty in the Pacific during WWII. And you did it without being served one drink. Wow! Who knew Happy ninety first belated birthday.

References

Auster, Simon. November 25, 2013. Telephone interview regarding his visit with Einstein in August, 1952.

Abrams, L.S., Anderson-Nathe, B., & Aguilar, J. (2008). Constructing masculinities in juvenile corrections. *Men and Masculinities, 11,* 22-28. Retrieved from http://jmm.sagepub.com/

Aerts, D., Apostel, L., De Moore, B. Hellemans, S., Maex, E., Van Belle, H., & Der Veken, V. (1994). World Views: from fragmentation to integration. Retrieved from http://pespmc1.vub.ac.be/

Akbar, N. (1985). *The Community of Self.* Tallahassee, FL: Mind Productions.

Alcoff, L. M. (2006). *Visible identities: Race, gender, and the self.* Retrieved from http://www.questia.com/

Alcorn, F.D. (1994*). Era of uncertainty, Resurgence of conflict confronting the 350 challenge of our multi-racial-ethnic presence.* Seattle, WA: Rockhill Press.

Aldridge, D. (2007, September 21). Reaction proves race is still an issue. *The Philadelphia Inquirer.* Retrieved from http://www.highbeam.com

Apps. J. W. (1985). *Improving practice in continuing education: Modern approaches for understanding the field and determining priorities.* San Francisco, Jossey-Bass.

Anderson, E. (Ed.). (2008). *Against the wall: Poor, young, Black and male.* Philadelphia: University of Pennsylvania Press.

Ani, M. (1994). Yurugu: *An Afrikan-centered critique of European cultural thought and behavior.* Trenton, NJ: African World Press.

Alexander, W.H. (2004). Homosexual and the racial identity conflicts and depression among African American gay males. *Trotter Review Scholarly Works*, 16, pp. 1-34.

Auerbach, C. & Silverstein, L.B. (2003). *Qualitative date: An introduction to coding and analysis.* New York, NY: New York Press.

Bakari, R. S. (1997). Epistemology from an Afrocentric perspective: Enhancing Black students' consciousness through an Afrocentric way of knowing. *Different Perspectives on Majority Rules, Paper 20.* Retrieved from http://digitalcommons.unl.edu/

Baker, H.A., Jr. (1995). Critical memory and the Black public sphere. *In The Black Public Sphere*, pp.7-37. Chicago, IL: The University of Chicago Press.

Baldwin, J.A. (1976. Black psychologist: Some issues for consideration. *Black Books Bulletin*, 4(3), 6-11.

Baldwin, J. (1962). *The fire next time.* New York, NY: Dell.

Barbour, F.B. (1970). Offensive mechanisms: The Black seventies. Boston, MA: Porter Sargent.

Belton, D. (1996). *Speak my name: Black men on masculinity and the American dream.* Boston, MA: Beacon Press.

Bentz, S., & Shapiro, J.J. (1998). *Mindful inquiry in social research.* Thousand Oaks, CA: Sage Publications.

Berger, P.L. & Luckmann, T. (2011) *The social construction of reality. A treatise in sociology of knowledge.* New York, NY: Open Road Integrated Media.

Bernal, G., & Saez-Santiago, E. (2006). Culturally centered psychological intervention). *Journal of Community Psychology*, 34, (2), 121-132. doi: 10.1002/

Bharmal, N., Kennedy, D., Jones-Lee, L., Johnson, C., Morris, D.A., Cardwell, B., Brown, A., Houston, T., Meeks, C., Vargas, R., Franco, I., Razzak, A.R., & Brown, A. (2012). Through our eyes: Exploring African-American men's perspectives on factors affecting transition to manhood. *Journal of International Medicine*, 27(2), doi: 10.1007/s11606-011-1836-0.

Billson, J.M. (1996). *Pathways to manhood: Young Black males struggle for identity.* New Brunswick, NJ: Transaction.

Bluestein, J. (2001). *Creating emotionally safe schools: A guide for educators and parents.* Deerfield Beach, FL: Health Communications.

Booker, C.B. (2000). *I wear no chain! A social history of African-African males.* Retrieved from http://www.questia.com/

Boris, E. (2003). From gender to racialized gender: Laboring bodies that matter. *Cambridge Journal*, 63, 9-13.

Boston, L. (1998). *Men of color: Fashion, history, and fundamentals.* Muskogee, OK: Artisan.

Bourdieu, P. (2001). *Masculine domination.* Palo Alto, CA: Stanford University Press.

Bourdieu, P. (1977). *Outline of theory and practice.* Cambridge: Cambridge University Press.

Bourdieu, P. (1984). *The field of cultural production: Essays on art and literature.* New York: Columbia University Press.

Breland, A.M. (1997). Airing dirty laundry: *Reasons and processes by which skin tone stratification continues to be a pervasive aspect of the African American community.* (Doctoral dissertation). Available from ProQuest Dissertations and Theses (ED431984).

Breland, A. M., Steward, R. J., Neil, D., Minami, T., Chan, C., Owen, D., & Wanda, S. C. (1999). Biracial individuals: Factors affecting racial identification. (Report No.143). Columbus, OH. (ED431156).

Bridges, E.M. (2011). Racial identity development and psychological coping strategies of undergraduate coping strategies of undergraduate and graduate African American Males, *Journal of African American Males in Education, 2,(2)*, 1-18.

Fries-Britt, S., & Griffin, K. (2007). The blackbox: How high achieving Black resist stereotypes about Black Americans. *Journal of Student Development*, 48(5), pp. 509-524

Brookfield, S.D. (1987). *Developing critical thinkers: Challenging adults to explore alternative ways of thinking and acting.* San Francisco, Jossey-Bass.

Brookfield, S. D. (2008). Radical questioning on the long walk to freedom: Nelson Mandela and the practice of critical reflection. *Adult Education Quarterly, 58*, 95-109. doi:10.1177/074/71360710150

Brown, T.J. (2005). Allan Iverson as America's most wanted: Black masculinity as a cultural site of struggle. *Journal of Intercultural Communication Research.* 34(1), pp. 65-87.

Brown, T. J. (2006). Welcome to the Terrordome: Exploring the contradictions of a hip-hop Black masculinity. In A.D. Mutua (Ed.)., *Progressive Black masculinities.* (pp. 191-213). New York, NY: Routledge.

Brown, T.J. (2011). Scripting the Black male athlete: Donovan McNabb and the double bind of the Black masculinity. In R.L. Jackson, II & M.C. Hopson, (Eds.). *Masculinity in the Black imagination Politics of Communicating Race and Manhood.* (pp. 147-166). New York, NY: Peter.

Bruner, J. (1990). *Acts of Meaning.* Boston: Harvard University Press.

Burrell, G., & Morgan, G. (1979). *Sociological paradigms an organizational analysis: Elements of the sociology of corporate life.* Portsmouth, NH: Heinemann Educational Books.

Burrell, T. (1997). Experiences and perceptions of interpersonal, environmental, and Institutional racism among African-American students in psychology graduate training. (Report No. 143). (ED4145440).

Burrell, T. (2010). *Brainwashed: Challenging the myth of Black inferiority.* New York, NY: SmileyBooks.

Butler, J. (1999). *Gender trouble-Feminism and the subversion of identity.* Retrieved from http://www.questia.com/

Bush, L. V. (1999). Am I a man?: A literature review engaging in the socio-historical dynamics of Black manhood in the United States. *The Western Journal of Black Studies, 23,(1),49-57.* Retrieved from http://web.ebscohost.com

Bush, L.V. (2004). How Black mothers participate in the development of manhood and Masculinity: What do we know about Black mothers and their sons? *Journal of Negro Education, 3,(4),*381-391. Retrieved from http://web.ebscohost/

Bynum, M.S., Best, C., Barnes, S.L. & Burton, E.T. (2008). Private Regard, Identity Protection and Perceived Racism among African American Males. *Journal of African American Studies,* 142-155. Retrieved from http://link.springer.com/

Byrd, R.P. & Guy-Sheftall, B. (Eds.). (2001). *Traps: African American men on gender and sexuality.* Bloomington, ID: Indiana University Press. Canada, G. (2000). *Reaching Up for Manhood.* Boston: Beacon Press.

Carby, H. V. (1998). *Race men.* Cambridge, MA: Harvard University Press.

Carkhuff, R. R. (1993). *The act of helping.* Amherst, MA: Resource Development Press.

Carr, W., & Kemmis, S. (1986). *Becoming critical: Education, Knowledge, and Action.* Deakin University Press.

Carroll, R. (Ed.). (1995). *Swing low: Black men writing.* New York, NY: Crown Trade.

Carruther, J.H. ((1994). *African or American: A question of intellectual allegiance.* Chicago: Kemetic Institute.

Center for Disease Control and Prevention. (2010). *A Closer Look at African American Men and High Blood Pressure Control: A Review of Psychological Factors and Systems-Level Intervention.* Atlanta: U.S Department of Health and Human Services. Retrieved from www. cdc. gov.

Carver, C. S. (1997). The internal-external scale confounds internal locus of control with expectancies of positive outcomes. *Personality Social Psychology Bulletin,* 23(16), 580-585.

Calmore, J.O. (2006). Reasonable and unreasonable suspects: The cultural construction of the anonymous Black man in Public space (here be dragons). In A. D. Mutua (Ed.), *Progressive Black masculinities.* (pp. 137-153). New York, NY: Routledge.

Chandler, K.J. (2011). How to Become a "Blackman:" Exploring African American Masculinities and the Performance of Gender. In R.L. Jackson, II & M.C. Hopson, (Eds.). *Masculinity in the Black imagination Politics of communicating race and manhood.* (pp. 55-88). New York, NY: Peter Lang.

Chandler, K.J. (2007). How to become a "Blackman:" Exploring African American masculinities and the performance of gender. (Doctoral dissertation). Available from ProQuest Dissertation and Theses database.

Clark, K. (2004). *Black Manhood in James Baldwin, Ernest J. Gaines, and August Wilson.* University of Illinois Press.

Chavez, R.C. & O'Donnell, J. (Eds.). (1998). *Speaking the unpleasant: The Politics of (non) engagement in the multicultural education terrain.* Albany, NY: SUNY Press.

Clandinin, D. J. (2007). *Handbook of narrative inquiry mapping a methodology.* Sage Publications.

Clandinin, D. J. & Connelly, F. M. (Ed.). (1990). Stories of experience and narrative inquiry, *Educational Researcher,* 19(5), pp. 2-14.

Clark, A. & Erickson, G. (2003). (Eds.). *Teaching inquiry: Living the research in everyday practice.* London: Routledge-Falmer.

Clatterbaugh, K, (1998) What is problematic about masculinities. *Men and Masculinities,* 1(1), pp. 24-45.

Coleman, K. (2005). *Power, money, and sexuality: The Black masculine paradigm* (Doctoral dissertation. Available from ProQuest Dissertation and Theses database.

Coles, T. (2009) Negotiating the field of masculinity, The production and reproduction of multiple dominant masculinities. *Men and Masculinities, 20,* 1-15. Retrieved from http://online.sagepub.com/

Collins, P.H. (2006). A telling difference: Dominance, strength, and Black masculinities. In A.Mutua, (Ed.). *Progressive Black Masculinities.* (pp. 73-97). New York, NY: Routledge.

Collins, P. H. (2000). *Black feminist thought: Knowledge, consciousness, and the politics of empowerment.* New York: Routledge.

Collins, P.H. (1998). Intersection of race, class, gender, and nation: Some implications a Black family study. *Comparative Family Studies.* 29(1), pp. 27-36.

Compton-Lilly, C. (2009). *The Development of habitus over time.* Working Paper: (WCER-2009-7). Madison, WI: Wisconsin Center for Education Research. University of Wisconsin-Madison. Retrieved from http://www.wcer.wisc.edu.

Cooper, F.R. (2006). Race, sex, and working identities, against bipolar Black masculinity: intersectionality, assimilation, identity performance, and hierarchy. *U.S. Davis, Law Review, 39,* 855-901. Retrieved from http://www.lexisnexis.com/

Courtenay, W. H. (2000). Constructions of masculinity and their influence on men's well-being: A theory of gender and health. Social *Science & Medicine, 50,* 1385-1401.

Crenshaw, K. (1989). Demarginalizing the intersection of race and sex: A Black feminist critique of antidiscrimination doctrine, feminist theory and antiracist politics. *Feminist Theory & Antiracist Politics*, pp. 139-167. Chicago, IL: University of Chicago Legal Forum

Crenshaw, K. (1991). Mapping the margins: Intersectionality, identity politics, and violence against women of color. *Stanford Law Review, 43*, 1241-1299.

Cross, M. & Naidoo, D. (2012). Race, diversity pedagogy: Mediated learning experience for transforming racist habitus and predispositions. *The Review of Education, Pedagogy, and Cultural Studies, 34*, 227-244. doi: 10.1080/10714413.2012.7355588

Cross. T. (1987). *The Black power imperative: Racial inequality and the politics of nonviolence.* New York: Faulkner Books.

Dalal, F. (2002). *Race, colour and the processes of racialization: New perspectives from group analysis, psychoanalysis and sociology.* New York, NY: Brunner-Routledge.

Davidson, A.L. (1996). *Making and molding identity in schools: Student narratives on race, gender, and academic engagement.* Albany, New York: State University of New York Press.

Delgado, R, & Stefancic, J. (2001). *Critical race theory: An introduction.* New York, NY: New York Press.

DeMause, L. (1975). *The New Psychohistory.* New York: Psychohistory Press.

Deonna, J.A. (2006). Emotion, perception and perspective. *Dialectica, 60,(1),* 20-46.

Diamond, J. B. & Spillane, J. P. (2004). Teachers' expectations and sense of responsibility for student learning: The importance race, class, and organizational habitus. *Anthropology and Education Quarterly,* 35(1), 75-98.

247770803

Doss. D.R. (2008). *African-American men and masculinity: A case study of young adult African-American men.* (Doctoral dissertation). Retrieved from ProQuest Dissertation and Theses Database.

Dubois, W.E.B. (1903). *The souls of Black folks.* Chicago: A.C. Mclurg.

Dyson, E.M. (1996*). Between God and gangsta rap. Bearing witness to Black culture.* New York, NY: Oxford Press.

Dyson, E.M. (2007). Know what I mean: Reflections on hip hop. New York: Basic Books.

Dyson, E.M. (October, 2008, 23). America as post-racial or post racist? Retrieved from http://youtube.com.

Eckert, P., & McConnell-Ginet, S. (1995). Constructing meaning, constructing ourselves: Snapshots of language, gender, and class from Belten High. In Hall, K., & Buchholtz, M., (Eds.). *Gender articulated: Arrangements of language and the socially constructed self* (pp. 469-507). London and New York: Routledge.

Edward, A. & Polite, C. K. (1992). *Children of the dream: The psychology of Black success.* New York, NY: Anchor Books.

Edmond, K. (1993). For the cool in you. [CD]. Los Angeles, CA: Epic Records.

Eisner, E. W. (1985). Aesthetic modes of knowing. In Eisner, E.W. (Ed.), *Learning and Teaching: The Ways of Knowing* (pp. 2-14). Chicago, IL: University of Chicago Press.

Eisner, E. W. (1998). *The enlightened eye: Qualitative inquiry and the enhancement of educational practice.* Columbus, OH: Merrill.

Elksnin, L. K., & Elksnin, N. (2003). "Fostering social-emotional intelligence in the classroom." *Education,* 124(1). www.questia.com

Ellison, R. (1990). *Invisible man.* New York, NY: Vintage International.

Epstein, T. (2000). Adolescents' perspectives on racial diversity in U.S.
history: Case studies from and urban classroom. *American Educational Research Journal, 37*(1), 185-214. doi:10.3102/002831203.

Eversley, S. (2004). *The real Negro: The question of authenticity in the twentieth-century African American literature*. London: Routledge.

Few, A. L. (2007). *Racialized gender. Black encyclopedia of sociology*. Retrieved from http://www/blackwellreference.com/

Finucane, M. L., Slovic, C., Mertz, K., Flynn, J., & Satterfield, T.A. (2000). Gender, race, and perceived risk: The "White male" effect. *Health, Risk & Society, 2*, 159-172. Retrieved from http://www.tandfonline.com/

Ford, K.A. (2011). Doing *fake* masculinity, being *real men*: Present and future constructions of Self among Black College Men. *Symbolic Interaction, 34*, 38-62. doi: 10.1525/

Fordham, S. (1996). *Blacked Out: Dilemma of race, identity, and success at Capital high*. Chicago, IL: University of Chicago Press.

Franklin, II, C.W. & Andre, M.C. (1995). Some factors influencing success among African-American men: A preliminary study. *Journal of Men's Studies, 3*, 191-197. Retrieved from http://proquest.umi.com/

Franklin, A.J. (1999). Invisibility syndrome and racial identity development in psychotherapy and counseling African American Men. *The Counseling Psychologist, 27, (6)*, 761-793. Doi:10.1/77/0011000099276002

Franklin, J.H. (1993). *The Color line: Legacy for the twenty-first century*. Columbia: University of Missouri Press.

Freire, P., & Faundez, A. (1987). *Learning to question: A pedagogy of liberation*. United Kingdom, UK: Blackwell Publishing.

Fuller, N., Jr. (1971). *The United Independent Compensatory Code/System/Concept: A textbook/workbook for thought, speech and/or action for victims of racism (white supremacy).* Publisher: Author.

Fusco, C. (1995*). English is broken here: Notes on cultural fusion in the Americas.* New York, NY: The New Press.

Fusco, C.& Wallis, B. (Eds.). (2003). *Only skin deep Changing Visions of the American Self.* New York, NY: Harry N. Abrams, Inc.

Garner, H., Haertel, G. D., & Walberg, H. J. (1993-1994). Synthesis of research: What helps students learn. *Educational Leadership,* 51(4), pp. 74-79.

Gates, H.L., Jr. (Ed.). (1997). *Thirteen ways of looking at a Black Man.* New York, NY: Vintage Books.

Gause, C.P. (2005). The ghetto sophisticates: Performing Black masculinity, saving lost souls, and serving the leaders of the new school. *The Journal of Culture and Education,* 9 (1) 17-31.

Gray, H. (1995). *Watching: Television and the Struggle for Blackness.* Minneapolis, University of Minnesota Press.

Greenlee, S. (1969). *The spook who sat by the door.* London, UK: Allison and Busby.

Greenwood, D., & Levin, M. (1998). *Introduction to action research: Social research for social change.* Thousand Oaks, CA: Sage Publications.

Grenfell, M. & James, D. (1998). Bourdieu and education: Acts of practical theory. Retrieved from http://www.questia.com.

Gooding, V.A., Sr. (2012). *Managing Multi-generational anger in African American males,* Family & Corrections Network. Retrieved from http://www.fenetwork.org/

Goldberg, S. C. (1999). The psychology of epistemology of self-knowledge. *Synthese, Kluwer Academic Publishers,* 118, 165-199.

Goldman, D. (1995). *Emotional intelligence: Why it can matter more than IQ.* New York, NY: Bantum.

Gibb, J. T. (1988). *Young Black and male in America: An endangered species.* Westport, CT: Auburn House.

Gibbs, J. T. (1999). The social construction of race, ethnicity, and culture. In Garrod, A, Ward, J. V., & Robinson, R. K. (Eds.). *In Souls looking Black: Portraits of growing up Black* (pp. 77-98). Retrieved from http://www.questia.com.

Gibson, J. R. (2009). *Why Black men don't teach and why we should: Understanding the existing African-American male teacher shortage.* Amazon Digital Services: KITABU.

Gilbert, R., & Gilbert, P. (1998). *Masculinity goes to school.* Florence, KY: Routledge.

Grant, C.A. & Ladson-Billings, G. (Eds.). (1997). *Dictionary of multicultural education.* Phoenix, AZ: Oryx Press.

Grier, W. H. & Cobbs, P. M. (1968) *Black rage: Two Black psychiatrists reveal the full dimensions of the inner conflicts and the desperation of Black life in the United States.* New York, NY: Basic Books.

Guinier, L. (2010). Introduction. In Parks, G.S. & Hughey, M. W. (Eds.). , *Twelve angry men: True stories of being a Black man in America today.* New York: The New Press.

Hall, E. T. (1990). *The hidden dimension.* Anchor Books.

Hall, R. E. (1997). Human Development across the Lifespan as Identity Model for Biracial Males. *Journal of African American Men, 2,* 65-80. doi: 10.1007/s12111-977-1017-8

Hall, R.E. (2007). Racism as health risk for African American males: Correlations between hypertension and skin color. *Journal of African American Studies.* doi: 10.1007/s12111-007-9081-1

Hammond, W.P., & Mattis, J.S. (2005). Being a man about it: Manhood meaning among African American men. *Psychology of Men & Masculinity. 6*, (2), 114-126.

Hargrow, A.M. (2001). Racial identity development: The Case of Mr. X, an African American. Journal of Mental Health Counseling, 23,(3), 1-10. Retrieved from http://www.questia.com/

Harper, P.B. (1996). *Are we not men? Masculine anxiety and the problem of African-American identity.* New York, NY: Oxford University Press.

Head, J. (2004). *Black Men and Depression: Saving lives, healing our families and friends.* New York, NY: Harlem Moon.

Hecht, M.L., Collier, M.J.,& Ribeau, S.A. (1993). *African American communication: ethnic identity and cultural interpretation.* Newbury Park, CA: Sage Publications.

Hegelian dialectic. *Journal of Black Studies, 27*, 731-750. doi.10.1177/002193479700601

Hemmings, A. (1998). The self-transformation of African American achievers. *Youth Society, 29*, 330-368. Retrieved from http://yas.sagepub.com/

Hogan, P.C. (2001). *The Culture of Conformism Understanding Social Consent. Understanding Social Consent.* Durham, NC: Duke University Press.

Holloway, J.E. (Ed.). (1991). *Africanisms in American Culture.* Bloomington, IN: Indiana University Press.

Hooks, B. (1992). *Black looks: Race and representation.* Boston: South End Press.

Hooks, B. (2004). *We Real Cool, Black Men and Masculinity.* London, England: Routledge.

Hopkinson, N. & Moore, N.Y. (2006). *Deconstructing Tyrone A New Look at Black Masculinity in the Hip Hop Generation.* San Francisco, CA: Cleis Press, Inc.

Horvat, E. M. & Antonio, A. L. (1999). "Hey those shoes are out of uniform:" African American girls in an elite high school and the importance of habitus. *Anthropology and Education Quarterly.* 30(3), pp. 317-342.

Howard, L. C. (2006). *Doin'me: Eight urban adolescent African American males understanding of masculinity.* (Doctoral Dissertation). Available from Proquest Dissertation and These database. (AAT 3221603)

Hurt, B. P. (Producer) (1998). [DVD] *I am a man: Black masculinity in America.* Newark, NJ: God Bless the Child Productions.

Hurt, B. P. (2008, November 9). *Barrack and Curtis: Examining Black Masculinity* [Video file]. Retrieved from http://www.bhurt.com

Hunter A.G. & Davis, J.E. (1994). Hidden voices of Black men: The meaning, structure, and complexity of manhood. *Journal of Black Studies, 25,* 20-38. Retrieved from http://jbs.sagepub.com/

Johnson, R. B., & Onwuegbuzie, A. J. (2004). Mixed methods research: A research paradigm whose time has come. *Educational researcher,* 33(7), 14-26.

Kawash, S. (1997). *Dislocating the colorline: Identity, hybridity, and singularity, in African-American narrative.* Palo-Alto, CA: Sanford University Press.

Kilson, M. (2000). *Claiming place: Biracial young adults of the post-civil rights era.* Westport, CT: Bergin and Garvey.

Kiwana, B. (2002). *Young Black and the crisis in African American culture: The hip hop generation.* New York: Basic Books.

Lemelle, A. J. (1997) *Black male deviance.* West Port, CT: Praeger

Pena, Gomez-G. (2006). *Border hysteria and the war against difference.* Retrieved from www2.ucsc.edu/raza/pipeline/border.pdf.

Pierre, M.R., & Mahalik, J.R. (2005). Examining African self-consciousness and Black racial identity as predictors of Black men's psychological well-being. *Cultural Diversity and Ethnic Psychology*, 11(1), 28-40

Pleck, E. H. & J. H. Pleck (1980). *The American man.* Englewood Cliffs, NJ: Prentice Hall.

Jackson, R.L., II, & Dangerfield, C.L. (2004). Defining Black masculinity as cultural property: Toward an identity negotiation paradigm. *African American communication & identities. Essential Readings, 197*, 120-130.

Jackson, R.L.II, (2002). Introduction: Theorizing and analyzing the nexus between cultural and gendered identities and the body. *Communication Quarterly*, 50(3), 245-250.

Jackson, R.L., II, (2005). *Scripting the Black masculine body: identity, discourse, and racial politics in popular media.* Albany, N.Y.: SUNY Press.

Jackson, R.L., II, & Hopson, M.C. (Eds). (2006). Introduction. *Masculinity in the Black imagination: Politics of communicating race and manhood.* New York, NY: Peter Lang.

Jackson, R.L. II, & Hopson, M.C. (Eds.). (2011). *Masculinity in the Black imagination: Politics of communicating race and manhood.* New York, NY: Peter Lang.

Jackson, R.L., II. (2002). Introduction: Theorizing and analyzing the nexus between cultural and gender identities and the body. *Communicating Quarterly, 50,(2)*, 245-249.

Johns, D.J. (2007). *Re-imaging Black masculine identity: an Investigation of the "problem" surrounding the construction of Black masculinity in America.* Retrieved from http://www.questia.com/

Johnson, R. R. (2003). Autobiography and transformative learning: Narrative in search of self.

Journal of Transformative Education, 1, 227-244. Retrieved from http://jtd.sagepub.com/

Joiner, V.E., Jr., & Walker, R.L. (2002). Construct validity of a measure of acculturative stress in African Americans. *Psychological Access, 14*, 462-466.

Kearney, M. (1984). *World View*. Novato, CA: Chandler & Sharp.

Kennedy, L. (1996). Alien nation: White male paranoia and imperial culture in the United States. *Journal of American Studies*, 30(1), pp. 87-100.

Kofer, B. K. (2008). Personal epistemology and culture. In M. S. Khine (Ed.). *Knowing, knowledge, and beliefs* (pp. 3-22). Retrieved from http://www.questia.com/

Koltko-Rivera, M.E. (2004). The psychology of worldviews. *Review of General Psychology, 8,(1),*-3-58. doi: 10.1037/1089-2680.8.1.3

Korgen. K. O. (1998). *From Black to Biracial Transforming Racial identity among Americans.* Retrieved from http://www.questia.com/

Koroma, M.A. (2003). "Black" or "African American?" *National Association of Black Journalists, 21,* 1-3. Retrieved from http://search.proquest.com/

Lau, R. W. K. (2004). Habitus and the practical logic of practice: An interpretation. *Sociology, 38(2),* 369-387. doi:10.1177/0038038504040870

Laubscher, L. (2005). Toward a (de) constructive psychology of African American men. *Journal of Black Psychology, 31,* 111-129. Retrieved from http://jbp.sagepub.com/

Leary, J.D. (2005). *Post traumatic slave syndrome America's legacy of enduring injury and healing.* Milwaukie, OR: Uptone Press.

Lefcourt, H. M. (1982). *Locus of control: Current trends in theory and research.* Hillsdale, NJ: Lawrence Erlbaum.

Lemelle, A. J. Jr., (1995). *Black male deviance.* Westport, CT: Praeger.

Lemelle, A. J. Jr., (2010). *Black masculinity and sexual politics.* New York, NY: Taylor & Francis.

Livingston, J. A. (2011). Metacognition: An overview. Retrieved from gse.buffalo.edu/

Lubiano, W. (Ed.). (1998*). The house that race built: Original essays by Toni Morrison, Angela Y. Davis, Cornel West, and others on Black Americans and politics in America today.* New York, NY: Vintage Books.

Lum, C. M. K. (1991). Communication and cultural insularity: The Chinese immigrant experience. *Critical Studies in Mass Communication,* 8, 91-101.

Madhibuti, H. R. (1991). *Black men: Obsolete, single, dangerous?* The Afrikan American family in transition. Chicago, IL: Third World Press.

Maddow, R. (2012, August, 12). *Reproductive rights and women's health.* Retrieved from http://www.msnbc.com

Marshall, J. (2004). Living systemic thinking: Exploring quality in first-person action research. Action Research, 2(3), 305-325. doi:10.77/1476750304045945.

Mahik, J.R., Pierre, M.R., & Wan, S.S.C. (2006). Examining racial identity and masculinity as correlates of self-esteem and psychological distress in Black men. Journal of Multicultural Counseling and Development, 34,(2), 94-104.

Martin, B.E. & Harris, F., III. (2006). Examining productive conceptions of masculinities lessons learned from academically driven African American male student-athletes. *Journal of Men's Studies, 14,(3),* 359-378.

Maton, K. (2008). Habitus. In M. Grenfell (Ed.), *Pierre Bourdieu: Key concepts* (pp. 49-66). UK: London, Acumen.

McDonald, M. & Wingfield, A. H. (2008). (In)visibility blues: The paradox of institutional racism. *Sociological Spectrum*, 29(1), pp. 28-50.

McDonough, P. M. (1997). *Choosing Colleges: How social class and schools structure opportunity.* Albany, NY: State University of New York Press.

Merida, K. (2007). *Being a Black man: At the corner of progress and peril.* New York, NY: PublicAffairs.

Meyers, L. J. (1988). *Understanding an Afrocentric world view: Introduction to an optimal psychology.* Dubuque, IA: Kendall/Hunt.

Miller, R. L. (1992). The human ecology of multiracial identity. In M.P.P. Root (Ed.), *Racially mixed people in America* (pp. 24-36). Newbury Park, CA: Sage Publications.

Mills, C. (1997). *The racial contract.* Ithaca, NY: Cornell University Press.

Mistry, J., and Rogoff, B. (1994). Remembering in cultural context. In Lonner, W.J., and Malpass, R. S. (Eds.), *Psychology and Culture* (pp. 139-144). Needham Heights, MA: Allyn and Bacon.

Mirza, H. S. (1999). Black masculinities and schooling: A Black feminist response. British Journal of Education. 20(1), pp. 137-147.

Molesworth, C., (Ed.). (2012*). The works of Alain Locke (The collective Black`writings).* New York, NY: Oxford University Press.

Moore, L. (2010). *Fine specimens of manhood: The Black boxer's body and the avenue to equality racial advancement, and manhood in the nineteenth century.* MELUS, 35.(4). pp. 59-84. Retrieved from http://www.questia.com/

Mutua, A.D. (Ed.). (2006). *Progressive Black masculinities.* New York, NY: Routledge.

Najarian, A. (2005). Discuss in what ways does one's habitus and cultural capital affect the relationship between schooling and work? Retrieved from http://stickyatlas.com.

Nedhari, A. (2009) In search of manhood: The Black male's struggle for identity and power. *Student Pulse, 1,(11),* 1-7. Retrieved from: http://www.studentpulse.com/

Nichols, E. (1988). *Philosophical aspects of cultural differences.* Publisher: Author.

Nightingale, D. J., & Cromby, J. (1999*). Social Constructionist Psychology: A critical analysis of theory.* Maidenhead, UK: Open Press University.

Nobles, W.W. (1990). The infusion of African and African American content: A question of content and intent. In A.G., Hilliard, III, L. Payton-Steward, & Williams, (Eds.), *Infusion of African American content in school curriculum.* (pp. 5-22). Morristown, NJ: Aaron Press.

Nobles, W.W., Goddard, L.L., Cavil, W.E., & George, P.Y. (1987). *African-American families: Issues, insights, and directions.* Oakland, CA: A Black Family Institute Publication.

Norguera, P.A. (1997). Reconsidering the "crisis" of the Black male in America. Social Justice, pp. 2-13. Retrieved from http://proquest.umi.com/

O'Donnell, S. Meyer, I. H. & Schwartz, S. (2011). Increased risk of suicide attempts among Black and Latino lesbians, gay men, and bisexuals. *American Journal of Public Health, 101,(6),* 1051-1060. doi:10.2105/AJPH.2510.300032

Oliver, W. (2006). "The streets:" An alternative Black male socialization institution. *Journal of Black Studies, 36,(6),* 918-937. Retrieved from http://jbs.sagepub.com/

Parham, T.A., & McDavis, R. (1987). Black men, An endangered species: Who's really pulling the trigger? *Journal of Counseling and Development, 66,* 24-27. Retrieved from http://web.ebscohost.com/

Parks, G.S., & Hugley, M.W. (2010). *12 angry men: true stories of being a Black man in America today.* New York, NY: The New Press.

Palmer, B.E.F., II. (2012). *Integrating African-centered worldview and acculturation as predictor of positive psychological outcomes in African Americans.* (Doctorial dissertation). Available from ProQuest Dissertation and Theses database.

Pascoe, C.J. (2003) Multiple Masculinities? Teenage Boys Talk about Jocks and Gender? *American Behavioral Scientist, 46, 10,* 1423-1438. Retrieved from http://abs.sagepub.com/

Pateman, C. & Mills, C. (2007). *Contract and domination.* Cambridge, UK: Polity Press.

Perkins, E. (1991). *Home is a dirty street The social oppression of Black children.* Chicago, IL: Third World Press.

Petin, M.A. (2011). "Are you in the brotherhood?" Humor, Black masculinity, and queer identity on prime-time television. In Jackson, R.L.,(II), & Hopson, M.C. (Eds.), *Masculinity in the Black imagination: Politics of communicating race and manhood* (pp. 89-102). New York,NY: Peter Lang.

Philogene, G. (2000). Blacks as serviceable other. *Journal of Community & Applied Social Psychology, 10,* 139-401.

Philogene, G. (1999). *From Black to African American: A new social representation.* Westport, CT: Praeger Publishers.

Pierre, C. M. (1970). Offensive Mechanisms: *The Black seventies.* In Barbour, F. (Ed.) (pp. 265-282). Boston, MA: Porter Sargent Publishing.

Pierre, M.R., & Mahalik, J.R. (2005). Examining African self-consciousness and Black racial identity as predictors of Black men's psychological well-being. *Cultural Diversity and Ethnic Minority Psychology, 11,(1)*,28-40. doi: 10.1037/1099-9809.

Poulson-Bryant, S. (2005). *Hung: A meditation on the measure of Black men in America.* New York, NY: Doubleday.

Poussaint, A. F. & Alexander, A. (2000). *Lay my burden down. Unraveling suicide and the mental health crisis among African Americans.* Boston, MA: Beacon Press.

Price, J. N. (2000). (Ed.). *Lesson from against the odds: The meaning of school and relationship in the lives of six young African-American men.* Stanford, CT: Ablex Publishing.

Ransby, B., & Matthews, T. (1993). *Black popular culture and the transcendence of patriarchal illusions.* In Race & Class Black America the street and campus (57-68). Thousand Oaks, CA: Sage Publications.

Rennallis, P. A. (2006). *Black middle school students perceptions of success and their influence on academic performance.* (Doctoral dissertation). Retrieved from Proquest UMI dissertations 32175771

Rich, A.C. (1986). *Blood, bread, and poetry: Selected prose, 1979-1985.* New York, NY: Norton.

Richardson, R. (2007). *Black masculinity and the U.S. South from Uncle Tom to gangsta.* Athens: University of Georgia Press.

Rios, V.M. (2009). The Consequences of the criminal justice pipeline on Black and Latino masculinity. *The Annals of the American Academy of Political and Social Science, 623*, 150-162. doi: 10.1177/0002716208330489

Roberts, D. (2011). *Fatal Invention how science, politics, and big business re-create race in the twenty-first century.* New York, NY: The New Press.

Robinson, E. (2010). *Disintegration The splintering of Black America.* New York, N.Y.: Doubleday.

Robinson, J., & Biran, M. (2006). Discovering self relationships between African identity and academic achievement. *Journal of Black Studies, 37,(1),* 46-68. doi:10.1177/0021934704272149.

Robinson, S. (2000). *Marked men: White masculinity in crisis.* Retrieved from http://www.questia.com/

Romanine, S. (1999). *Communicating gender.* Mahwah, N.J.: Lawrence Erlbaum Associates.

Rome, D. (2004). Black demons: The Media's depiction of the African American male criminal stereotype. Retrieved from: http//www.questia.com/

Rogers, J.A.(1967). *Sex and Race-Volume I.* St. Petersburg, FL.: Helga M. Rogers.

Root, M.P.P. (Ed.). (1992). Racially mixed people in America. Newbury Park, CA: Sage Publications.

Ross, M.P.P. (1998). In search of Black men's masculinities. *Feminist Studies, 24,* 599-626.

Rotter, J. B. (1990). Internal vs. external control of reinforcement: A case history of a variable. *American Psychologist, 45*(4), pp. 489-493.

Royster, F. T. (2011). Here's Chance to dance our way out of our constrictions: P-Funk's Black masculinity and the performance of imaginative freedom. Poroi, *An Interdisciplinary Journal of Rhetorical Analysis and Intervention, 7,(2),* 1-42. Retrieved from http://ir.uiowa.edu/

Saint-Aubin, A. F. (1994). The dis-ease of Black men in White supremacist, patriarchal culture. Callaloo, 17,(4), 1054-1073. Retrieved from http://fgul.idm.oclc.org/

Saint-Aubin, A.F. (2002) A grammar of Black masculinity: A body of science. *Journal of Men's Studies, 10,(3)*, 247-270.

Sagor, R. (1992). *How to conduct collaborative action research.* Alexandria, VA: Association for Supervision and Curriculum Development.

Sauza, D. (1995). *End of Racism.* New York: Free Press.

Schostak, J. F. (2005). Interviewing and representation in qualitative research. Berkshire, UK: Open University Press.

Sewell, T. (1997*). Black masculinities and schooling: How Black boys survive modern schooling.* Staffordshire, England: Trentham Books.

Shade, B. J. R. (1997). *Culture, style, and the educative process: Making schools work for racially diverse students.* Springfield, IL: Charles C. Thomas.

Shelton, J.N. & Sellers, R. M. (2000). Situational stability and variability in African American racial identity. *Journal of Black Psychology, 26*, 27-48. doi:10.1177/0095798400026001002

Shen, W. & Dumani, S. (2013). The complexity of marginalized identities: The social construction of identities, multiple identities, and the experience of exclusion. *Industrial and Organizational Psychological, 6,(1)*, 84-87. Retrieved from onlinelibary.wiley.com/doi/10.1111/

Shkedi, A. (2005). *Multiple case narrative: A qualitative approach to studying multiple populations.* Amsterdam: John Benjamin's Publishing.

Shrilling, C. (2003). *The body in social theory.* Thousand Oaks, CA: Sage Publications.

Shujaa, M.J. (1993). Education and schooling: You can have one without the other. *Urban Education, 27*, 328-351. Retrieved from http://uex.sagepub.com/

Shujaa M.J. (1994). *Too much schooling, too little education: The paradox of Black life in White Societies.* Trenton, NJ: African World Press.

Simone, T. M. (1989) *About race: Race in postmodern America.* Brooklyn, NY: Autonomedia.

Sinyangwe, S. (2012). The Significance of mixed-race: Public perception of Barack Obama's race and the effects of Obama's race on public support for his presidency. *Social Science Research Network*, pp. 1-35. doi: 10.2139/ssrn.1910209

Smith, D.T. (2012). Don't be too Black, Mr. President: The racial effect of President Obama's performance in the 2012 Presidential Debates. Retrieved from www.darronsmith.com/

Smith, E. J. (2006). Strength-based counseling model. *The Counseling Psychologist*, 34(1), 13-79. doi: 10.1177/0011000000.

Smith, W.A., Hung, M. & Franklin, J.D. (2011*). Racial battle fatigue and the misEducation of Black men: Racial microaggressions, societal problems, and environmental stress.* (pp.1-16). Retrieved from http://www.questia.com/

Spradley, P. (2001). *Strategies for educating the adult Black male in college.* Washington, DC: Off ice of Educational Research and Improvement (ED). Retrieved from ERIC database. (ED464524.

Spraggins, D.J., Jr. (1999). African American masculinity: Power and expression. *Journal of African American Men, 4,(3),* 45-72. Retrieved from http://iibp/chadwyck.com/

Spivey, D. (1978). *Schooling for the new slavery Black industrial education,* 1868-1915. Westport, CT: Greenwood Press.

Squires, C. R. (2002). Rethinking the Black public sphere: An alternative vocabulary for multiple public spheres. *Communication Theory, 24,(4),* 446-468.

Staples, R. (1982). *Black male's role in American society.* San Francisco, CA: The Black Scholar Press.

Slater, J. J. (1996). *Anatomy of a collaboration: A study of a college education and public school partnership.* Routledge.

Steele, C.M. (1997). A threat in the air: How stereotypes shape intellectual test performance of African Americans. *Journal of Personality and Social Psychology,* 52, 613-629.

Steele, C.M. & Anderson, A. (1995). Stereotype threat and the intellectual test performance of African Americans. *Journal of Personality and Psychology,* 16(5), 792-811.

Stephan, C. W. (1992). Mixed-heritage individuals: Ethnic-identity and trait characteristics. In Root, M.P.P. (Ed.), *Racially mixed people in America* (pp. 50-63). Newbury Park, CA: Sage Publications.

Stephens, T. Braithwaite, H., Johnson, L., Harris, C., Katkowsky, S.& Troutman, A. (2008). Cardiovascular risk reduction for African American men through health empowerment and anger management. *Health Education Journal, 67,* 208-218. Doi:10.1177/0017896908094638

Stevenson, H.C. (1997). Managing anger: Protective, proactive, or adaptive racial socialization identity profiles and African-American manhood development. *Journal of Preventive Intervention in the Community, 6,(1),2,*35-61.

Stevenson, H.C., Jr. (2002) Wrestling with destiny: The cultural socialization of anger and healing in African American males. *Journal of Psychology and Christianity. 21 (3),* 357-364.

Stewart, E.C. & Bennett, M.J (1991). *American cultural patterns: A cross-cultural perspective.* Yarmouth, ME: Intercultural Press.

Stowe, H. B. (1952). *Uncle Tom's Cabin.* Mead and Company.

Sue, D.W., Capodilupo, C.M., Torina, G.C., Bucceri, J. M., Holder, A.M.B., Nadal, K. L., & Esquilin, M. (2007). Racial miscroaggressions in everyday life, implications for clinical practice. *American Psychologist, 62,(4),* 272-286. doi: 10.1037/0003.066X62.4.271

Sue, D. W. (1981). *Counseling the culturally different: Theory and practice.* New York: Wiley.

Sue, D.W. (2003). Dismantling the myth of a color-blind society. *Diverse Issues in Higher Education.* Retrieved from http://diverseducation.com.

Summers, M. (2004). *Manliness and its discontents: The Black middle class and the transformation of masculinity, 1900-1930.* Retrieved from http://www.questia.com/

Steele, C. M. (1999). Thin ice: Stereotype threat and Black college students. *Journal of Black Studies, 16,(3),* 1-10. Retrieved from http://www.jstor.org/

Swartz, D.L.(2002). The sociology of habit: The perspective of Pierre Bourdieu. *The Occupational Therapy Journal of Research, 22,*615-695.

Tilly, C. (1998). *Durable Inequality.* Berkley and Los Angeles, CA: University of California Press.

Thompson-Miller, R., & Feagin, J. R. (2007). Continuing injuries of racism: Counseling in a racist context. The Counseling Psychologist, 35,106-115. doi: 10.1177/0011000006294664

Thompson, E.H. Jr., & Whearty, P.M. (2004). Older men's sociological participation: The importance of masculinity ideology. *Journal of Men's Studies, 13,(1),*1-19. Retrieved from http://www.questia.com/

Tough, P. (2009, December 13). The Obama effect. *New York Times Magazine.* Retrieved from http://www.nytime.com/

Tyree, T. C.M., Byerly, C., & Hamilton, K.A. (2012). Representations of (new) Black masculinity: A news-making case study. *Journalism, 13,* 467-481. doi: 10.1177/1464884911421695

Upchurch, C. (1997). *Convicted in the womb: One man's journey from prisoner to peacemaker.* New York, NY: Bantam Books.

Vasquez, J.M. (2010). Blurred borders for some but not "others:" Racialization "flexible ethnicity," gender, and third-generation Mexican American identity. *Sociological Perspective, 53,(1)*, 45-71, doi: 10.11525/

Wacquant, L.J.D. (1993). From ruling class to field of power: An interview with Pierre Boudieu on La Noblesse, d' Etat. Theory, Culture, and Society, 10, 19-44. doi:10.1177/026327693010003002.

Wade, J.C., & Rochlen, A. B. (2013). Introduction: Masculinity, identity, and the health and well-being of African American men. *Psychology, Men, & Masculinity, 3*,1-6. Retrieved from http://www.apa.org/

Wang, M.C., & Haertel, G.D. (1993-1994). What helps students learn? *Synthesis of Research*, 51(4), pp. 74-79. Retrieved from http:www.ascd.org.

Walden, D. L. (2008). *"I'm gonna let you define me:" A qualitative investigation of racial development in Black men.* (Doctoral dissertation). Retrieved from retrieved from http://search.proquest.com

Walker, L., Butland, D, & Connell, R.W. (2000). Boys on the road: Masculinities car culture and road safety education. *Journal of Men's Studies*, 8(2) pp. 153-169.

Wallace, M. O. (2002). *Constructing the Black masculine: Identity and ideality in African American men's literature and culture, 1775-1995.* Durham, NC: Duke University Press.

Wallace, T. (1984). *Bloods: Black veterans of the Vietnam War: An oral history.* New York: Random House.

Watkins, D. C. (2012). Depression over the adult life course for African American men: Toward framework for research and practice. *American Journal of Men's Health, 6*,(3), 194-210. Retrieved from http://jmh.sagepub.com/

Weinhold, B., & Elliott, L. (1979). *Transpersonal Communication: How to establish contact with yourself and others.* Englewood, NJ: Prentice Hall.

West, C. (1993). *Race matters.* Boston: Beacon Press.

Wells, T.L. (1992). *Learned effectiveness: An empirical validation.* Retrieved from ERIC data base. (ED367919).

White, J.L. & Cones, J.H., III. (Ed.). (1999) *Black man emerging facing the past and seizing a future in America.* New York, NY: Routledge.

Whiting, G. W. & Lewis, T. (2008). On Manliness: Black masculinity revisited. *The Journal of Black Masculinity, 6,(1),*1-13. Retrieved from http://www.blackmasculinity.com/

Wideman, J. E. (1994). *Fatheralong: A meditation of fathers and sons, race and society.* New York, NY: Patheon Books.

Wilkins, A. (2012). "Not out to start a revolution:" Race, gender, and emotional restraint among Black university men. *Journal of Contemporary Ethnography, 41, (1),* 31-65. Retrieved from http://sagepub.com/

Williams, D.R. & Williams-Morris, R. (2000)/ Racism and mental health: The African American experience. *Ethnicity and Health, 5 (3/4),* 243-268.

Winant, H. (1994). *Racial conditions: Politics, theory, comparisons.* Minneapolis, MN: University of Minnesota Press.

Winant, H. (1998). Racial dualism at century's end. In W. Lubiano (Ed.). *The House that Race Built,* (pp. 87-111). New York, NY: Vintage Books.

Winant, H. (1994). *Racial formation in the United States: From the 1960's to the 1990's.* New York, NY: Routledge.

Wise, T. (2011). *White like me: Reflections on race from a privileged son.* Berkeley, CA: Soft Skull Press.

Witkin, H.A., & Goodengough, M. D. R. (1977). Field dependent and field independent cognitive styles and their educational implications. *Review of Educational Research*, 47(1), pp.1-64.

Wolcott, H.F. (2004). The *Ethnographic Autobiography, Auto/Biography, 12*, 93-106

Woodland, M.H. (2004). *Ethnocultural exposure as a predictor of academic achievement, Academic self-concept and self-reliance in Black college males* (Doctorial dissertation). Available from Proquest Dissertation and Theses database.

Woodson, C.G. (1933). *The Miseducation of the Negro*. New York, NY: AMS Press.

Wright, C. (1989). Wittgenstein's later philosophy of mind: Sensation, privacy, and intention. *Journal of Philosophy*, 89, 622-634.

Wright, C. A. (2005). Educational schizophrenia: Black middle class students making sense of hyper-racialization and de-racialization. Retrieved from http://www.allacademic.com/

Young, A.A., Jr. (2011). The Black Masculinities of Barack Obama: Some implications for African American men. *Daedadus, MIT Press Journal, 140, (2)*, 206-214. doi:10.1162

Young, V.A. (2007). *Your average nigga: Performing race, literacy, and masculinity*. Detroit, MI: Wayne State University Press.

Zimmerman, B.J., Bandura, A., & Martinez-Pons, M. (1992). Self-motivation for academic attainment: The role of self-efficacy beliefs and personal goal setting. *American Educational Research Journal*, 29(3), pp. 663-676. Retrieved from http://aerj.aera.net/

Index

www.ingramcontent.com/pod-product-compliance
Lightning Source LLC
Chambersburg PA
CBHW050409280326
41932CB00013BA/1789

* 9 781622 730803 *